D0997894

CROSSWORD COMPENDIUM

igloobooks

igloobooks

Published in 2017
by Igloo Books Ltd
Cottage Farm
Sywell
NN6 0BJ
www.igloobooks.com

HUN001 1017
2 4 6 8 10 9 7 5 3
ISBN 978-1-78557-855-7

Cover designed by Nicholas Gage

Puzzle compilation, typesetting and design by:
Clarity Media Ltd, http://www.clarity-media.co.uk

Printed and manufactured in China

Contents

Puzzle 1

Across

4 Large insect (6)
6 Fixes the result (4)
7 Annoy (3)
8 Sword handle (4)
9 At a distance (4)
10 Pub (3)
11 Group of players; side (4)
12 Hard tooth coating (6)

Down

1 Giddiness (9)
2 Nautical (8)
3 Made short and sharp turns (9)
5 US state (8)

Puzzle 2

Across

4 Set up for a purpose (9)
6 Frying pan (3)
8 Equine animal (5)
9 Merchandise; possessions (5)
10 Wily (3)
12 Someone worthy of imitation (4,5)

Down

1 Game played on horseback (4)
2 Homeliest (anag) (9)
3 Protects (6)
5 All (5)
6 Gamble (5)
7 Small hills (6)
11 Right to hold property (4)

Crossword

Puzzle 3

Across

1 A wine shop (6)
6 Athletic contest (9)
7 Destroy (4)
8 Large underground chamber (4)
9 Undisguised and shameless (9)
11 Left (6)

Down

1 Garment worn after a shower (8)
2 Cocktail (8)
3 Obtained (3)
4 Neat and smart (5-3)
5 Planned (8)
10 Mend (3)

1 B	O	2 D	E	3 G	A			
A		A		O		4 E		5 I
6 T	R	I	A	T	H	L	O	N
H		Q				E		T
7 R	O	U	T		8 C	A	V	E
O		I				N		N
9 B	A	R	E	10 F	A	C	E	D
E		I		I		U		E
			11 E	X	I	T	E	D

Puzzle 4

Across

1 Received by genetic transmission (9)
5 Stencils (9)
8 Hank of wool (5)
9 Perceptive (5-4)
12 Succinctly (9)

Down

1 Belonging naturally (9)
2 Cut of pork (3)
3 Very small child (3)
4 Cowardly and despicable (9)
6 Card game (5)
7 Nimble (5)
10 Goal (3)
11 Nevertheless (3)

1 I	N	2 H	E	R	I	3 T	E	4 D
N		A				O		A
5 T	E	M	6 P	L	7 A	T	E	S
R			O		G			T
I		8 S	K	E	I	N		A
N			E		L			R
9 S	H	10 A	R	P	E	11 Y	E	D
I		I				E		L
12 C	O	M	P	A	C	T	L	Y

Puzzle 5

Across

4 Secret (6)
6 Large wading bird (4)
7 Food item from a hen (3)
8 Chicken (4)
9 Bird of prey (4)
10 Opposite of in (3)
11 Yellow and black insect (4)
12 Wrongdoer (6)

Down

1 Speech sound that is not a vowel (9)
2 Grows more mature (8)
3 Fresh precipitation (9)
5 Constricts (8)

Puzzle 6

Across

1 Dismissed as insignificant (9)
5 Adolescents (9)
8 Venomous snake (5)
9 Rhetorics (anag) (9)
12 Way of living (9)

Down

1 Pertaining to plants (9)
2 False statement (3)
3 Strong alkaline solution (3)
4 Release from a duty (9)
6 Lowest point (5)
7 Dull colours (5)
10 Lout (3)
11 Your (poetic) (3)

Crossword

Puzzle 7

Across

1 Hold a position or job (6)
6 Watch (9)
7 Roll of photographic film (4)
8 Curl one's hair (4)
9 Anomaly (9)
11 Not written in any key (of music) (6)

Down

1 Exclamations of protest (8)
2 Start (8)
3 Fizzy drink (3)
4 Act of removal (8)
5 End of a railway route (8)
10 Place (3)

Puzzle 8

Across

4 Leap on one foot (3)
6 Seedless raisin (7)
7 Quickly (7)
8 Rid of something unpleasant (7)
10 Yearbook (7)
11 Queen ___ : fairy in Romeo and Juliet (3)

Down

1 Banishment from a group (9)
2 Flutter (4)
3 Reveries (9)
4 Hard to make out; indistinct (4)
5 Contrition (9)
8 Decapod crustacean (4)
9 ___ Simone: US singer (4)

Puzzle 9

Across

1 Emergency vehicle (9)
5 Brett ___ : Australian fast bowler (3)
7 Shine like a star (7)
8 Commercials (7)
11 Female pronoun (3)
12 Very lifelike (9)

Down

1 Semiaquatic reptile (9)
2 Plant with an edible root (4)
3 ___ Grimshaw: DJ (4)
4 Unconventional (of a person) (9)
6 Levels; ranks (5)
9 Entry document (4)
10 Hots (anag) (4)

Puzzle 10

Across

1 Hairstyle (8)
5 Numerical fact (9)
6 Smooth; groom (5)
7 Edifices (9)
9 Not curly (of hair) (8)

Down

1 Bed for a baby (3)
2 Among other things (Latin) (5,4)
3 Promoting the growth of (9)
4 Guardians (7)
5 People who copy out documents (7)
8 Stomach (3)

Crossword

Puzzle 11

Across

1 Geek (4)
3 Ancient France (4)
5 Location for indoor exercise (9)
6 Occurring every three years (9)
8 Responding to (9)
10 Currency of Italy and Spain (4)
11 Crush with a sharp blow (4)

Down

1 Discuss the terms of a deal (9)
2 Simpleton (5)
3 Eg oxygen (3)
4 Glare of publicity (9)
7 Conventions (5)
9 Court (3)

Puzzle 12

Across

1 Composer or singer (8)
5 Large digging machine (9)
6 Removes the skin from (5)
7 Recurring again and again (9)
9 Least clean (8)

Down

1 Blend together (3)
2 Declaration (9)
3 Demanding situation (9)
4 Small Arctic whale (7)
5 Fled from captivity (7)
8 What painters create (3)

Puzzle 13

Across

4 Unwind (6)
6 Wild mountain goat (4)
7 Mouthpiece attached to a bridle (3)
8 Leave out (4)
9 Large deer (pl) (4)
10 Pro (3)
11 In ___ : in place of (4)
12 Migratory grasshopper (6)

Down

1 Someone who cannot sleep (9)
2 Uncertain (8)
3 Morning meal (9)
5 Ability to read (8)

Puzzle 14

Across

4 Diminishing (9)
6 Excavated soil (3)
8 Dressed to the ___ : elaborately clothed (5)
9 Shine brightly (5)
10 Put down (3)
12 Damaged by ultraviolet rays (of skin) (9)

Down

1 Holier than ___ : phrase (4)
2 Of one mind (9)
3 Gesture (6)
5 Blowing in puffs (of wind) (5)
6 Edgar ___ : French artist (5)
7 Putting lawns in golf (6)
11 Imitated (4)

Crossword

Puzzle 15

Across

1 Assigned (9)
5 Green vegetable (9)
8 Move to music (5)
9 Person who takes bets (9)
12 Brought to an end (9)

Down

1 Occurring in the absence of oxygen (9)
2 Remove branches (3)
3 Pull at (3)
4 Felt hopeless (9)
6 Taken ___ : surprised (5)
7 Capital of Ghana (5)
10 Possess (3)
11 Child (3)

Puzzle 16

Across

4 Unrefined (6)
6 Religious sisters (4)
7 Annoy continuously (3)
8 Fixed costs (4)
9 River in England (4)
10 Pear-shaped fruit (3)
11 Broad (4)
12 Meaner (anag) (6)

Down

1 Bruise (9)
2 Move to another place (8)
3 Theatrical form of entertainment (9)
5 Pleasing and captivating (8)

Puzzle 17

Across

1 Tip the hat (4)
3 Loud noise (4)
5 These are kicked by soccer players (9)
6 Undivided opinion (9)
8 Vaccinate (9)
10 Fleet of ships (4)
11 Male children (4)

Down

1 Dispersal (9)
2 Japanese mattress (5)
3 Bleat of a sheep (3)
4 Accompaniment to fish and chips (5,4)
7 Beasts of burden (5)
9 Bashful; reluctant to give details (3)

Puzzle 18

Across

1 Roused from sleep (8)
5 Process of being brought to an end (9)
6 Piece of broken pottery (5)
7 Bright stage lamp (9)
9 Concise (8)

Down

1 Mock (3)
2 Concerned with beauty (9)
3 Blackmail (9)
4 Stinted (anag) (7)
5 Distinct sentence parts (7)
8 Head covering (3)

Crossword

Puzzle 19

Across

4 Having a body (9)
6 Ground condensation (3)
8 Artifice (5)
9 Bundle of wheat (5)
10 Roll of bank notes (3)
12 Material used to make glass reflective (9)

Down

1 Loose flowing garment (4)
2 Deeply embarrassed (9)
3 Formal assessment (6)
5 Found agreeable (5)
6 Flat circular plates (5)
7 Occurring every seven days (6)
11 ___ Hathaway: actress (4)

Puzzle 20

Across

1 Paul ___ : former England footballer (4)
3 Italian acknowledgement (4)
5 Disgusting (9)
6 Walking unsteadily (9)
8 Large body of troops (9)
10 Fencing sword (4)
11 Earth (4)

Down

1 Easily angered (9)
2 Pick out; choose (5)
3 Mountain pass (3)
4 Eight-sided (9)
7 Parts in a play (5)
9 Definite article (3)

Puzzle 21

Across

1 Relating to dissension (8)
5 Change dramatically (9)
6 Work of fiction (5)
7 Derived from experience (9)
9 Purple quartz (8)

Down

1 Not near (3)
2 Make narrower (9)
3 Physical weakness (9)
4 Strongly influencing later developments (7)
5 Crisp plain fabric (7)
8 Suitable (3)

Puzzle 22

Across

4 Method; road (3)
6 Make bigger (7)
7 Type of conference (7)
8 Rounded domes (7)
10 Dribble (7)
11 State (3)

Down

1 Incessant (9)
2 Bivalve sea creature (4)
3 Formula One race (5,4)
4 Low dam across a river (4)
5 Child (9)
8 Large town (4)
9 Find pleasant (4)

Crossword

Puzzle 23

Across

- **1** Flashy (6)
- **6** Suggest indirectly (9)
- **7** Edible fat (4)
- **8** This covers your body (4)
- **9** Small space (9)
- **11** Walks slowly (6)

Down

- **1** Severe traffic congestion (8)
- **2** Carve words on something (8)
- **3** School of Mahayana Buddhism (3)
- **4** Finance something (8)
- **5** Enthusiasm (8)
- **10** Sweet potato (3)

1 G	L	2 I	T	3 Z	Y	■	■	■
R	■	N	■	E	■	4 B	■	5 K
6 I	N	S	I	N	U	A	T	E
D	■	C	■	■	■	N	■	E
7 L	A	R	D	■	8 S	K	I	N
O	■	I	■	■	■	R	■	N
9 C	U	B	B	10 Y	H	O	L	E
K	■	E	■	A	■	L	■	S
■	■	■	11 A	M	B	L	E	S

Puzzle 24

Across

- **4** Removed from sight (3)
- **6** Discharge from a hole in a pipe (7)
- **7** Large public rooms on ships (7)
- **8** Set up (7)
- **10** Rower (7)
- **11** Bread roll (3)

Down

- **1** Source of a brief burst of bright light (9)
- **2** Pull something heavy (4)
- **3** Movement requiring skill and care (9)
- **4** Mesh (anag) (4)
- **5** Demeaning (9)
- **8** Fail totally (4)
- **9** Barriers to hold back water (4)

1 F	■	2 H	■	3 M	■	4 H	I	5 D
6 L	E	A	K	A	G	E	■	E
A	■	U	■	N	■	M	■	G
7 S	A	L	O	O	N	S	■	R
H	■	■	■	E	■	■	■	A
B	■	8 F	O	U	N	9 D	E	D
U	■	L	■	V	■	A	■	I
L	■	10 O	A	R	S	M	A	N
11 B	A	P	■	E	■	S	■	G

Puzzle 25

Across

4 Having a repeated design (9)
6 Chatter (3)
8 Believer in a supreme being (5)
9 Double fold in a garment (5)
10 Plaything (3)
12 Anxiously (9)

Down

1 Celebration; festivity (4)
2 Performance (9)
3 Procure; sign up (6)
5 Simple song (5)
6 Tokyo is the capital here (5)
7 Sailing barge (6)
11 Look at amorously (4)

Puzzle 26

Across

1 Shoe with a wooden sole (4)
3 Hew (4)
5 US state (9)
6 Design plan (9)
8 Having equality of measure (9)
10 Thread (4)
11 Loud cry (4)

Down

1 Famous person (9)
2 Objection; complain (5)
3 22nd Greek letter (3)
4 Feasible (9)
7 Irritable (5)
9 Male person (3)

Crossword

Puzzle 27

Across

1 Flood (6)
6 Relating to the stomach (9)
7 Steals from (4)
8 Fertile type of soil (4)
9 Traders (9)
11 Concurs (6)

Down

1 Simplified drawings (8)
2 Spotted beetle (8)
3 Jewel (3)
4 Proclaim (8)
5 Spies (8)
10 Embrace (3)

1 D	E	2 L	U	3 G	E	■	■	■
I	■	A	■	E	■	4 A	■	5 C
6 A	B	D	O	M	I	N	A	L
G	■	Y	■	■	■	N	■	I
7 R	O	B	S	■	8 L	O	A	M
A	■	I	■	■	■	U	■	P
9 M	E	R	C	10 H	A	N	T	S
S	■	D	■	U	■	C	■	E
■	■	■	11 A	G	R	E	E	S

Puzzle 28

Across

✓1 Getting onto a ship (8)
5 Profound transformation (3,6)
✓6 Liberates (5)
✓7 Divergence from a course (9)
9 Lofty peak (8)

Down

✓1 Farewell remark (3)
✓2 Musical instrument (9)
3 Enquiry into metaphysical contradictions (9)
4 Imaginary mischievous sprite (7)
5 Type of comedy (5-2)
✓8 Lyric poem (3)

■	1 B	O	2 A	R	3 D	I	N	4 G
■	Y	■	E	■	I	■	■	R
5 S	E	A	C	H	A	N	G	E
T	■	■	O	■	L	■	■	M
A	■	6 F	R	E	E	S	■	L
N	■	■	D	■	E	■	■	I
7 D	E	V	I	A	T	I	8 O	N
U	■	■	A	■	I	■	D	■
9 P	I	N	N	A	C	L	E	■

Puzzle 29

Across

- **1** Wine-bottle opener (9)
- **5** Craze (3)
- **7** Alan ___ : footballer (7)
- **8** Ban on trade with a country (7)
- **11** How (anag) (3)
- **12** One to whom a letter is directed (9)

Down

- **1** Type of restaurant (9)
- **2** Fishing sticks (4)
- **3** Raise (4)
- **4** Tiresome (9)
- **6** Strange (5)
- **9** Tie together (4)
- **10** Possesses (4)

1 2 3 4 5 6 7 8 9 10 11 12

Puzzle 30

Across

- **1** Believed (a lie) (9)
- **5** Merchants who sell goods (9)
- **8** Distorts (5)
- **9** Disorganised (9)
- **12** Increase rapidly (9)

Down

- **1** Extends one's body (9)
- **2** Towards the stern (3)
- **3** Great distress (3)
- **4** Harm the reputation of (9)
- **6** Covered with water (5)
- **7** City in Bolivia (2,3)
- **10** Layer of a folded material (3)
- **11** Ancient boat (3)

1 2 3 4 5 6 7 8 9 10 11 12

Crossword

Puzzle 31

Across

- **1** Pierce (9)
- **5** Unit of current (3)
- **7** Next after sixth (7)
- **8** Suggested but not stated explicitly (7)
- **11** Division of a play (3)
- **12** Nanny (9)

Down

- **1** Grouselike game bird (9)
- **2** Bites at (4)
- **3** Related by blood (4)
- **4** Spellbound (9)
- **6** Preclude (5)
- **9** Platform leading out to sea (4)
- **10** Facts and statistics collectively (4)

Puzzle 32

Across

- **1** A long way away (3,3)
- **6** Correctness (9)
- **7** Spherical object (4)
- **8** Heavenly body (4)
- **9** Discovery (9)
- **11** Reveal (6)

Down

- **1** Portend (8)
- **2** Control (8)
- **3** In good health (3)
- **4** Neutral particle with negligible mass (8)
- **5** Keep at a distance (8)
- **10** Person who steers a boat (3)

Puzzle 33

Across
- **4** Knock vigorously (3)
- **6** Break between words (in verse) (7)
- **7** Elate (7)
- **8** Violinist (7)
- **10** Statement of transactions (7)
- **11** A man; fellow (3)

Down
- **1** Education (9)
- **2** Unit of heredity (4)
- **3** Under judgement (3,6)
- **4** Showing vigour or spirit (4)
- **5** All future generations (9)
- **8** Wear away (4)
- **9** Noisy (4)

Puzzle 34

Across
- **4** Country in Central America (6)
- **6** Jump (4)
- **7** Make a choice (3)
- **8** Scottish singer-songwriter (4)
- **9** Skin irritation (4)
- **10** Eg use a chair (3)
- **11** Small mountain (4)
- **12** Songlike cries (6)

Down
- **1** Mammal with a pouch (9)
- **2** Excellently (8)
- **3** Irritable (9)
- **5** Height (8)

Crossword

Puzzle 35

Across

1 Feeling resentment (9)
5 Technical equipment (9)
8 Type of military operation (5)
9 Went underwater (9)
12 Eg floods and earthquakes (4,2,3)

Down

1 Inability to feel pain (9)
2 Empty space between two objects (3)
3 Animal doctor (3)
4 Went down (9)
6 Self-evident truth (5)
7 Foresee or predict (5)
10 Nocturnal mammal (3)
11 Performance by a musician (3)

Puzzle 36

Across

1 A mechanical failure (9)
5 Belonging to us (3)
7 Takes into custody (7)
8 Occurs (7)
11 Fruit of a rose (3)
12 Something that is revealing (3-6)

Down

1 Parts of earth supporting life (9)
2 ___ Pound: US poet (4)
3 Blades for rowing a boat (4)
4 A periodical that is usually daily (9)
6 Doctrine (5)
9 Stride; rate of moving (4)
10 Cut of beef from the leg (4)

Puzzle 37

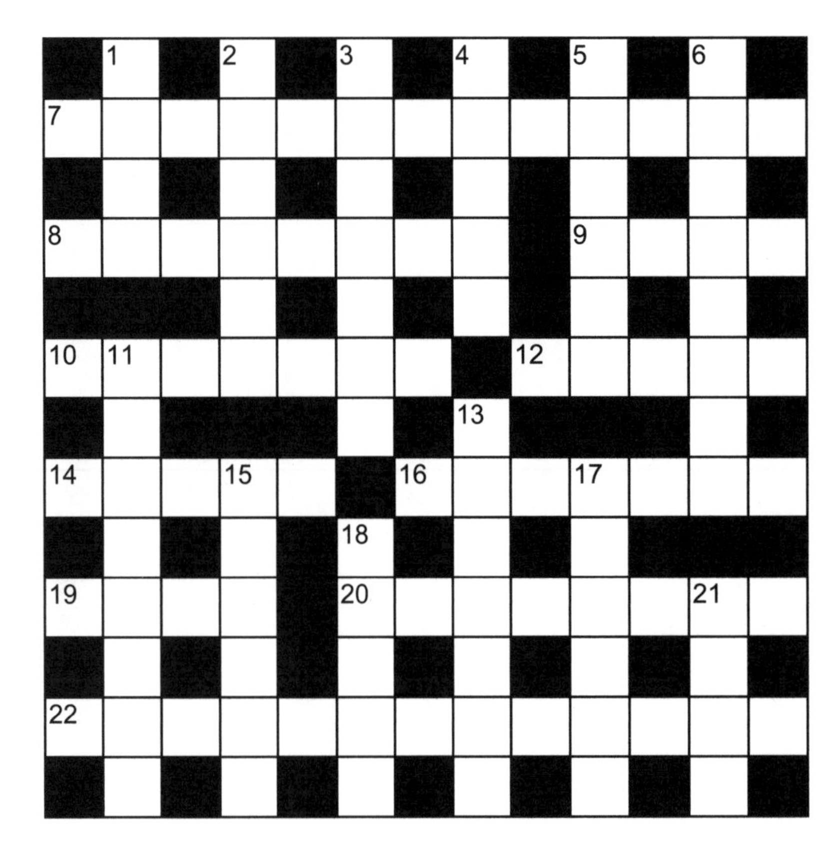

Across

7 Shape or arrangement (13)
8 Scornful negativity (8)
9 Cook in the oven (4)
10 Imitator (7)
12 Receive and pass on a message (5)
14 Wander off track (5)
16 Cantered (7)
19 Halt (4)
20 00:00 on a 24-hour clock (8)
22 Rude and discourteous (13)

Down

1 Torso (4)
2 Representation of a person (6)
3 Contrary to (7)
4 Packs tightly (5)
5 Firmly fixed (6)
6 Piece of furniture (8)
11 Surpass (8)
13 Held a baby (7)
15 Aim to achieve something (6)
17 Distorts (6)
18 Entertain (5)
21 Sixty minutes (4)

Crossword

Puzzle 38

Across

1 Engages in an argument (5)
4 Skin marks from wounds (5)
10 Remains (7)
11 Vacillate (5)
12 Small flashing dot on a radar screen (4)
13 Surrounded on all sides (8)
16 Banished (6)
17 Squirt a liquid in short bursts (6)
20 Infectious (8)
21 Clever remark (4)
23 Mark of repetition (5)
25 Irregularity (7)
26 Monastery church (5)
27 Eg Wordsworth and Keats (5)

Down

2 Person who expects the worst (9)
3 Travelled by horse (4)
5 Marsh marigolds (8)
6 Increase the running speed of an engine (3)
7 Multiply by three (6)
8 Existing (5)
9 Network of lines (4)
14 Incentive; substance like caffeine (9)
15 Remove a monarch (8)
18 Current of air (6)
19 Go stealthily or furtively (5)
20 Closing section of music (4)
22 Extinct bird (4)
24 Bat (anag) (3)

Puzzle 39

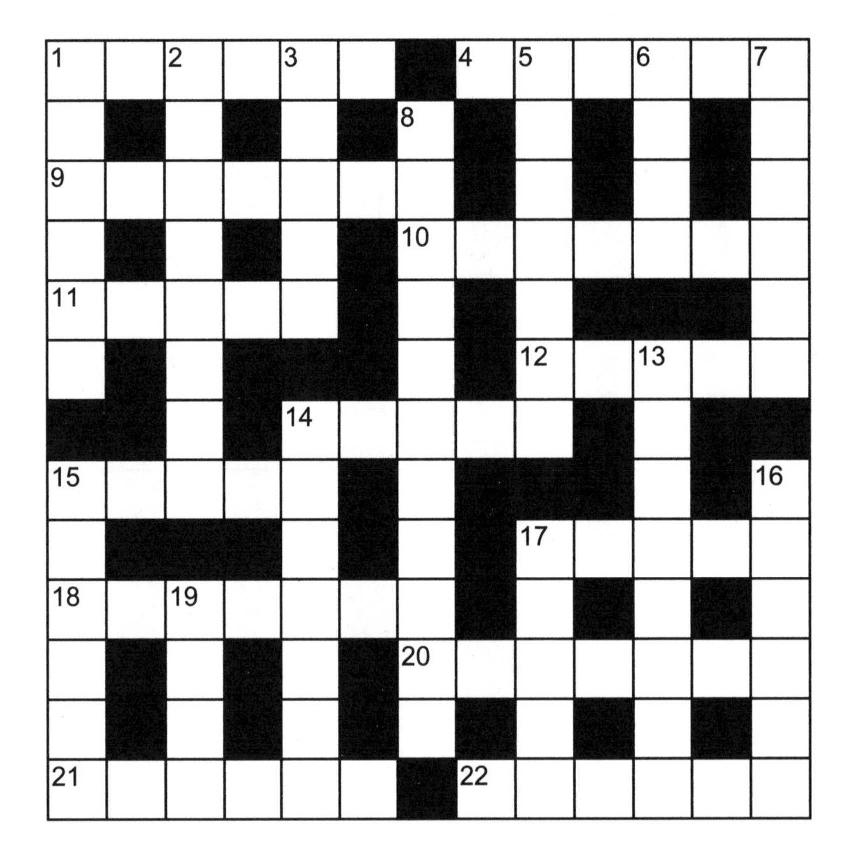

Across

1 Revolve (6)
4 Tropical American lizard (6)
9 Long-lasting and recurrent (7)
10 Cheer (7)
11 Clod of turf (5)
12 Stroll (5)
14 Relocated (5)
15 Baby carriage (5)
17 Recipient of money (5)
18 Disciple (7)
20 Snuggles (7)
21 History play by Shakespeare (5,1)
22 Makes fun of someone (6)

Down

1 Withdraw; gradually diminish (6)
2 Prospering (8)
3 Principle or belief (5)
5 Knight of King Arthur (7)
6 Encourage in wrongdoing (4)
7 Geneva (anag) (6)
8 Accomplishment (11)
13 Two-wheeled vehicles (8)
14 Puzzle (7)
15 Make white by removing colour (6)
16 Glasses contain these (6)
17 Out of fashion (5)
19 Augury (4)

Crossword

Puzzle 40

Across

1 One who presides over a meeting (11)
9 Ring solemnly (5)
10 Item for catching fish (3)
11 Bequeath an income to (5)
12 Wireless (5)
13 Pursuit of high principles (8)
16 Horse of light tan colour (8)
18 Behaved (5)
21 Looks slyly (5)
22 Make a mistake (3)
23 Eg from Athens (5)
24 Highly destructive (11)

Down

2 Receiver (7)
3 Writing fluid holder (7)
4 Small folds in clothing (6)
5 Measuring stick (5)
6 Possessed (5)
7 Makes better (11)
8 Awfully (11)
14 Box of useful equipment (7)
15 Male blaze fighters (7)
17 Season of the Church year (6)
19 Curt (5)
20 School of thought (5)

Puzzle 41

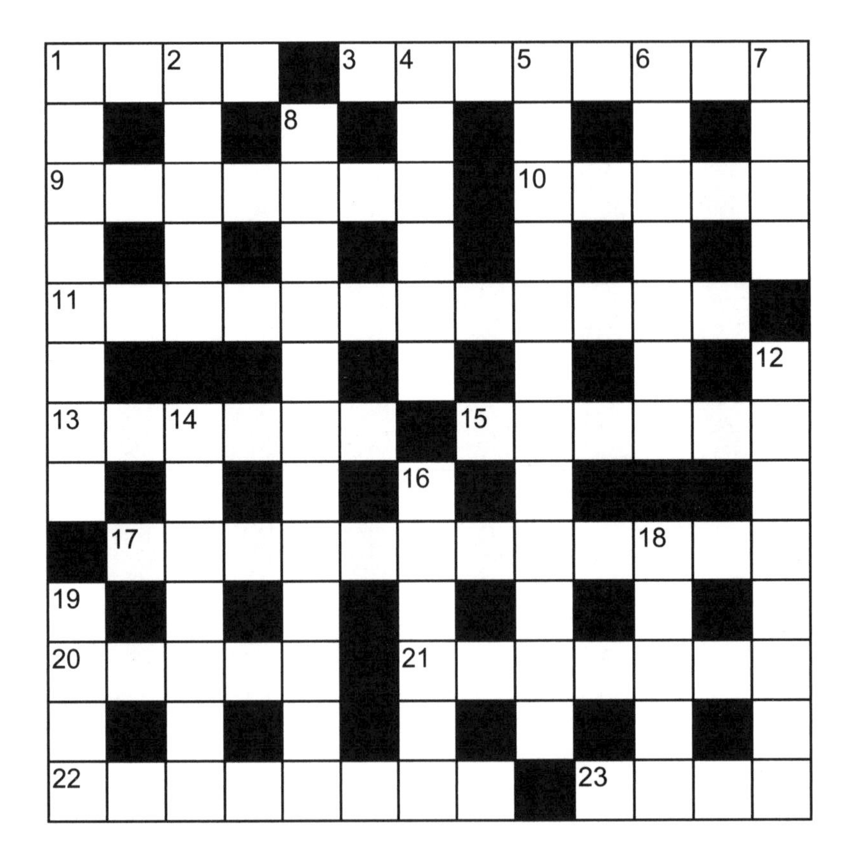

Across

1 Vessel (4)
3 Fugitives (8)
9 Small house (7)
10 Temporary police force (5)
11 Not on purpose (12)
13 Floating freely (6)
15 Deceives; finest (anag) (6)
17 Insubordination (12)
20 ___ Maradona: footballer (5)
21 Featured in the leading role (7)
22 Preserve or hold sacred (8)
23 Long-running dispute (4)

Down

1 Card game (8)
2 ___ Camera: band (5)
4 The rear parts of ships (6)
5 Pertaining to letters (12)
6 Fifth Greek letter (7)
7 Slanting; crooked (4)
8 Bride's primary attendant (4,2,6)
12 Climbed (8)
14 Marauders (7)
16 Period of instruction (6)
18 Care for; look after (5)
19 Indolent (4)

Crossword

Puzzle 42

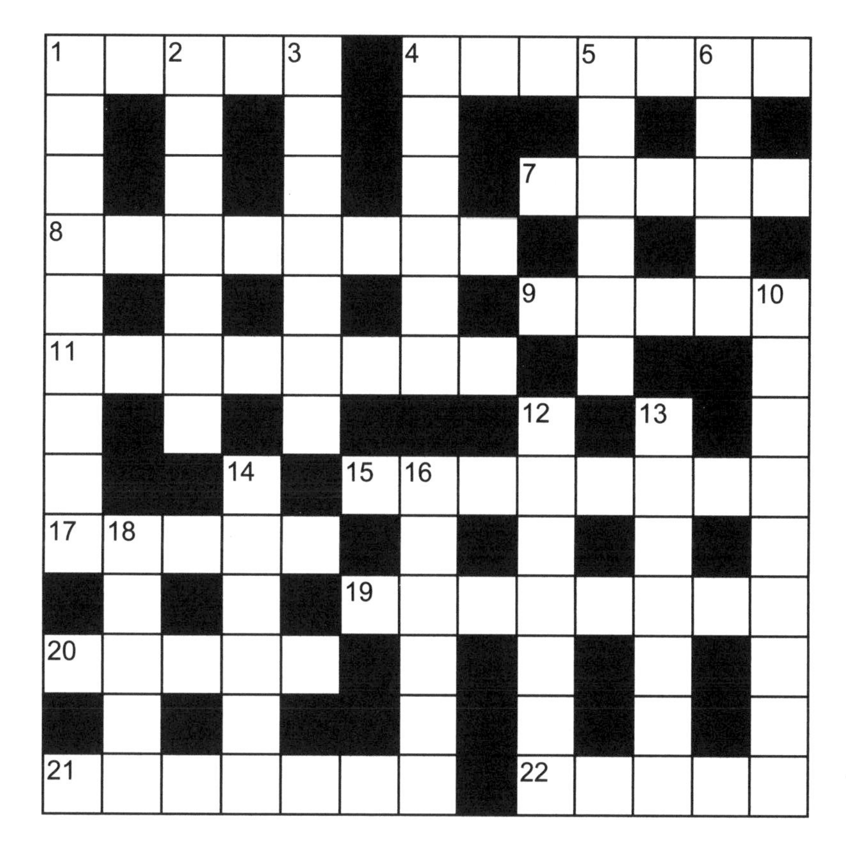

Across

1 Inert gas found in air (5)
4 Sleeps lightly (7)
7 Ancient harps (5)
8 Mixture used to flavour food (8)
9 Triangular river mouth (5)
11 A division between people (8)
15 Church rules (5,3)
17 Threads or fibres (5)
19 User; purchaser (8)
20 Fruits of the palm (5)
21 Sellers (7)
22 Late (5)

Down

1 Feeling of ill will (9)
2 Immature fruit of a cucumber (7)
3 Freshness (7)
4 Workroom of a painter (6)
5 Gas we breathe (6)
6 Dismiss from office (5)
10 Fit to fly (of an aeroplane) (9)
12 Random criticism (7)
13 Strident noise (7)
14 In truth; really (6)
16 Makes more attractive (6)
18 Not asleep (5)

Puzzle 43

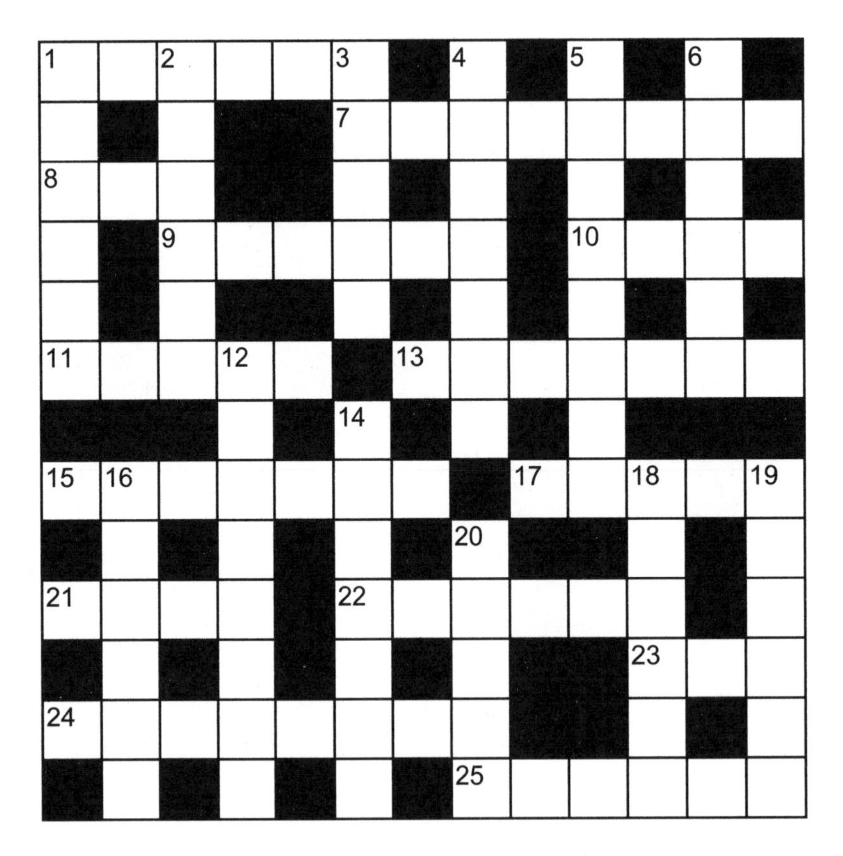

Across

1 Lifting devices (6)
7 Cornerstone (8)
8 Drunkard (3)
9 Notable inconvenience (6)
10 Reflection of sound (4)
11 Unpleasant giants (5)
13 Precis (7)
15 Beetroot soup (7)
17 Layabout (5)
21 Guinea pig (4)
22 Bird with a massive bill (6)
23 Clothing needed for an activity (3)
24 Leave the ground (of a space rocket) (5,3)
25 Livestock food (6)

Down

1 Building for gambling (6)
2 ___ Conan Doyle: author (6)
3 Break into pieces (5)
4 Secret place (7)
5 Admired and respected (8)
6 More precisely (6)
12 Author (8)
14 Stand for small items (7)
16 Mouthpiece of the gods (6)
18 Connected (6)
19 Bird of prey (6)
20 Tuft of hair (5)

Crossword

Puzzle 44

Across

1 Totally (5)
4 Good at (5)
10 Open-minded; given freely (7)
11 Core group; basic unit (5)
12 Tense (4)
13 Cold Spanish tomato soup (8)
16 Concealed from view (6)
17 Oceanic seabird (6)
20 Sorting (8)
21 Pertaining to the Isle of Man (4)
23 Full of life (5)
25 Vehicle towed by another (7)
26 Fixes (5)
27 Raucous (5)

Down

2 Unlimited (9)
3 Engage in spirited fun (4)
5 Interpret the meaning of (8)
6 Seed vessel (3)
7 Malfunction (6)
8 Puff up; swell (5)
9 Brave person; idol (4)
14 Cut short (9)
15 Informed upon (8)
18 State of great comfort (6)
19 Midges (5)
20 Seep; exude (4)
22 Type of starch (4)
24 ___ Barker: former tennis player (3)

Puzzle 45

Across

1 Fleshes out unnecessarily (4)
3 Adhering to closely (8)
9 Irreverence (7)
10 Essential (5)
11 Newt (3)
12 Type of spear (5)
13 Facial protuberances (5)
15 Sea duck (5)
17 Climbing shrubs (5)
18 Move up and down on water (3)
19 Jewelled headdress (5)
20 Destructive (7)
21 Flower-shaped competition awards (8)
22 Fever or shivering fit (4)

Down

1 Head of the government (5,8)
2 Storage place (5)
4 Lymphoid organ (6)
5 Public official (5,7)
6 Recites as a chant (7)
7 50th anniversary of a major event (6,7)
8 Medicine taken when blocked-up (12)
14 Winding shapes (7)
16 Feasible (6)
18 Confuse or obscure (5)

Crossword

Puzzle 46

Across

1 Paired (anag) (6)
7 Assimilate again (8)
8 Compete (3)
9 Gambol (6)
10 ___ Sharif: actor (4)
11 Sends an SMS (5)
13 Persevere with (7)
15 Immature and childish (7)
17 Having nothing written on (of paper) (5)
21 Male sheep (pl) (4)
22 Fierce or domineering woman (6)
23 Marry (3)
24 Mathematically aware (8)
25 Lovingly (6)

Down

1 Return to a former condition (6)
2 Title placed before a name (6)
3 Bore into (5)
4 Connoisseur (7)
5 Marriage ceremony (8)
6 Cracks; loses control (6)
12 Beat easily (8)
14 Pertaining to a river (7)
16 Planet (6)
18 Declared (6)
19 Pleasant and agreeable (6)
20 Great sorrow (5)

Puzzle 47

Across

- **1** Aromatic annual herb (4)
- **3** Monitors (8)
- **9** Settled oneself comfortably (7)
- **10** Path or road (5)
- **11** Easy targets (7,5)
- **14** Type of vase (3)
- **16** Crucial person or point; axis (5)
- **17** ___ de Cologne: perfume (3)
- **18** Ate excessively (12)
- **21** Eyelashes (5)
- **22** Ancient wise king (7)
- **23** Praising highly (8)
- **24** Become less bright over time (4)

Down

- **1** Enormous extinct creature (8)
- **2** Franz ___ : Hungarian composer (5)
- **4** Primary colour (3)
- **5** Luckily (12)
- **6** Laugh (7)
- **7** Cook slowly in liquid (4)
- **8** Crucial (3,9)
- **12** Acknowledged; assumed (5)
- **13** Direction; general help (8)
- **15** Short story (7)
- **19** Third Greek letter (5)
- **20** Unit of land area (4)
- **22** What our planet orbits (3)

Crossword

Puzzle 48

Across

1 Having only magnitude (6)
5 Feline animal (3)
7 Genuflect (5)
8 Impassive (7)
9 US state (5)
10 Become part of a solution (8)
12 Solent (anag) (6)
14 Takes up (6)
17 Choosing from various sources (8)
18 Evergreen trees (5)
20 Overturned (7)
21 Derisive smile (5)
22 Long-leaved lettuce (3)
23 Shun (6)

Down

2 Live together (7)
3 Endorsed (8)
4 Round before the final (abbrev) (4)
5 Clear mess away (5,2)
6 Crowds of people (7)
7 Rogue; scoundrel (5)
11 Laziness (8)
12 Cynic (7)
13 Strangeness (7)
15 Ancient galley (7)
16 Take place; happen (5)
19 Ooze (4)

Puzzle 49

Across

1 Body of water (4)
3 Discard; abandon (8)
9 Taste (7)
10 Cake decoration (5)
11 Marksman (12)
13 Moved at an easy pace (6)
15 Small piece of food (6)
17 Notwithstanding (12)
20 Foot joint (5)
21 Large tent (7)
22 Removing from office (8)
23 Scores (a goal) (4)

Down

1 Longevity of an individual (8)
2 Australian arboreal marsupial (5)
4 Hearty (anag) (6)
5 Mathematics of triangles (12)
6 Arachnids (7)
7 Near (4)
8 Entirety (12)
12 Fabric strips for covering wounds (8)
14 Disperse (5,2)
16 Part of a flower (6)
18 Short musical composition (5)
19 Unit of transmission speed (4)

Crossword

Puzzle 50

Across

1 Small bunch of flowers (4)
3 Cutting instrument (8)
9 Draws forth (7)
10 Sends out in the post (5)
11 Last Greek letter (5)
12 Formal speech (7)
13 Becomes subject to (6)
15 Spain and Portugal (6)
17 Sharply (7)
18 City in Tuscany (5)
20 Garbage or drivel (5)
21 Salvaged (7)
22 Christmas season (8)
23 Immobilise (4)

Down

1 Principally (13)
2 Take hold of (5)
4 Tradition (6)
5 Sleepwalker (12)
6 Laurence ___ : English actor (7)
7 Thelma & Louise actress (5,8)
8 Conflict of opinion (12)
14 Critical (7)
16 Composite of different species (6)
19 Outer layer of bread (5)

Puzzle 51

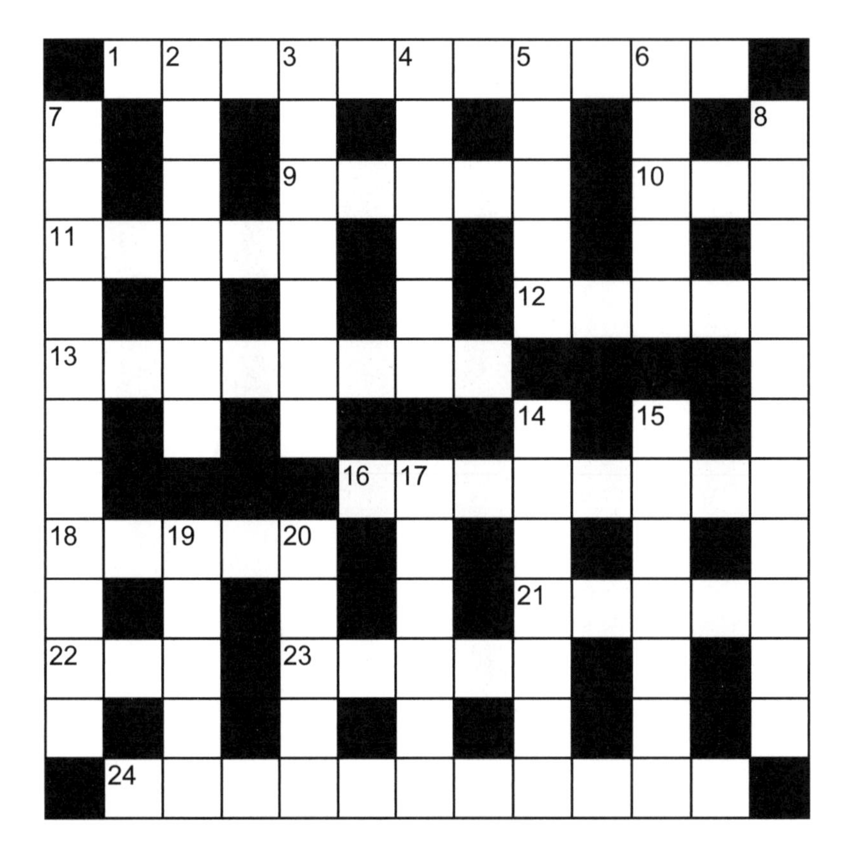

Across

1 Computation (11)
9 Benefactor (5)
10 Chopping tool (3)
11 Danger (5)
12 Use inefficiently (5)
13 Vertical flues (8)
16 Nobel ___ : winner of a Nobel Prize (8)
18 Sum; add up (5)
21 Chop meat into very small pieces (5)
22 Tree that bears acorns (3)
23 Chambers (5)
24 Link together (11)

Down

2 Sour in taste (7)
3 Type of cooking apple (7)
4 Missing human interaction (6)
5 Chuck (5)
6 Ellipses (5)
7 Belief something will happen (11)
8 Helpless (11)
14 Red colour (7)
15 Serious and sincere (7)
17 Nimble (6)
19 Capital of Japan (5)
20 Expressing emotions (of poetry) (5)

Crossword

Puzzle 52

Across

1 Type of bag (8)
5 Woes (4)
9 Radio receiver (5)
10 Giraffes have long ones (5)
11 Given for free (2,3,5)
14 Timothy ___ : James Bond actor (6)
15 Imperative (6)
17 Pacify; make calm (10)
20 Mark ___ : Samuel Langhorne Clemens (5)
21 Single-edged hunting knife (5)
22 Long grass (4)
23 Moved backwards (8)

Down

1 Skit (anag) (4)
2 ___ Karenina: novel by Tolstoy (4)
3 Scallions (6,6)
4 Trapped (6)
6 University teacher (8)
7 Believes tentatively (8)
8 Unkind; unsympathetic (12)
12 Teacher (8)
13 Lengthen (8)
16 Shuffle playing cards (6)
18 Is indebted to pay (4)
19 Curve in a road (4)

Puzzle 53

Across

1 Makes musical sounds (5)
4 Post (5)
10 Disentangle (7)
11 Nairobi is the capital here (5)
12 Smacks (4)
13 Raider (8)
16 Putrid (6)
17 Tropical fruit (6)
20 Pertaining to hearing (8)
21 Song for a solo voice (4)
23 Well cared for (5)
25 Had faith in (7)
26 Petite (5)
27 Tennis score (5)

Down

2 Vexed (9)
3 Hand over (4)
5 Convenience meal (4-4)
6 Relations (3)
7 Writer (6)
8 Ask for earnestly (5)
9 This grows on your head (4)
14 Eg an accent or cedilla (9)
15 Advocating abstinence from alcohol (8)
18 Prizes (6)
19 Worries (5)
20 Seabirds (4)
22 Silent (4)
24 Mother (3)

Crossword

Puzzle 54

Across

1 Quotidian (8)
5 Highly excited (4)
8 Comedian (5)
9 Sheikdom in the Persian Gulf (7)
10 Not as old (7)
12 Divisions between groups of people (7)
14 Extremely shocking things (7)
16 European country (7)
18 Musical composition (7)
19 Lazed (5)
20 Run quickly (4)
21 Warily (8)

Down

1 Engrave; carve (4)
2 Entangle (6)
3 Sailor of a light vessel (9)
4 Church buildings (6)
6 House with farm buildings (6)
7 Unselfish (8)
11 Moving to a higher class (9)
12 Showing mettle; fiery (8)
13 Loose protective garments (6)
14 US state of islands (6)
15 Stableman (6)
17 In a tense state (4)

Puzzle 55

Across

1 Applaud (4)
3 Hot and humid (8)
9 Up-and-down movement (7)
10 Noble gas (5)
11 Blends; mixtures (12)
14 First woman (3)
16 Leaf of parchment (5)
17 Military commander or official (3)
18 Vain (12)
21 Hawaiian greeting (5)
22 Active during the day (7)
23 Male singer (8)
24 Midge (4)

Down

1 Small bays (8)
2 Collection of songs (5)
4 Piece of cloth (3)
5 Penny-pinching (12)
6 Virtuoso solo passage (7)
7 Fabric used to dress wounds (4)
8 Germicide (12)
12 Collection of maps (5)
13 Knight of the round table (8)
15 Inspire with love (7)
19 Mortise partner (5)
20 Clothing (4)
22 Loud noise (3)

Crossword

Puzzle 56

Across

1 Brass instrument (4)
3 Sports grounds (8)
9 One event in a sequence (7)
10 Speech sound (5)
11 Coloured fluid used for writing (3)
12 Recycle (5)
13 Tests (5)
15 Section of a long poem (5)
17 Find the solution (5)
18 Perceive (3)
19 Mother-of-pearl (5)
20 Most poorly lit (7)
21 Qualified for by right (8)
22 Hunted animal (4)

Down

1 Horror film directed by M. Night Shyamalan (3,5,5)
2 Open and close the eyes quickly (5)
4 ___ Barlow: actress (6)
5 Designed to distract (12)
6 Relaxed (7)
7 Obviously (4-9)
8 Beginning (12)
14 Ask for; try to obtain (7)
16 Pasta strip (6)
18 Remove wool from sheep (5)

Puzzle 57

Across

- **1** Not genuine (6)
- **5** Before the present (3)
- **7** Eg gateaus (5)
- **8** Abandon hope (7)
- **9** Town in Surrey; sheer (anag) (5)
- **10** Study the night sky (8)
- **12** Recount (6)
- **14** Soldier who keeps guard (6)
- **17** Close friend (8)
- **18** Evenly balanced (5)
- **20** Increases a deadline (7)
- **21** Brown earth pigment (5)
- **22** Hill (3)
- **23** Ukrainian port (6)

Down

- **2** Type of staff (7)
- **3** Game played on a chessboard (8)
- **4** Island of the Inner Hebrides (4)
- **5** Road or roofing material (7)
- **6** Give too much money (7)
- **7** Insane (5)
- **11** Discovered (8)
- **12** Cheese on toast (7)
- **13** Sweet alcoholic spirit (7)
- **15** Retreats (7)
- **16** Penny-pincher (5)
- **19** Part of the ear (4)

Crossword

Puzzle 58

Across

1 Book introduction (8)
5 Moat (anag) (4)
9 Maurice ___ : French composer (5)
10 Words that identify things (5)
11 Recompense (10)
14 Permits (6)
15 Less attractive (6)
17 Metric unit of length (10)
20 Complete trust (5)
21 Not containing anything (5)
22 Company symbol (4)
23 Excited or annoyed (8)

Down

1 Blaze (4)
2 Wander (4)
3 Boxing class division (12)
4 Commotion or disturbance (6)
6 Giant ocean waves (8)
7 People who provide massages (8)
8 Clothing such as a vest (12)
12 Observant (8)
13 Eg putting a sapling in the ground (8)
16 Observing (6)
18 Small fight (4)
19 Coloured (4)

Puzzle 59

Across

1 Thick cord (4)
3 Scrawl (8)
9 Agitate (7)
10 Short treatise (5)
11 Efficient (12)
13 Pictorial representations (6)
15 Inexpensive restaurant (6)
17 Modestly (12)
20 Large intestine (5)
21 ___ Carlisle: US singer (7)
22 Magician (8)
23 Part of the foot (4)

Down

1 Type of state (8)
2 Cat sounds (5)
4 Eg Picasso or Braque (6)
5 Comprehensible (12)
6 Bed covering (7)
7 Consumes (4)
8 Most perfect example of a quality (12)
12 Hairstyle (8)
14 Ring-shaped (7)
16 Mix up (6)
18 Spirit in a bottle (5)
19 Performs in a play (4)

Crossword

Puzzle 60

Across

1 Defect in the eye (11)
9 Long rods (5)
10 Criticise strongly (3)
11 One of the senses (5)
12 Reduce prices substantially (5)
13 Male relation (8)
16 Force lifting something up (8)
18 Loosened (5)
21 Touch on; mention (5)
22 Also (3)
23 Stringed instrument (5)
24 Dehydration (11)

Down

2 Motorcycle attachment (7)
3 Burst inwards (7)
4 Alyssa ___ : Phoebe in Charmed (6)
5 Tries out (5)
6 Dark brown colour (5)
7 Homework tasks (11)
8 Not having a written constitution (11)
14 Cigar (7)
15 Bison (7)
17 Meal eaten in the fresh air (6)
19 Breathe heavily at night (5)
20 One of the United Arab Emirates (5)

Puzzle 61

Across

1 Cipher (4)
3 Disease caused by a lack of thiamine (8)
9 Spouts (7)
10 Relating to a city (5)
11 Cease (3)
12 Foolishly credulous (5)
13 Small open pies (5)
15 Stares at amorously (5)
17 Fourth month (5)
18 Sound of a dove (3)
19 Lazes; does nothing (5)
20 Render utterly perplexed (7)
21 Letting off (8)
22 Small horse (4)

Down

1 Very thoughtful (13)
2 Bewildered; stunned by a blow (5)
4 Simpler (6)
5 Not staying the same throughout (12)
6 Desiring what someone else has (7)
7 Recoils unduly (anag) (13)
8 Decomposition by a current (12)
14 Modern type of paint (7)
16 John ___ : one of the Beatles (6)
18 Stringed instrument (5)

Puzzle 62

Across

1 Eg sketches (8)
5 Flightless birds (4)
8 Of the nose (5)
9 Wine merchant (7)
10 Zeroes (7)
12 Snipping (7)
14 Made a monarch (7)
16 ___ May: Prime Minister (7)
18 Kettledrums (7)
19 Shire (anag) (5)
20 Beach constituent (4)
21 Children beginning to walk (8)

Down

1 ___ beetle: insect (4)
2 Support; help (6)
3 Unreadable (9)
4 Donating (6)
6 Eg March and May (6)
7 Accented (8)
11 Unhandled (9)
12 Short musical compositions (8)
13 Speech given in church (6)
14 Coarse cloth (6)
15 Indigenous (6)
17 Egyptian goddess of fertility (4)

Puzzle 63

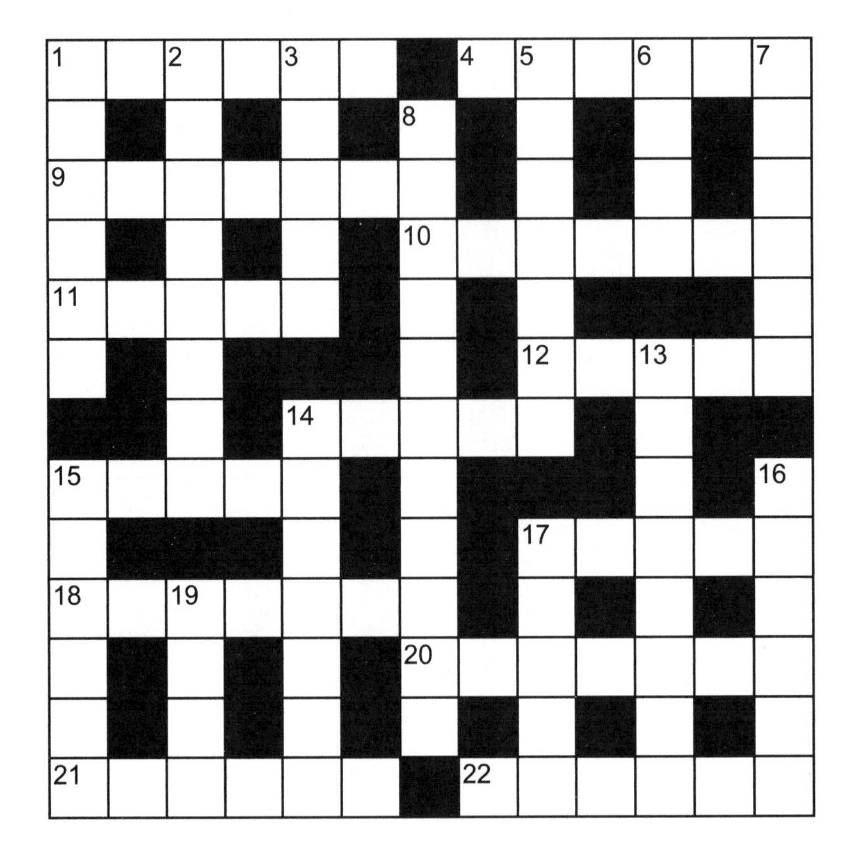

Across

1 Symbolise (6)
4 Nonsense (6)
9 Aromatic herb (7)
10 Unfurls (7)
11 Mexican plant fibre (5)
12 Walk (5)
14 Recurrent topic (5)
15 Wrathful (5)
17 Egg-shaped (5)
18 Mends (7)
20 Pasta dish (7)
21 Nervously (6)
22 Incidental remarks (6)

Down

1 Selfishness (6)
2 Formal approval (8)
3 Speak in a slow manner (5)
5 Tearing (anag) (7)
6 Thwart (4)
7 Wiped out (6)
8 Generously; liberally (11)
13 Increased in size (8)
14 Average (7)
15 Wear away (6)
16 Floors of a building (6)
17 Fertile spots in deserts (5)
19 Self-righteous person (4)

Crossword

Puzzle 64

Across

1 There (anag) (5)
4 Flamboyant confidence of style (7)
7 Severe (5)
8 Distinction; high status (8)
9 Growing thickly (5)
11 One liquid dispersed in another (8)
15 Aggressor (8)
17 Floor of a building (5)
19 Ballroom dance (8)
20 Cinders (5)
21 Acknowledgement of payment (7)
22 Extinct birds (5)

Down

1 Transitory (9)
2 Large marine flatfish (7)
3 Go backwards (7)
4 Mexican cloak (6)
5 Increase over time (6)
6 Snag; minor problem (5)
10 Annual compendiums of facts (9)
12 Female pub worker (7)
13 Thick-___ : insensitive to criticism (7)
14 Remove; excise (6)
16 Particularly strong ability (6)
18 Result; follow (5)

Puzzle 65

Across

- **1** Of doubtful honesty (informal) (5)
- **4** Burn (5)
- **10** Govern badly (7)
- **11** Tycoon (5)
- **12** Sailing vessel (4)
- **13** Disregards (8)
- **16** Ploys (6)
- **17** Tiny fish (6)
- **20** Country in E Africa (8)
- **21** Regretted (4)
- **23** Tropical American tree (5)
- **25** Runs out (7)
- **26** Manipulate dough (5)
- **27** Growl with bare teeth (5)

Down

- **2** Person who studies the past (9)
- **3** Stern and forbidding (4)
- **5** Grumble (8)
- **6** Piece of wood (3)
- **7** Among (6)
- **8** Less (5)
- **9** Mountain system in Europe (4)
- **14** Victor (9)
- **15** US state (8)
- **18** Broadest (6)
- **19** Person who goes underwater (5)
- **20** Thoughtfulness (4)
- **22** Puns (anag) (4)
- **24** Metal container; is able to (3)

Crossword

Puzzle 66

Across

1 Support or foundation (4)
3 Formal evening dress (5,3)
9 Smoothing clothes (7)
10 Remnant of a dying fire (5)
11 Lexicons (12)
13 Refund (6)
15 Concerned with sight (6)
17 Reckless; ready to react violently (7-5)
20 Longest river in Europe (5)
21 A very skilled performer (7)
22 Estrange (anag) (8)
23 School bedroom (abbrev) (4)

Down

1 People who construct things (8)
2 Indifferent to emotions (5)
4 Fable (6)
5 Mentally acute (5-7)
6 Group of figures representing a scene (7)
7 Auditory receptors (4)
8 Break up into pieces (12)
12 Recreational area for children (8)
14 Thief (7)
16 Language spoken in Berlin (6)
18 Paved courtyard (5)
19 Days before major events (4)

Puzzle 67

Across

1 Touches gently (4)
3 Evading (8)
9 Tranquil (7)
10 Delicious (5)
11 Characteristic of the present (12)
14 Grassland (3)
16 Armistice (5)
17 Depression (3)
18 Build up again from parts (12)
21 Come with (5)
22 Anxious (7)
23 Oblique (8)
24 Medium-sized feline (4)

Down

1 Immediately (8)
2 Water container (5)
4 ___ Kilmer: famous actor (3)
5 Middleman (12)
6 Secured against loss or damage (7)
7 Men (4)
8 An idea that is added later (12)
12 Rains heavily (5)
13 Supplemental part of a book (8)
15 United States (7)
19 Oneness (5)
20 Falls back (4)
22 Came first in a race (3)

Crossword

Puzzle 68

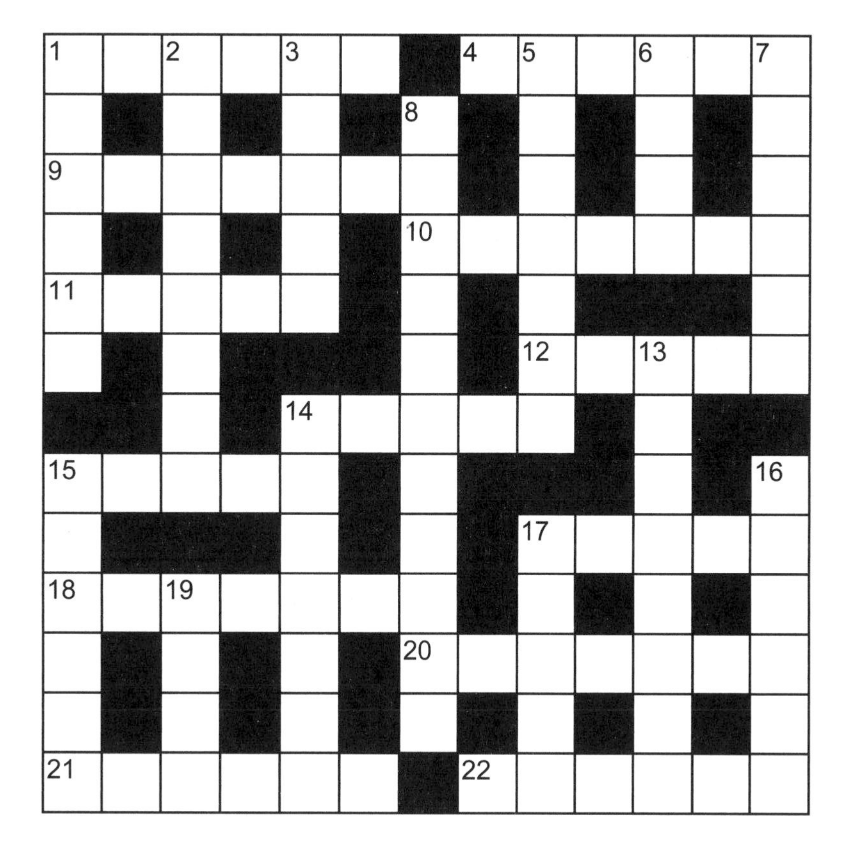

Across

1 Leg bone (6)
4 Frightens (6)
9 Pear-shaped fruit (7)
10 Broad knife (7)
11 Francis ___ : English statesman (5)
12 Staggers (5)
14 Locates or places (5)
15 Excuse or pretext (5)
17 Bird droppings used as fertiliser (5)
18 Things that evoke reactions (7)
20 Citrus fruits (7)
21 Cause to become (6)
22 Person to whom a lease is granted (6)

Down

1 Overweight (6)
2 Green vegetable (8)
3 Discover (5)
5 Agrees (7)
6 Garden implement (4)
7 Toffees or chocolates (6)
8 Contest (11)
13 Makes bigger (8)
14 Put in a certain position (7)
15 Reply (6)
16 Whipped cream dessert (6)
17 Elegance; class (5)
19 Metallic element (4)

Puzzle 69

Across

1 Female chickens (4)
3 Relinquish a throne (8)
9 Hassles; prickles (7)
10 Conditions (5)
11 Science of deciphering codes (12)
14 Cover with steam (of a glass surface) (3)
16 Leaves (5)
17 In favour of (3)
18 Caused by disease (12)
21 Traveller on horseback (5)
22 Regeneration (7)
23 Relating to the Middle Ages (8)
24 Ancient city (4)

Down

1 Shackle (8)
2 Destitute (5)
4 Form of public transport (3)
5 Inflexible (12)
6 Zeppelin (7)
7 Otherwise (4)
8 Framework for washed garments (7,5)
12 Question intensely (5)
13 Unsporting activity (4,4)
15 Protected (7)
19 Crouch down in fear (5)
20 Baby carriage (4)
22 Chris ___ : English singer (3)

Crossword

Puzzle 70

Across

1 Hating (8)
5 Remnant (4)
8 Clergyman (5)
9 Spanish beverage (7)
10 Given; bequeathed (7)
12 Smartened up (7)
14 Acute suffering (7)
16 Examine (7)
18 Henry David ___ : US author and poet (7)
19 Unreliable (5)
20 Roster (4)
21 Uses again (8)

Down

1 Tax (4)
2 Heavy metal weight used by a ship (6)
3 Cyclone (9)
4 Tensed (anag) (6)
6 Propels through the air (6)
7 Wave or flourish in display (8)
11 Insect (9)
12 Sliver of wood (8)
13 Classify (6)
14 Acclimatise or accustom (6)
15 Country in the Middle East (6)
17 Hair colourants (4)

Puzzle 71

Across

- **1** Emulates (6)
- **7** One in charge of a gaming table (8)
- **8** Religious sister (3)
- **9** Substance found in wine (6)
- **10** Dairy product (4)
- **11** First Greek letter (5)
- **13** Dishonesty (7)
- **15** Roof flue (7)
- **17** Go away from quickly (5)
- **21** Public transport vehicle (4)
- **22** Treatises (6)
- **23** Belonging to him (3)
- **24** Feud (8)
- **25** Noisily (6)

Down

- **1** Ottawa is the capital here (6)
- **2** Closely held back (4-2)
- **3** View; picture (5)
- **4** Injured (7)
- **5** Precise and clear (8)
- **6** Brought up (6)
- **12** Created in the house (8)
- **14** Having a valid will (7)
- **16** Rounded up animals (6)
- **18** Hurried (6)
- **19** Waterlogged (6)
- **20** Wild and untamed (5)

Crossword

Puzzle 72

Across

1 Physical weakness (8)
5 Silvery-white metallic element (4)
8 Large group of insects (5)
9 Innocently (7)
10 Last in a series (7)
12 Swam like a dog (7)
14 Edible marine molluscs (7)
16 Large fast warship (7)
18 Illegally in advance of the ball (in football) (7)
19 Embarrass (5)
20 Badger's home (4)
21 Totally uninformed (8)

Down

1 Circular storage medium (4)
2 Made a loud and harsh sound (6)
3 Boundless (9)
4 Intend (anag) (6)
6 Refrigerator compartment (6)
7 Solids with regularly ordered atoms (8)
11 Squander (9)
12 Of great value (8)
13 Meal where guests serve themselves (6)
14 Trying experience (6)
15 Gas with formula C2H6 (6)
17 Therefore (4)

Puzzle 73

Across

1 Next after third (6)
5 Aggressive dog (3)
7 Partly melted snow (5)
8 Overly conceited and arrogant (5-2)
9 Machine for shaping wood or metal (5)
10 Reduction in price (8)
12 Book of the Bible (6)
14 A husband or wife (6)
17 Fighters (8)
18 Needing to be scratched (5)
20 Difficult to catch (7)
21 ___ on: urged; encouraged (5)
22 Head movement showing assent (3)
23 HMS ___ : boat Darwin sailed on (6)

Down

2 Acquires (7)
3 Assume control of (4,4)
4 Quieten down (4)
5 Country house (7)
6 Be given (7)
7 Used up; exhausted (5)
11 An opening (8)
12 Brighten up (7)
13 Duped (7)
15 Wither (7)
16 Scraped at (of an animal) (5)
19 Hindu spiritual discipline (4)

Crossword

Puzzle 74

Across

1 Russian country house (5)
4 Refine metal (5)
10 Ancient jar (7)
11 Triangular wall part (5)
12 Cut of meat (4)
13 Rigorous investigation (8)
16 Robinson ___ : novel (6)
17 Craned (anag) (6)
20 Ornamental climbing plant (8)
21 Retail store (4)
23 Oily organic compound (5)
25 Alike (7)
26 Pointed weapon (5)
27 Hilary ___ : US actress (5)

Down

2 Maximum extent of a vibration (9)
3 Owl cry (4)
5 Ferdinand ___ : Portuguese navigator (8)
6 Research place (abbrev) (3)
7 Characteristically French (6)
8 Precipitates (5)
9 Barrels (4)
14 Artificial sweetener (9)
15 Bowl-shaped strainer (8)
18 Fast-flowing part of a river (6)
19 Ice hockey buildings (5)
20 Cry out (4)
22 Understand; realise (4)
24 Animal foot (3)

Puzzle 75

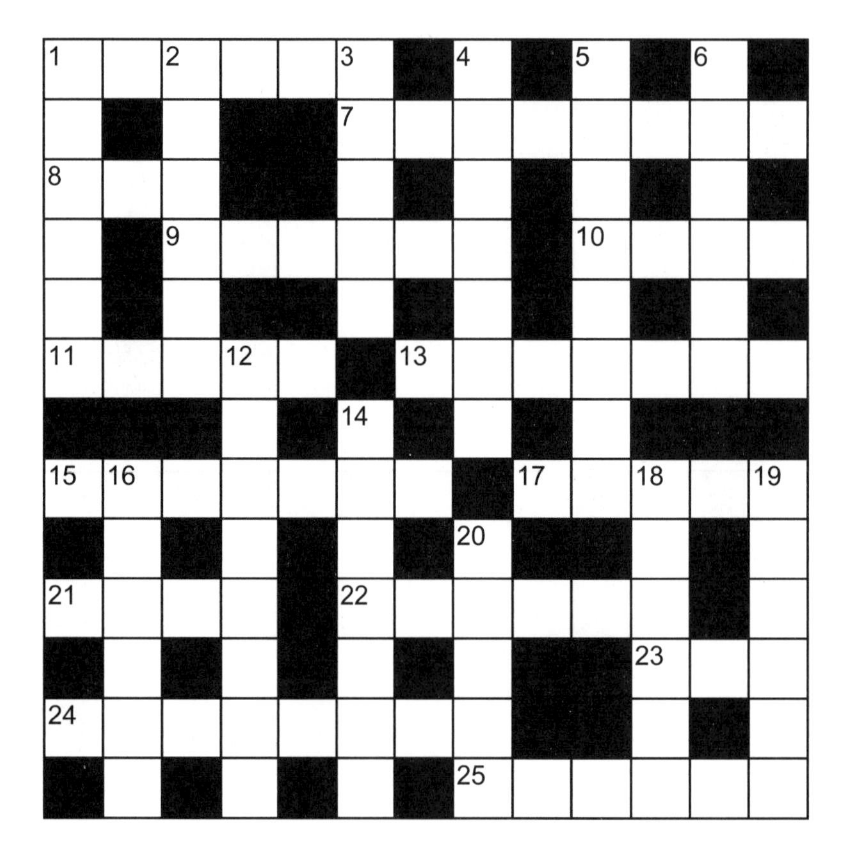

Across

- **1** Spanish festival (6)
- **7** Follower (8)
- **8** Muhammad ___ : boxing great (3)
- **9** Area of flat unforested grassland (6)
- **10** Scheme (4)
- **11** Feeling of boredom (5)
- **13** Moved away from the right course (7)
- **15** Befuddle (7)
- **17** Thigh bone (5)
- **21** Beers (4)
- **22** Academy Awards (6)
- **23** North American nation (abbrev) (3)
- **24** Confined as a prisoner (8)
- **25** Move apart; open out (6)

Down

- **1** European country (6)
- **2** Thomas ___ : US inventor (6)
- **3** Select; formally approve (5)
- **4** Characteristics (7)
- **5** Take over the role of (8)
- **6** Break apart (6)
- **12** Undo; loosen (8)
- **14** Shock with wonder (7)
- **16** Lubricating (6)
- **18** Utilise wrongly (6)
- **19** Recompense for hardship (6)
- **20** Rushes along; skims (5)

Crossword

Puzzle 76

Across

1 Frank and sincere (6)
5 Hog (3)
7 Group of shots (5)
8 Veracity (7)
9 Distinctive design (5)
10 Edible snail (8)
12 Wince (6)
14 Exclusive stories (6)
17 Completes a race (8)
18 Rustic (5)
20 Plain and clear (7)
21 Henrik ___ : Norwegian dramatist (5)
22 Joke (3)
23 ___ Holden: English actress (6)

Down

2 Act of awakening from sleep (7)
3 Teach (8)
4 Poor city district (4)
5 Type of porch (7)
6 Boisterous laughs (7)
7 Church council (5)
11 Radioactive element (8)
12 Sudden outburst of something (5-2)
13 Firmly fix in a person (7)
15 Deer pen (anag) (7)
16 Ascended (5)
19 Tilt to one side (4)

Puzzle 77

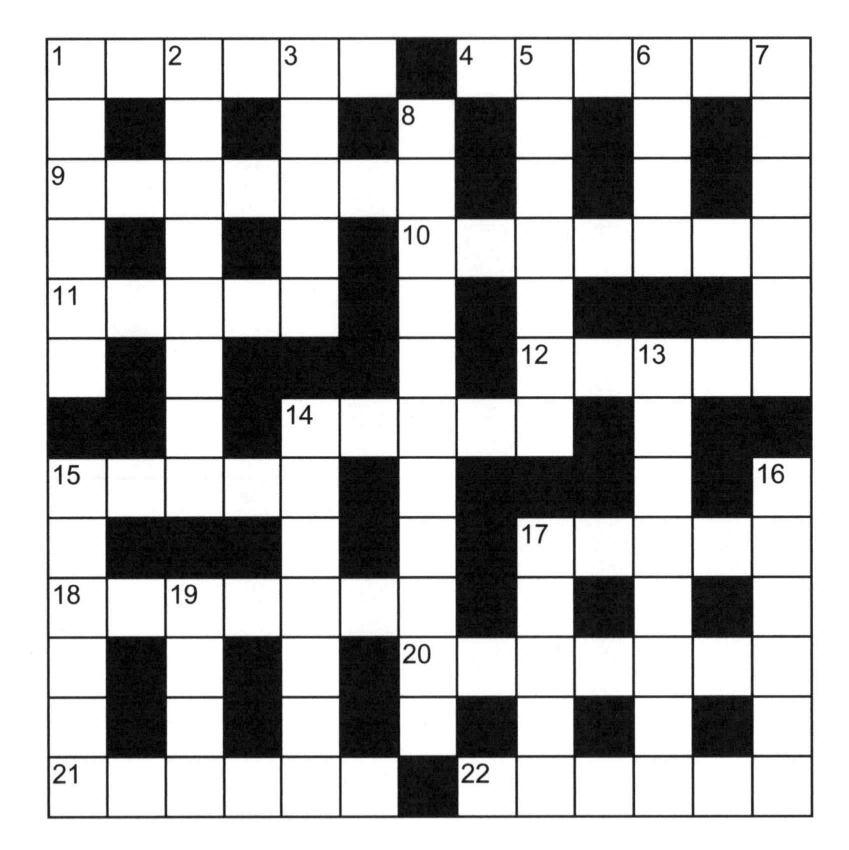

Across

1 Winner (6)
4 Cause to feel upset (6)
9 Taller and thinner (7)
10 Small bone (7)
11 Seven (anag) (5)
12 Make a physical or mental effort (5)
14 Make available for sale (5)
15 Verse form (5)
17 Shed (5)
18 A parent's mother (7)
20 Fabric (7)
21 Promises solemnly (6)
22 Sayings (6)

Down

1 Person who prices things (6)
2 Musical pieces for solo instruments (8)
3 Leaves out (5)
5 Nervous excitement (7)
6 Heroic poem (4)
7 Hate (6)
8 Multiply (11)
13 Abiding (8)
14 Located in the fresh air (7)
15 Scottish dish (6)
16 Capital of Greece (6)
17 Blended (5)
19 Assistant (4)

Crossword

Puzzle 78

Across

1 Not achieving the desired result (11)
9 Rise to one's feet (3,2)
10 Male aristocrat (3)
11 Emerge from an egg (5)
12 Swift (5)
13 Financially ruined (8)
16 Overflowing with praise (8)
18 Simple aquatic plants (5)
21 Roman cloaks (5)
22 Domestic bovine animal (3)
23 Asian country (5)
24 Property professional (6,5)

Down

2 One of the planets (7)
3 Warning device for ships (7)
4 Catch or snare (6)
5 Come to a point (5)
6 Greek writer of fables (5)
7 Occupancy (11)
8 One who held a job previously (11)
14 Small hardy range horse (7)
15 Central bolt (7)
17 Violin (6)
19 Loose garments (5)
20 ___ Dushku: actress (5)

Puzzle 79

Across

1 Dispose of (5)
4 No longer fresh (of food) (5)
10 Confident (7)
11 Eg Amir Khan (5)
12 Run away (4)
13 Stacy ___ : Black Eyed Peas singer (8)
16 Muggy (6)
17 Flat-bottomed rowing-boat (6)
20 Lose (8)
21 ___ and cons: pluses and minuses (4)
23 Recreational activity (5)
25 Grew tired (7)
26 Gave out playing cards (5)
27 Schemes (5)

Down

2 Make-up (9)
3 Askew (4)
5 Sledge (8)
6 Negligent (3)
7 Blunders (6)
8 Borders (5)
9 Sci-fi film with Jeff Bridges (4)
14 Common garden herb (9)
15 Emaciated (8)
18 Favourable aspect of something (6)
19 Unpleasant facial expression (5)
20 Has to (4)
22 Appendage (4)
24 Single in number (3)

Crossword

Puzzle 80

Across

1 Residents (11)
9 A moving part of a generator (5)
10 Stimulus (3)
11 Stage name of Mark Althavean Andrews (5)
12 Language of the Romans (5)
13 Towns with harbours (8)
16 Broadening (8)
18 Stove (anag) (5)
21 The Norwegian language (5)
22 Illumination unit (3)
23 Island in the Mediterranean Sea (5)
24 Pretentious display (11)

Down

2 Male reporter (7)
3 Container releasing a fine spray (7)
4 Meaning; purpose (6)
5 Pertaining to the ear (5)
6 Implied (5)
7 Compulsively (11)
8 Unintelligible (11)
14 Bring a law into effect again (2-5)
15 Wavering vocal quality (7)
17 Charge with a crime (6)
19 US state where one finds Houston (5)
20 Glisten (5)

Crossword

Puzzle 81

Across

1 Searching for prey (8)
5 Musical group (4)
8 Excessively mean (5)
9 Large Israeli city (3,4)
10 Put up with (7)
12 Climbing plant (7)
14 Exacted retribution (7)
16 Meals (7)
18 Secretion of an endocrine gland (7)
19 Suffuse with colour (5)
20 Hardens (4)
21 Most precipitous (8)

Down

1 Agreement (4)
2 Body of work (6)
3 Sweets on sticks (9)
4 Talk idly (6)
6 Promotional material (6)
7 Money paid to shareholders (8)
11 Misleading (9)
12 Places of worship (8)
13 Ghost (6)
14 State confidently (6)
15 Speak rapidly (6)
17 Joke (4)

Crossword

Puzzle 82

Across

1 Ship used by Jason and followers (4)
3 The armed forces (8)
9 Vacuum flask (7)
10 Cylinder of smoking tobacco (5)
11 In a persuasive manner (12)
13 Put briefly into liquid (6)
15 Flowering plant with a prickly stem (6)
17 The dispersal of goods (12)
20 Quantitative relation between two amounts (5)
21 A rich mine; big prize (7)
22 Laughably small (8)
23 Examine quickly (4)

Down

1 Come before in time (8)
2 Obtain information from various sources (5)
4 Six-legged arthropod (6)
5 Irrelevant (12)
6 A Roman Catholic devotion (7)
7 City in North Yorkshire (4)
8 Able to use both hands well (12)
12 Starchy banana-like fruit (8)
14 Artist (7)
16 Warm up (6)
18 Type of chemical bond (5)
19 Parched (4)

Crossword

Puzzle 83

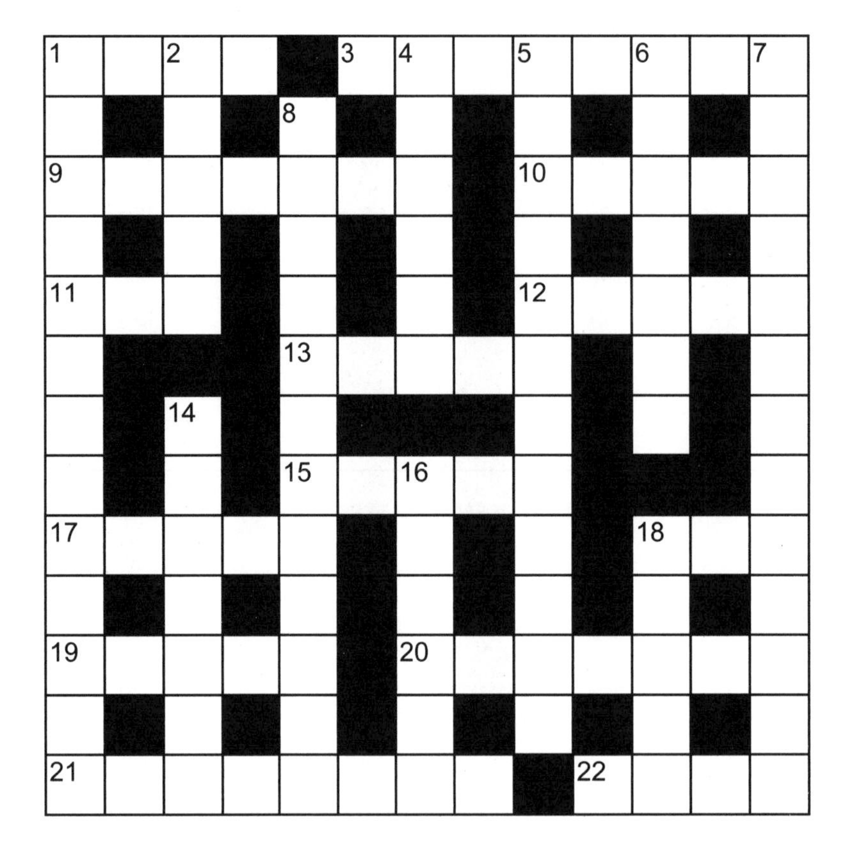

Across

1 US state (4)
3 Disdainful rejection (5-3)
9 Opposite (7)
10 Country whose capital is Tripoli (5)
11 Friend (3)
12 Gate fastener (5)
13 ___ Berry: actress (5)
15 Underside of a projecting roof (5)
17 Damien ___ : modern English artist (5)
18 Type of statistical chart (3)
19 Simple (5)
20 Whipping (7)
21 Lens for improving vision (8)
22 Dispatched (4)

Down

1 Totally trustworthy (13)
2 Auditory ossicle (5)
4 Expressing regret (6)
5 Altruism (12)
6 Passing around a town (of a road) (7)
7 Boxing class division (13)
8 Relating to numeric calculations (12)
14 Envisage (7)
16 Bowed string instruments (6)
18 Open up (5)

Crossword

Puzzle 84

Across

1 Act of sticking together (8)
5 Matured (4)
9 Very masculine (5)
10 Thick slices (5)
11 Eg cooking in a wok (4-6)
14 Sloping (of a typeface) (6)
15 Quick look (6)
17 Study of the mind (10)
20 Ethos (anag) (5)
21 Sing like a bird (5)
22 Conceal (4)
23 Favourably disposed towards (8)

Down

1 Temporary living quarters (4)
2 Access illegally (4)
3 Myopic (5-7)
4 Strong public protest (6)
6 Slope (8)
7 Creator (8)
8 Relating to horoscopes (12)
12 Send off to a destination (8)
13 Infancy (8)
16 Large bottle for wine (6)
18 Oven or furnace (4)
19 Travelled too quickly (4)

Puzzle 85

Across

1 Be aggrieved by (6)
7 Be heavier than (8)
8 Mauna ___ : Hawaiian volcano (3)
9 Drinking vessel (6)
10 Sea eagle (4)
11 Carer (anag) (5)
13 Word opposite in meaning to another (7)
15 More saccharine (7)
17 Woody tissue (5)
21 Give up one's rights (4)
22 Person after whom a discovery is named (6)
23 Knot with a double loop (3)
24 Make fun of (8)
25 Series of prayers (6)

Down

1 Long swelling wave (6)
2 Not moving (6)
3 Come into direct contact with (5)
4 Regular salary (7)
5 Dominance by one group over others (8)
6 Business organisation (6)
12 Critical explanation (8)
14 Income (7)
16 Beetle that damages grain (6)
18 11th Greek letter (6)
19 Towards the middle of something (6)
20 Garden tool for cutting grass (5)

Crossword

Puzzle 86

Across

7 Abandoned (8)
8 ___ Duncan Smith: politician (4)
9 Grey-haired with age (4)
10 Copycat (8)
11 Parcel (7)
12 Small woodland (5)
15 Attractive (5)
17 Concern; implicate (7)
20 Set free (8)
22 ___ Macpherson: Australian model (4)
23 Repeat an action (4)
24 Made untidy with rubbish (8)

Down

1 Spanish title for a married woman (6)
2 Tall type of furry hat (8)
3 Part of an orchestra (7)
4 Mingle with something else (5)
5 ___ Minnelli: US actress (4)
6 People who fly aeroplanes (6)
13 Device recording distance travelled (8)
14 Turns upside down (7)
16 Voiles (anag) (6)
18 Principles (6)
19 Shopping centres (US) (5)
21 Greek god of love (4)

Puzzle 87

Across

1 Vex (4)
3 Dead end (3-2-3)
9 Adult (5-2)
10 Viewpoint (5)
11 Pay tribute to another (12)
13 Consider to be true (6)
15 Sear (6)
17 Changes to a situation (12)
20 Totem (anag) (5)
21 Not limited to one class (7)
22 Notes (8)
23 Dull heavy sound (4)

Down

1 Sorcerer (8)
2 Scowl (5)
4 Self-important; arrogant (6)
5 Action of moving a thing from its position (12)
6 Break into pieces (7)
7 Pretty (4)
8 Someone who sets up their own business (12)
12 Made a high-pitched sound (8)
14 Makes (7)
16 Cause bafflement (6)
18 ___ Jones: American singer-songwriter (5)
19 Eg bullets (abbrev) (4)

Puzzle 88

Across

1 Chess piece (6)
7 Socialist part of a political party (4,4)
8 Large dark antelope (3)
9 Black Sea peninsula (6)
10 Place where a wild animal lives (4)
11 Crevices (5)
13 Intoxicating element in wine (7)
15 Hopes to achieve (7)
17 Try (5)
21 Pack carefully and neatly (4)
22 Rich cake (6)
23 Fishing pole (3)
24 Angel of the highest order (8)
25 Seem (6)

Down

1 Famous London clock (3,3)
2 Plaster for coating walls (6)
3 Long cloud of smoke (5)
4 In a friendly manner (7)
5 Migratory birds (8)
6 Deep blue colour (6)
12 Woollen clothing (8)
14 Distances (7)
16 Long-haired breed of dog (6)
18 Place of origination (6)
19 Over there (6)
20 Minute pore in a leaf (5)

Puzzle 89

Across

1 Unattractive (4)
3 Forceful (8)
9 Suggested a course of action (7)
10 Pied ___ of Hamelin: legendary person (5)
11 Scoundrel (3)
12 Historic nobleman (5)
13 Between eighth and tenth (5)
15 Crouch (5)
17 Hard and durable (5)
18 Range of knowledge (3)
19 ___ Willis: Unbreakable actor (5)
20 Form a mental picture (7)
21 Individual things (8)
22 Relax and do little (4)

Down

1 Inexplicable (13)
2 Cherished (5)
4 Make angry (6)
5 Conjectural (12)
6 Art of clipping shrubs decoratively (7)
7 Person who writes letters regularly (13)
8 Amazement (12)
14 Bunch of flowers (7)
16 Not sensible (6)
18 Cutting instrument (5)

Crossword

Puzzle 90

Across

1 Small crustacean (6)
7 To some degree (8)
8 Canine (3)
9 Strong-smelling bulb (6)
10 ___ Forever: Spice Girls hit (4)
11 Network points where lines intersect (5)
13 Foolish (7)
15 Supreme fleet commander (7)
17 Synthetic fabric (5)
21 Knowledge (abbrev) (4)
22 Soft white fibre (6)
23 Edible nut (3)
24 Suggestive remark (8)
25 Grinding tool (6)

Down

1 Make unhappy (6)
2 Tattered (6)
3 Sacred hymn or song (5)
4 Lap of a track (7)
5 Courtesy towards women (8)
6 Hand protectors (6)
12 Concluding section (8)
14 Immunising agent (7)
16 Act of eating out (6)
18 Surgical knife (6)
19 Gnaw (6)
20 Device used to sharpen razors (5)

Puzzle 91

Across

1 Adds (4)
3 Authorises (8)
9 Triumph (7)
10 Unit of weight (5)
11 Pond-dwelling amphibians (5)
12 Inflamed (a feeling) (7)
13 Jumped on one leg (6)
15 Yellow fruit (6)
17 Ugly building (7)
18 Upright (5)
20 Blood vessels (5)
21 Short moral story (7)
22 Recently married (5-3)
23 Inspires fear and wonder (4)

Down

1 State of extreme happiness (7,6)
2 Parrot (5)
4 Bribe (3-3)
5 Large Brazilian city (3,2,7)
6 Ice cream flavour (7)
7 Loyalty in the face of trouble (13)
8 In a carefree manner (12)
14 Trailer (7)
16 Place of worship (6)
19 Arm joint (5)

Crossword

Puzzle 92

Across

1 Unit of linear measure (4)
3 Grammatical case (8)
9 Litter (7)
10 Spin quickly (5)
11 Popular edible fish (3)
12 Very informal phrases (5)
13 Arduous search for something (5)
15 Loft (5)
17 Eg the Thames (5)
18 Animal enclosure (3)
19 Flat-bottomed boat (5)
20 Slanting (7)
21 Revealing a truth (8)
22 Encounter; come across (4)

Down

1 Irretrievable (13)
2 Raised to the third power (5)
4 Act properly (6)
5 In a creative manner (12)
6 Copy; mimic (7)
7 The ___ : intellectual movement (13)
8 Squint harder (anag) (12)
14 Attempt to hide the truth (5-2)
16 Confused or disconcerted (6)
18 Wound the pride of (5)

Puzzle 93

Across

1 Bay (4)
3 Without fortune (8)
9 Refiles (anag) (7)
10 In a slow tempo (of music) (5)
11 Denise van ___ : English actress (5)
12 Three-pronged weapon (7)
13 Fillings (6)
15 Toxin (6)
17 Changed gradually (7)
18 Capital of Egypt (5)
20 Eg Pacific or Atlantic (5)
21 Fish-eating birds of prey (7)
22 Gives strength to (8)
23 Remain in the same place (4)

Down

1 Period of the Paleozoic era (13)
2 Personal attendant (5)
4 Surprise results (6)
5 Children's toy (12)
6 People who make money (7)
7 Impulsively (13)
8 US state (12)
14 Slackens (7)
16 Border (6)
19 Inactive (5)

Crossword

Puzzle 94

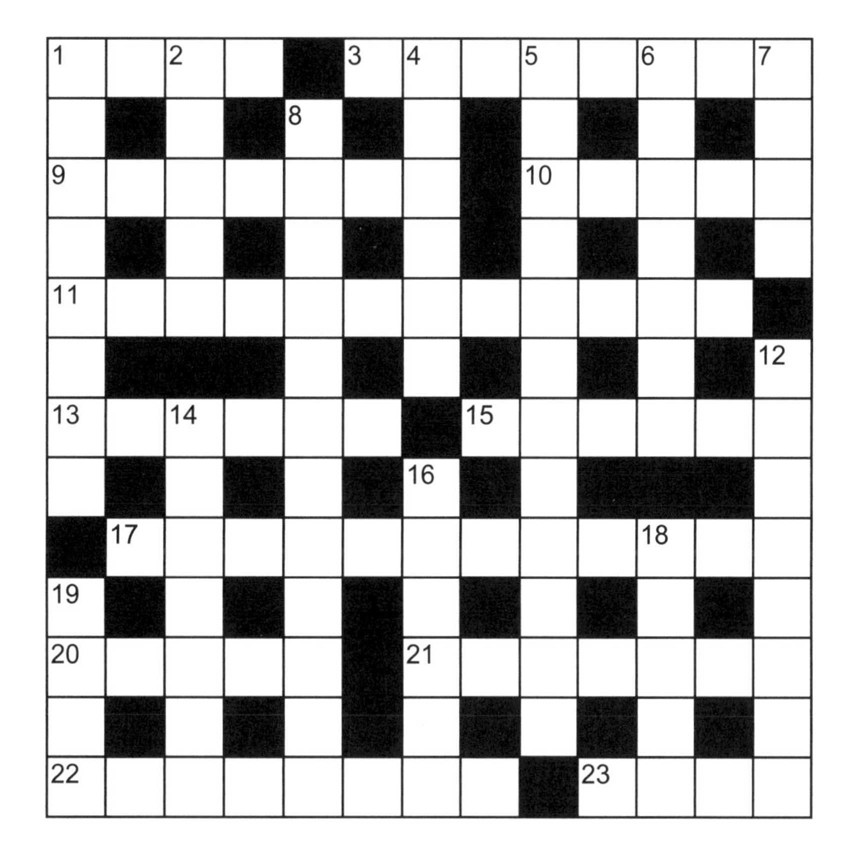

Across

1 Hens lay these (4)
3 Work outfits (8)
9 Mocking (7)
10 Surprise result (5)
11 Total destruction (12)
13 Light volcanic rock (6)
15 Dinner jacket (6)
17 Awkward (12)
20 Masculine in appearance (5)
21 Nasal opening (7)
22 Musical composition (8)
23 In an inactive way; with no particular purpose (4)

Down

1 Measure of the heat content of a system (8)
2 Speck of food (5)
4 Small worry; irritate (6)
5 Productivity (12)
6 Reinstate (7)
7 Locate or place (4)
8 Garments worn in bed (12)
12 Inn (8)
14 The small details of something (7)
16 Flattened out (6)
18 Long-___ owl: bird (5)
19 Seal of the Archbishop of York (4)

Crossword

Puzzle 95

Across

1 Segment of the spinal column (8)
5 Con; swindle (4)
8 Crazy (5)
9 Country in N Africa (7)
10 Division of the UK (7)
12 Burdened (7)
14 Writes untidily (7)
16 Decipher (7)
18 Malady (7)
19 ___ Lewis: British singer (5)
20 Deities (4)
21 Getting away from (8)

Down

1 Plant of the grape family (4)
2 Plump (6)
3 The origin of a word (9)
4 Decayed (6)
6 Relaxed and informal (6)
7 Wanders (of a stream) (8)
11 ___ Cilmi: Australian singer (9)
12 Sailing swiftly (8)
13 Climbed (6)
14 Stagnation or inactivity (6)
15 ___ Goldberg: US actress (6)
17 Feeling of hunger (4)

Crossword

Puzzle 96

Across

1 Spherical objects (4)
3 Musical composition (8)
9 Constantly present (7)
10 Fits of violent anger (5)
11 Erase trumpet (anag) (12)
14 Umpire (abbrev) (3)
16 Runs at a moderate pace (5)
17 Secret agent (3)
18 Capable of being moved (12)
21 Mortal (5)
22 Country in West Africa (7)
23 Extreme reproach (8)
24 Gossip (4)

Down

1 Capsize (8)
2 Darken (5)
4 Mythical monster (3)
5 Restrict within limits (12)
6 Return to a former state (7)
7 Kiln for drying hops (4)
8 Impudence (12)
12 Remote in manner (5)
13 Always in a similar role (of an actor) (8)
15 Supervisory worker (7)
19 Time when life begins (5)
20 Stylish (4)
22 One circuit of a track (3)

Puzzle 97

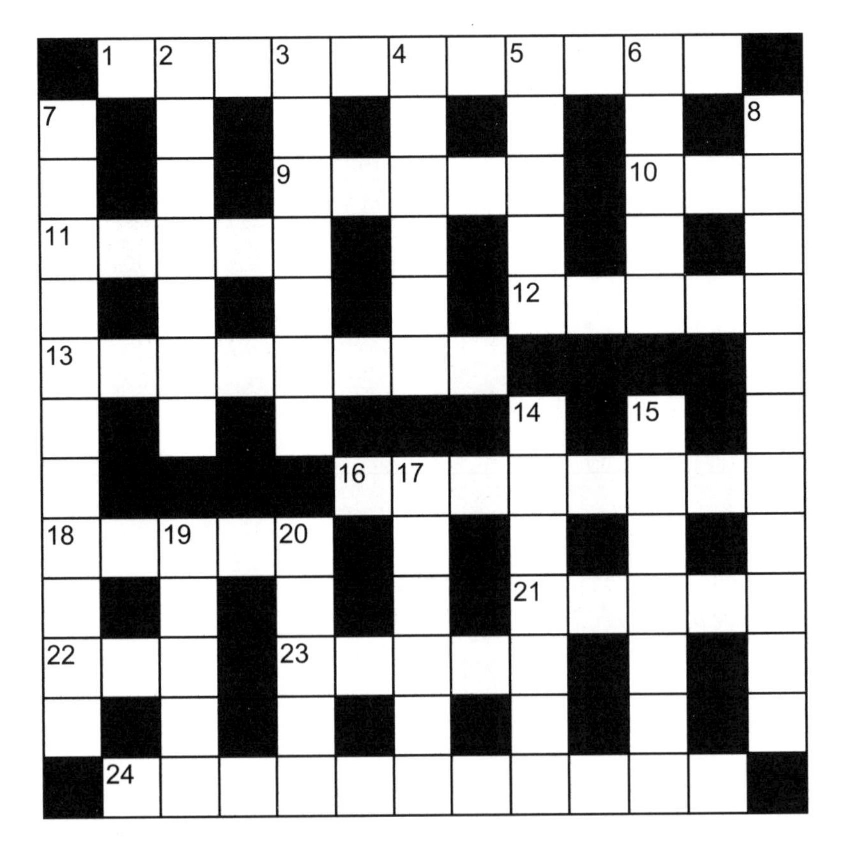

Across

1 Flower (6-2-3)
9 Bond or connection (5)
10 Posed (3)
11 Debate in a heated manner (5)
12 Focused light beam (5)
13 Capital of Chile (8)
16 Small crustacean (8)
18 Hear a court case anew (5)
21 Use to one's advantage (5)
22 Nothing (3)
23 Bart's father in the Simpsons (5)
24 Amazing (11)

Down

2 Starting points (7)
3 Book of the Bible (7)
4 Difficult (6)
5 Self-supporting wooden frame (5)
6 Fertile area in a desert (5)
7 Diaphanous (11)
8 Narrator (11)
14 Dig out of the ground (7)
15 Eight-sided polygon (7)
17 Former students (6)
19 Leans at an angle (5)
20 Loutish person (5)

Crossword

Puzzle 98

Across

1 Ancient boats (4)
3 Speak unfavourably about (3-5)
9 Soothsayer (7)
10 Position or point (5)
11 Perceptions (12)
14 Vehicle (3)
16 Venomous snake (5)
17 Opposite of no (3)
18 Unpleasant (12)
21 Mistaken (5)
22 Reveals (anag) (7)
23 Plummet (8)
24 Goad on (4)

Down

1 Come nearer to (8)
2 Understands; realises (5)
4 Small social insect (3)
5 Agreed upon by several parties (12)
6 Mysterious (7)
7 Silence (4)
8 Cheated someone financially (5-7)
12 Natural yellow resin (5)
13 Evaluator (8)
15 Destructive (7)
19 High-pitched tone (5)
20 Link a town with another (4)
22 ___ Tyler: actress (3)

Puzzle 99

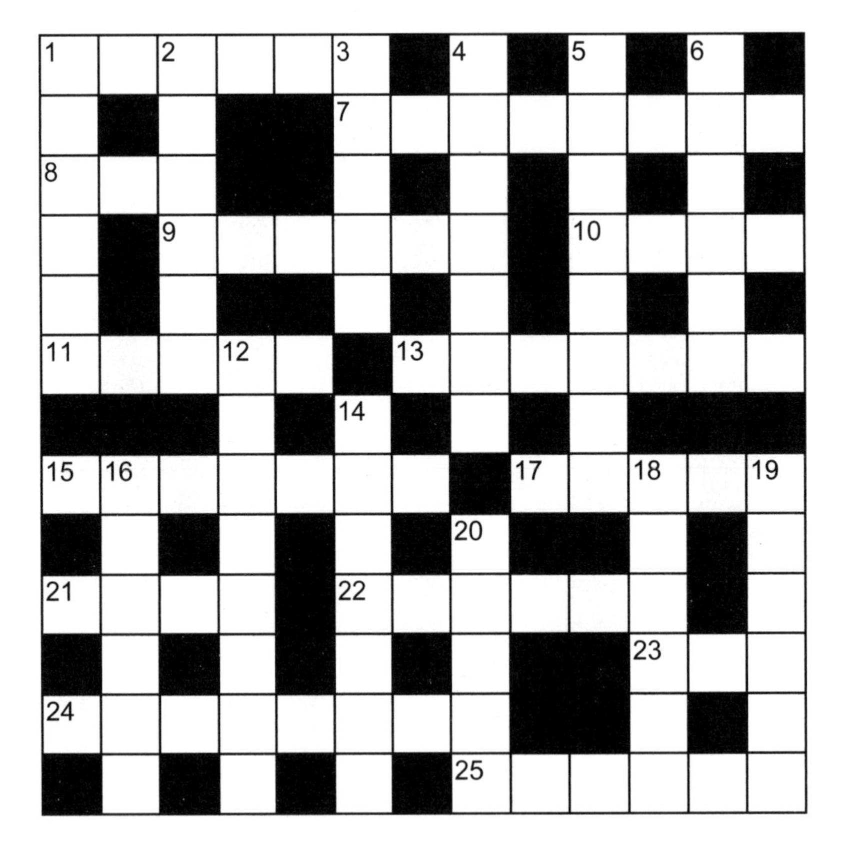

Across

1 Type of tent (6)
7 Undo a shirt (8)
8 Blade for rowing a boat (3)
9 ___ Moon: Character in Frasier (6)
10 Curved (4)
11 Head over ___ : totally (in love) (5)
13 Choose and follow (7)
15 Implement (7)
17 One image within another (5)
21 South American country (4)
22 Large dark cloud (6)
23 Possesses (3)
24 Less dark (8)
25 Fine cloth (6)

Down

1 Loud rushing noise (6)
2 Belt worn round the waist (6)
3 Pulpy (5)
4 Alongside each other (7)
5 Resolute (8)
6 Activities a person engages in (6)
12 Tongue (8)
14 Composed or serious manner (7)
16 System of ideas to explain something (6)
18 Long strips of cloth (6)
19 Scrap (6)
20 Hurt; clever (5)

Crossword

Puzzle 100

Across

- **1** Shine (4)
- **3** Agreeable (8)
- **9** Prospered (7)
- **10** ___ Sarandon: US actress (5)
- **11** Study of human societies (12)
- **14** Diving bird (3)
- **16** Change; modify (5)
- **17** Net (anag) (3)
- **18** Impossible to achieve (12)
- **21** Relating to sound (5)
- **22** Talk tediously or at length (7)
- **23** Starved (8)
- **24** Require (4)

Down

- **1** Act of treachery (8)
- **2** Top degree mark (5)
- **4** Bottle top (3)
- **5** Completeness (12)
- **6** Clear perception (7)
- **7** Mob (4)
- **8** Unnecessarily careful (12)
- **12** Public square (5)
- **13** Set in from the margin (8)
- **15** Royal domain (7)
- **19** Hold responsible (5)
- **20** Child who has no home (4)
- **22** Female kangaroo (3)

Puzzle 101

Across

1 Exhausts (4)
3 Talking (8)
9 Discourse (7)
10 Cowboy exhibition (5)
11 Uptight (5)
12 Furry nocturnal carnivorous mammal (7)
13 Flowing back (6)
15 Enclosed recess (6)
17 Resistance to change (7)
18 Wedding official (5)
20 ___ Milan: Italian football club (5)
21 Cooked meat in the oven (7)
22 Provoking (8)
23 Catch sight of (4)

Down

1 Judgement that is not unanimous (5,8)
2 Brown nut (5)
4 Metrical writing (6)
5 Relating to farming (12)
6 Not outside (7)
7 Amiably (4-9)
8 Occult (12)
14 Respire (7)
16 Financier (6)
19 Dislikes intensely (5)

Puzzle 102

Across

1 Consideration of the future (11)
9 Outdo (5)
10 Sticky substance (3)
11 Liquid essential for life (5)
12 Birds lay their eggs in these (5)
13 Last (8)
16 Symmetrical open plane curve (8)
18 Cuban folk dance (5)
21 Country once ruled by Papa Doc (5)
22 Long period of time (3)
23 ___ Klum: supermodel (5)
24 Having greatest importance (11)

Down

2 Driving out (7)
3 Exceptional; not usual (7)
4 Homes (6)
5 Unfasten a garment (5)
6 Opposite of lows (5)
7 Dejected; discouraged (11)
8 Plant of the cabbage family (11)
14 Mode (7)
15 On the ___ : about to happen (7)
17 Chamber of the heart (6)
19 Lesser (5)
20 Small insect (5)

Puzzle 103

Across

1 Goodbye (Spanish) (5)
4 Climb (5)
10 Newness (7)
11 Performer (5)
12 Rank (4)
13 Vehicle with three wheels (8)
16 Sadness (6)
17 Dried grape (6)
20 Dregs (8)
21 Unpleasant smell (4)
23 Threshold (5)
25 Biggest (7)
26 Glasses (abbrev) (5)
27 Anxiety (5)

Down

2 Reduced (9)
3 Sound of a pig (4)
5 Form of carbon (8)
6 Allow (3)
7 For the time being (3,3)
8 Monster with nine heads (5)
9 At liberty (4)
14 Clients (9)
15 Having a strong smell (8)
18 Periods of darkness (6)
19 Went down on one knee (5)
20 Marine flatfish (4)
22 A parent's mother (4)
24 Soak up; wipe away (3)

Crossword

Puzzle 104

Across

1 Ten-cent coin (US) (4)
3 Spattered with liquid (8)
9 End result (7)
10 Rotates (5)
11 Malfunction or fail (of an electrical device) (5-7)
13 Small pit or cavity (6)
15 Support (6)
17 Unfriendly (12)
20 Eg motorways (5)
21 Pasta strips (7)
22 Enclosed area in a farm (8)
23 Hoofed grazing mammal (4)

Down

1 Sleepily (8)
2 Saying; slogan (5)
4 Event which precedes another (6)
5 Prediction or expectation (12)
6 Courageous woman (7)
7 Piece of office furniture (4)
8 Endlessly (12)
12 Peacemaker (8)
14 Mythical being (7)
16 Batsman who starts an innings (6)
18 Attractive young lady (5)
19 Dull (4)

Puzzle 105

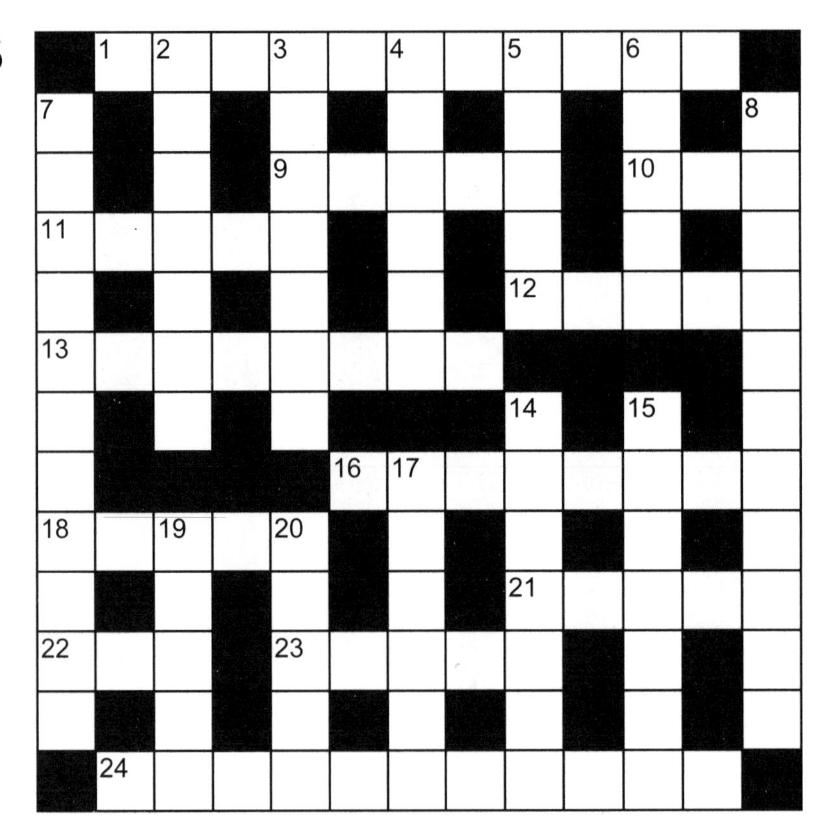

Across

1 Thing that may happen (11)
9 Island in the Bay of Naples (5)
10 Cry of disapproval (3)
11 Turf out (5)
12 Style of Greek architecture (5)
13 Small flesh-eating mammal (8)
16 Cruel (8)
18 Savour (5)
21 Warms up (5)
22 Consume food (3)
23 Young male horses (5)
24 Energetically (11)

Down

2 Choices (7)
3 Subdivision (7)
4 Go around (6)
5 Landowner (5)
6 Underground enlarged stem (5)
7 Item that measures temperature (11)
8 Witches (11)
14 Vivid purplish-red colour (7)
15 Sugar heated until it turns brown (7)
17 Central parts of cells (6)
19 Small pier (5)
20 Woody-stemmed plant (5)

Puzzle 106

Across

1 Ornamental structure in a pool (8)
5 Condemn to destruction (4)
8 Number in a trilogy (5)
9 Posting (7)
10 Person moved from danger (7)
12 Equalled (7)
14 Puzzling and obscure (7)
16 Gnawing animal (7)
18 Child's room (7)
19 U-shaped curve in a river (5)
20 Grind food (4)
21 Unequal; biased (3-5)

Down

1 Fundraising party (4)
2 Turbulence (6)
3 Cutting; incisive (9)
4 Given out (6)
6 Repulsive (6)
7 Very attractive (of personality) (8)
11 Containing no water (9)
12 Person who repairs cars (8)
13 Come into view (6)
14 Stick of coloured wax (6)
15 Murky (6)
17 Still to be paid (4)

Puzzle 107

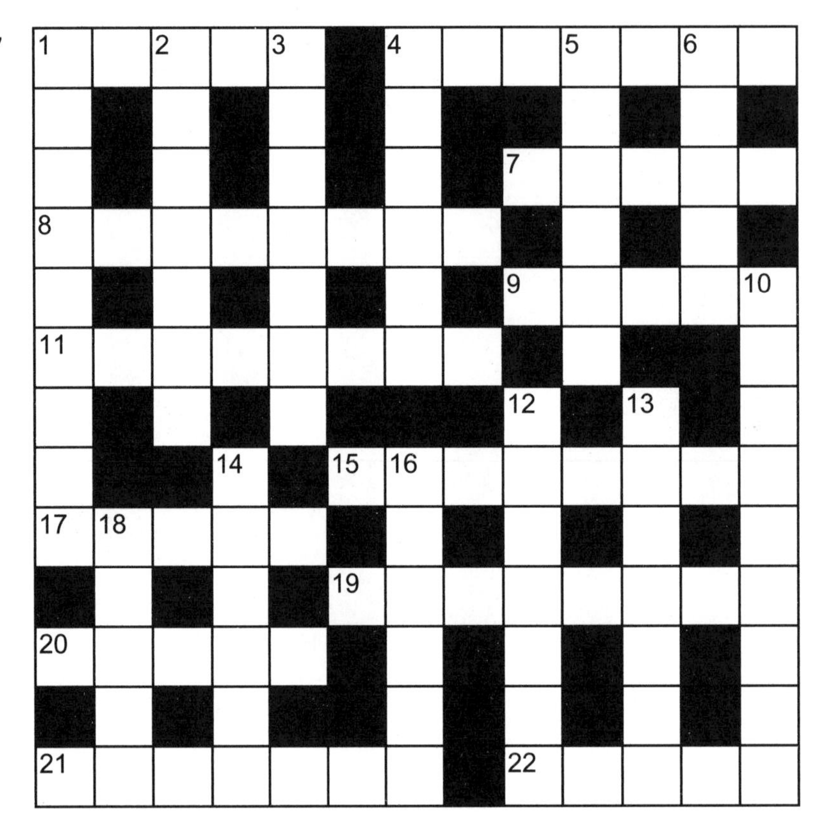

Across

1 Targeted (5)
4 Guglielmo ___ : radio pioneer (7)
7 Soothes (5)
8 Omission from speech of superfluous words (8)
9 Looks after oneself (5)
11 Casual (8)
15 Beginning (8)
17 Variety show (5)
19 Official document (8)
20 Unable to move (5)
21 Better for the environment (7)
22 Member of the weasel family (5)

Down

1 Small dish eaten before a meal (9)
2 Appease; placate (7)
3 Cook in hot fat (4-3)
4 Smallest quantities (6)
5 Pursues (6)
6 Titled (5)
10 Tiniest (9)
12 Betrays (slang) (7)
13 Italian dish (7)
14 Brawn; strength (6)
16 Person who buys and sells (6)
18 Trees (anag); organic compound (5)

Crossword

Puzzle 108

Across

1 ___ Plath: author of The Bell Jar (6)
7 Reinforce (8)
8 Saw (anag) (3)
9 Place of education (6)
10 Sound of a cat (4)
11 Less common (5)
13 Walks with long steps (7)
15 Vivid (7)
17 Obscure road (5)
21 Arthur ___ : former US tennis player (4)
22 Boiled sweet (6)
23 What you hear with (3)
24 Midwestern US state (8)
25 Of inferior quality (6)

Down

1 Woodcutter (6)
2 Not so important (6)
3 Head monk (5)
4 Eg Mo Farah (7)
5 Irritably (8)
6 On the beach; on land (6)
12 Strong type of coffee (8)
14 Soft metallic element (7)
16 World's largest country (6)
18 Gambles (6)
19 Annually (6)
20 Scope or extent (5)

Puzzle 109

Across
- **1** Figure of speech (6)
- **4** Fix (6)
- **9** Endure (7)
- **10** Observes (7)
- **11** Ten more than forty (5)
- **12** Supply with new weapons (5)
- **14** Nobleman (5)
- **15** Mosquito (5)
- **17** Small farm (5)
- **18** Natural environment (7)
- **20** Left out (7)
- **21** Oppose (6)
- **22** Instrument panel (6)

Down
- **1** Fills up (6)
- **2** Changed (8)
- **3** Truck (5)
- **5** Oriental (7)
- **6** ___ Stewart: ex-England cricketer (4)
- **7** Payment for the release of someone (6)
- **8** Snake (11)
- **13** Type of puzzle (8)
- **14** Insects with biting mouthparts (7)
- **15** Fibre from the angora goat (6)
- **16** Sporting venues (6)
- **17** Porcelain (5)
- **19** Wagers (4)

Crossword

Puzzle 110

Across

1 Splendid display and ceremony (4)
3 Moved at a fast canter (8)
9 Small fish (7)
10 Latin American dance (5)
11 Clearness (12)
13 Tune (6)
15 Electric generator (6)
17 Omit too much detail (12)
20 Meat and vegetables on a skewer (5)
21 Hurtful (7)
22 Feigns (8)
23 Run at a moderate pace (4)

Down

1 School break (8)
2 Variety of strong coffee (5)
4 Regardless (6)
5 As quickly as possible (7-5)
6 Remedy for everything (7)
7 Small drink of spirits (4)
8 Significant (12)
12 Knowing many languages (8)
14 Deserving affection (7)
16 Walked awkwardly (6)
18 Deduce or conclude (5)
19 Bypass (4)

Puzzle 111

Across

1 Pulled (a muscle) (8)
5 Affectedly dainty (4)
8 Competed in a speed contest (5)
9 Daydream (7)
10 Heist (7)
12 Yellow fruits (7)
14 Motivate (7)
16 Currents of air (7)
18 Vague and uncertain (7)
19 Skilled job (5)
20 Quantity of medication (4)
21 Choosing to take up or follow (8)

Down

1 South Asian garment (4)
2 Establish by calculation (6)
3 Security against a loss (9)
4 Mistakes (6)
6 Laboured (6)
7 All people (8)
11 Yellow flower (9)
12 Fashionable term (8)
13 Musical works (6)
14 Go up (6)
15 Opposite of an acid (6)
17 Adult male deer (4)

Crossword

Puzzle 112

Across

1 Form of accommodation (4)
3 Happened (8)
9 Compensates for (7)
10 Disgust (5)
11 Incessantly (12)
13 Morsels of food (6)
15 Tranquil (6)
17 Lacking courage (5-7)
20 Measure heaviness (5)
21 Gold or silver in bulk (7)
22 Reverie (8)
23 Clothed (4)

Down

1 Grow in a vigorous way (8)
2 Dreadful (5)
4 Fortified medieval building (6)
5 Not capable of reply (12)
6 Drive back by force (7)
7 Bob ___ : US politician (4)
8 Miser (5-7)
12 Made (a noise) less intense (8)
14 The world as it is (7)
16 Irrational fear (6)
18 Quavering sound (5)
19 Inspired by reverence (4)

Puzzle 113

Across

1 Taking away (8)
5 Move fast in a straight line (4)
8 Wounded by a wasp (5)
9 Mishits (7)
10 Departing (7)
12 Fashion anew (7)
14 Segmented worm (7)
16 Surpasses (7)
18 Cross-bred dog (7)
19 Camel-like animal (5)
20 Mend with rows of stitches (4)
21 In the open air (8)

Down

1 Justin ___ : golfer (4)
2 Cave openings (6)
3 Watchfulness (9)
4 Agile (6)
6 Child of your aunt or uncle (6)
7 Made with purpose; planned (8)
11 Friendly towards a younger person (9)
12 Uncovered; displayed (8)
13 Cricket statistician (6)
14 Relating to stars (6)
15 Residents of an area (6)
17 Roman censor (4)

Crossword

Puzzle 114

Across

1 Method; fashion (4)
3 Cause resentment (8)
9 Critiques (7)
10 Burrowing animals (5)
11 Very determined (6-6)
14 Type of viper (3)
16 ___ Piper: potato (5)
17 Blue ___ : bird (3)
18 Made (12)
21 Small cabin (5)
22 Enlarged; puffy (7)
23 Representative example (8)
24 Centre of rotation (4)

Down

1 Someone skilled in shooting (8)
2 Backless sofa (5)
4 Title of a married woman (3)
5 Vaccination (12)
6 Greatest in height (7)
7 Expose to danger (4)
8 Afraid to speak frankly (5-7)
12 ___ Sharapova: tennis player (5)
13 School pupils (8)
15 Large flat dish (7)
19 Loosen up (5)
20 Vessel (4)
22 Bulge downwards under pressure (3)

Puzzle 115

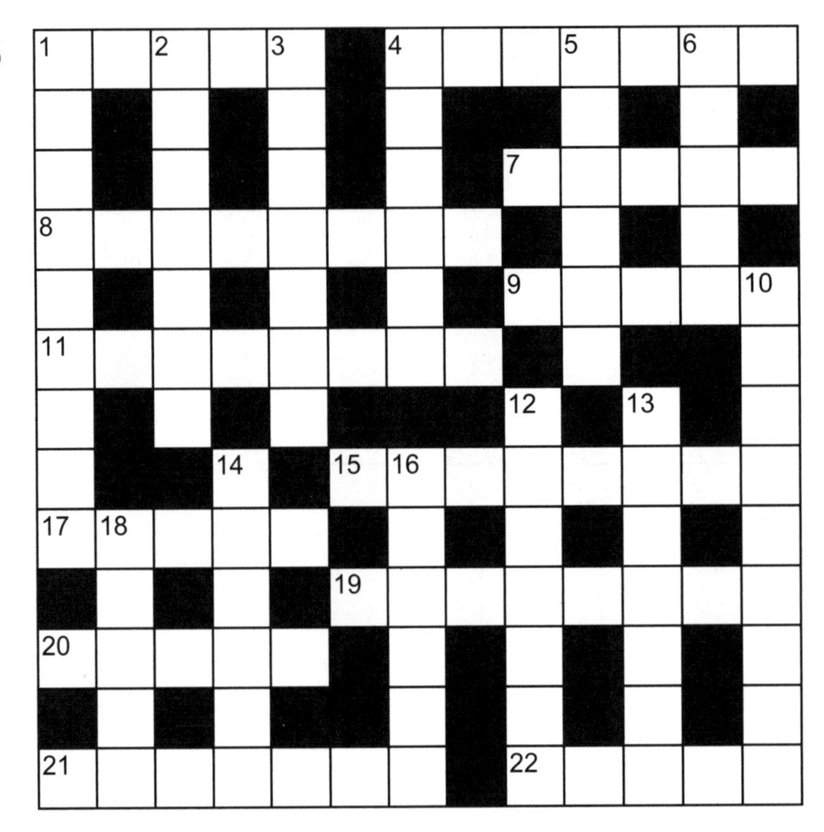

Across

1 Chaplain in the armed services (5)
4 Leader of a community (7)
7 Become subject to (5)
8 Grandiosity of language (8)
9 Cereal plant (5)
11 Extremely accomplished (8)
15 Tack with a large head (8)
17 Mountain cry (5)
19 Determined (8)
20 Military opponent (5)
21 Traversed (7)
22 Give up (5)

Down

1 Heritage (9)
2 Varied (7)
3 Laid open to view (7)
4 Mark ___ : Star Wars actor (6)
5 Daniel (anag) (6)
6 Humming (5)
10 Very sharp and perceptive (5-4)
12 Arsenal (7)
13 Minute cavity in organic tissue (7)
14 Assumed propositions (6)
16 Complied with orders (6)
18 Possessor (5)

Crossword

Puzzle 116

Across

1 Brilliant performers (8)
5 Russian monarch (4)
9 One who steals (5)
10 Hankered after (5)
11 Swimming stroke (10)
14 Inborn (6)
15 Plan of action (6)
17 City of London (6,4)
20 Series of linked metal rings (5)
21 Direct competitor (5)
22 Observed (4)
23 Dark colour that is virtually black (4,4)

Down

1 Ballot choice (4)
2 Liquid precipitation (4)
3 Uncomplimentary (12)
4 Eerie; sinister (6)
6 Educated (8)
7 Blushed (8)
8 Especially (12)
12 Cuts into bits (8)
13 Prevent heat loss (8)
16 Leaping antelope (6)
18 Egg-shaped (4)
19 ___ vera: used in cosmetics (4)

Puzzle 117

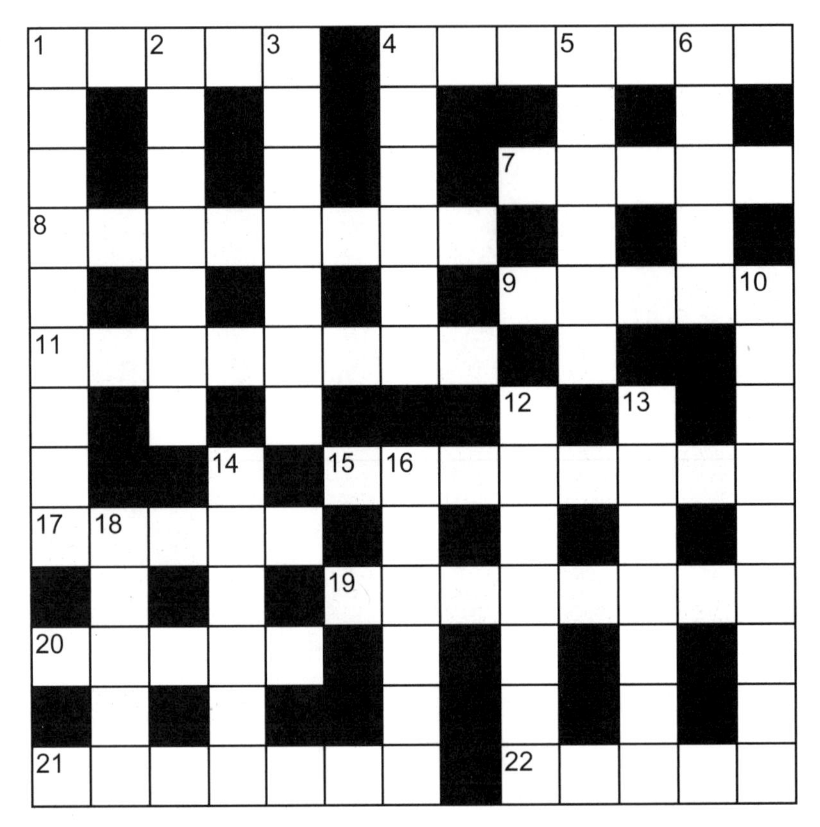

Across

1 Social division in some societies (5)
4 Embarrassed (7)
7 Loose fibre from old rope (5)
8 Sparkling (8)
9 Indian monetary unit (5)
11 Debilitated (8)
15 Recondite (8)
17 Chris ___ : tennis champion (5)
19 Unit of power (8)
20 Small island (5)
21 Musical composition (7)
22 Respected person in a field (5)

Down

1 Tsunami (5,4)
2 Language spoken in Rome (7)
3 Gave out (7)
4 Measure of electrical current (6)
5 Sculptured figure (6)
6 Escape from (5)
10 The skill of clear speech (9)
12 Bent forwards and downwards (7)
13 Widely (7)
14 Silver (literary) (6)
16 Mark of disgrace (6)
18 View (5)

Crossword

Puzzle 118

Across

1 Uncover (6)
7 Tidiness (8)
8 Hit high into the air (3)
9 Involuntary spasm (6)
10 Distinctive atmosphere created by a person (4)
11 Speed music is played at (5)
13 Sport with arrows (7)
15 Fastest animal on land (7)
17 Speak without preparation (2-3)
21 Soft cheese (4)
22 May one (anag) (6)
23 Mischievous sprite (3)
24 Relating to courts of law (8)
25 Desire or craving (6)

Down

1 Cause to fall from a horse (6)
2 Chaos (6)
3 Bump into (5)
4 Shelter for a vehicle (7)
5 Unclean (8)
6 Loan shark (6)
12 Goes before (8)
14 Infantile (7)
16 Agricultural implement (6)
18 Protective layer (6)
19 Exceptionally large or successful (6)
20 Single-decker bus (5)

Puzzle 119

Across

1 Seethe (4)
3 Dared to suggest (8)
9 Fighter (7)
10 Donor (5)
11 Completely unaware of (12)
13 Give a new and improved appearance to (6)
15 Swiss city (6)
17 A type of error in speech (8,4)
20 Swing audibly through the air (5)
21 Movement conveying an expression (7)
22 Extreme bitterness (8)
23 Immense (4)

Down

1 Second month (8)
2 Tiny insects (5)
4 Gained deservedly (6)
5 Fellowship (12)
6 Form of retaliation (7)
7 Challenge (4)
8 Reticent; secretive (12)
12 Most pleased (8)
14 Pierre ___ : French mathematician (7)
16 Move restlessly (6)
18 ___ Robson: British tennis player (5)
19 ___ Fisher: actress (4)

Crossword

Puzzle 120

Across

1 Murmured (8)
5 Coloured ring of feathers on a bird (4)
9 The ___ Roundabout: children's TV show (5)
10 Recently (5)
11 US state (10)
14 Happenings (6)
15 Each (6)
17 Unpaid helpers (10)
20 Fish basket (5)
21 Piece of wood that is thin and flat (5)
22 A performance by one person (4)
23 Genteel and feminine in manner (8)

Down

1 Mother (4)
2 Tows a vessel (4)
3 Bewitchingly (12)
4 Magical potion (6)
6 Unwelcome (8)
7 Insect trap (8)
8 Immeasurably (12)
12 Shots that start tennis points (8)
13 In a disorderly manner (4-4)
16 Source of caviar (6)
18 Hired form of transport (4)
19 Axe-like tool (4)

Puzzle 121

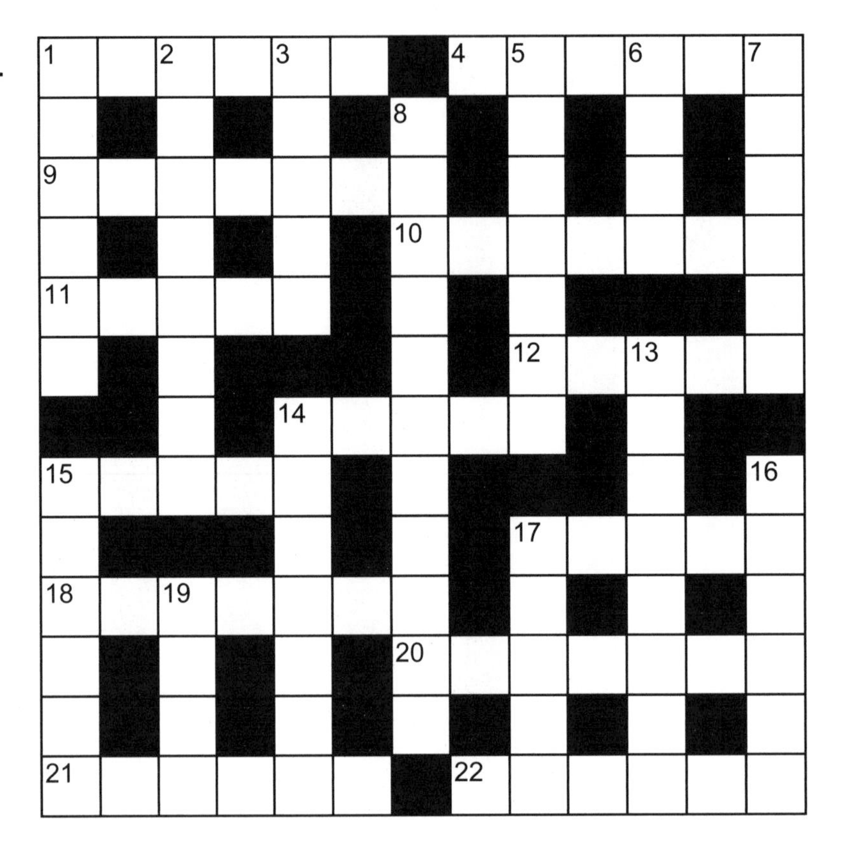

Across

1 Unique (3-3)
4 Characteristic (6)
9 Move something; agitate (7)
10 Effluence (7)
11 Calls out like a lion (5)
12 Kick out (5)
14 Female relatives (5)
15 Eg mallards (5)
17 Espresso coffee and steamed milk (5)
18 Japanese army officer (7)
20 Sheer dress fabric (7)
21 One or the other of two (6)
22 Spiny tree or shrub (6)

Down

1 Commands (6)
2 Extremely happy (8)
3 Smoke pipes (5)
5 Seats for more than one person (7)
6 Wicked (4)
7 Small gardening tool with a curved scoop (6)
8 Feeling of hatred (11)
13 Free from sensual desire (8)
14 Assign (7)
15 Discontinuance; neglect (6)
16 US state (6)
17 Reasoned judgement (5)
19 Ditch filled with water (4)

Crossword

Puzzle 122

Across

1 ___ Affleck: US actor (5)
4 Exhausted (4,3)
7 Samantha ___ : Irish singer (5)
8 Small pocket tool (8)
9 Deliberate; cogitate (5)
11 Curiosity (8)
15 Fence formed by bushes (8)
17 Circular in shape (5)
19 Ozzy ___ : Black Sabbath vocalist (8)
20 Bend forwards and downwards (5)
21 Eg Borneo and Java (7)
22 Male duck (5)

Down

1 Joint advocate (9)
2 Eg from Madrid (7)
3 Opening the mouth wide when tired (7)
4 Smells (6)
5 Zero (6)
6 Living in a city (5)
10 General erudition (9)
12 Paid no attention to (7)
13 Proportionately (3,4)
14 Long-haired variety of cat (6)
16 Pieces of writing (6)
18 Solemn promises (5)

Puzzle 123

Across

- **1** Arrive (4)
- **3** Give guidance to (8)
- **9** Pseudoscience (7)
- **10** Coarse rock used for polishing (5)
- **11** Commensurate (12)
- **14** And not (3)
- **16** Reject with disdain (5)
- **17** Tree of the genus Ulmus (3)
- **18** Discreditable (12)
- **21** Established custom (5)
- **22** Decorative altar cloth (7)
- **23** Frustrated (8)
- **24** Garden outbuilding (4)

Down

- **1** Applauding (8)
- **2** Extremely small (prefix) (5)
- **4** Animal fodder (3)
- **5** Knowledge of a future event (12)
- **6** Lift up (7)
- **7** 24 hour periods (4)
- **8** One who takes part in a protest (12)
- **12** Solid blow (5)
- **13** Driven to action (8)
- **15** Arc of coloured light (7)
- **19** Bungle (5)
- **20** Close (4)
- **22** Enemy (3)

Crossword

Puzzle 124

Across

1 Statuette (8)
5 Exploits (4)
8 Not illuminated (5)
9 ___ shorts: item of clothing (7)
10 Bored into (7)
12 Conveniently (7)
14 Played for time (7)
16 Legal inquiry (7)
18 Friendly (7)
19 Beast (5)
20 TV award (4)
21 Starlike symbol (8)

Down

1 Disgusting (4)
2 Unit of volume (6)
3 Fight back (9)
4 No one (6)
6 Violent gust of wind (6)
7 Reference point; norm (8)
11 Unable to do something (9)
12 Waver (8)
13 Writhe (6)
14 Soaks in liquid (6)
15 Lapis ___ : blue gemstone (6)
17 A quick look (4)

Puzzle 125

Across

1 Desire to act (4)
3 Gather together in one place (8)
9 Distinctive pattern; Scottish town (7)
10 Inapt (anag) (5)
11 Number after seven (5)
12 Perfect happiness (7)
13 Reason for not doing something (6)
15 Taxonomic groupings (6)
17 Burdensome work (7)
18 Leg bone (5)
20 Small fruit used for oil (5)
21 Pamphlet (7)
22 Formerly (8)
23 Large group of people (4)

Down

1 Not ostentatious (13)
2 Departing (5)
4 Intelligence activity (6)
5 Derived from past events (12)
6 Army unit (7)
7 Wastefully; lavishly (13)
8 First part of the Bible (3,9)
14 Skull (7)
16 Type of ski race (6)
19 Contradict (5)

Crossword

Puzzle 126

Across

1 Finely chopped (8)
5 Blue dye (4)
8 Friend (Spanish) (5)
9 Reconstruct (7)
10 Engraving (7)
12 The North Star (7)
14 Scottish national emblem (7)
16 Table support (7)
18 Responded to (7)
19 Alphabetical list in a book (5)
20 Foolish (4)
21 Dreariness (8)

Down

1 Total spread of a bridge (4)
2 Nasal (6)
3 Substance that reduces perspiration (9)
4 Eagles' nests (6)
6 Establish by law (6)
7 Emissary (8)
11 Inquisitiveness (9)
12 Ambled (8)
13 On ___ of: in the interests of (6)
14 Showing gentleness (6)
15 Walk laboriously (6)
17 Hatchets (4)

Puzzle 127

Across

1 Offered (8)
5 Mark left from a wound (4)
9 Agreeable sound or tune (5)
10 Brings up (5)
11 Increased greatly in number (10)
14 Pull back from (6)
15 East ___ : where one finds Norfolk (6)
17 Glasses (10)
20 Unit of light (5)
21 ___ Adkins: singer (5)
22 Clarets (4)
23 Places in position (8)

Down

1 Duration (4)
2 Food (informal) (4)
3 Intensely painful (12)
4 Fourscore (6)
6 Collarbone (8)
7 Remaining (8)
8 Surpassing in influence (12)
12 Fighter in close combat (8)
13 Shouted very loudly (8)
16 Stress mark (6)
18 Roman emperor (4)
19 Areas of ground for growing plants (4)

Crossword

Puzzle 128

Across

1 Large heavy book (4)
3 Examines in detail (8)
9 More than enough (7)
10 Courageous (5)
11 Laudatory (12)
14 Be in debt (3)
16 Trembling poplar (5)
17 Male offspring (3)
18 Orcas (6,6)
21 Ball of lead (5)
22 Imaginary scary creature (7)
23 ___ hour: the latest possible moment (8)
24 School test (4)

Down

1 Cutlery used to stir a drink (8)
2 Mediterranean island country (5)
4 Negative vote (3)
5 Intricate and confusing (12)
6 Breaks into pieces (7)
7 Perceives (4)
8 Impregnable (12)
12 Car windscreen cleaner (5)
13 Very small unit of length (8)
15 Connoisseur; gourmet (7)
19 Water and rubber mix (5)
20 Church recess (4)
22 Floor covering (3)

Puzzle 129

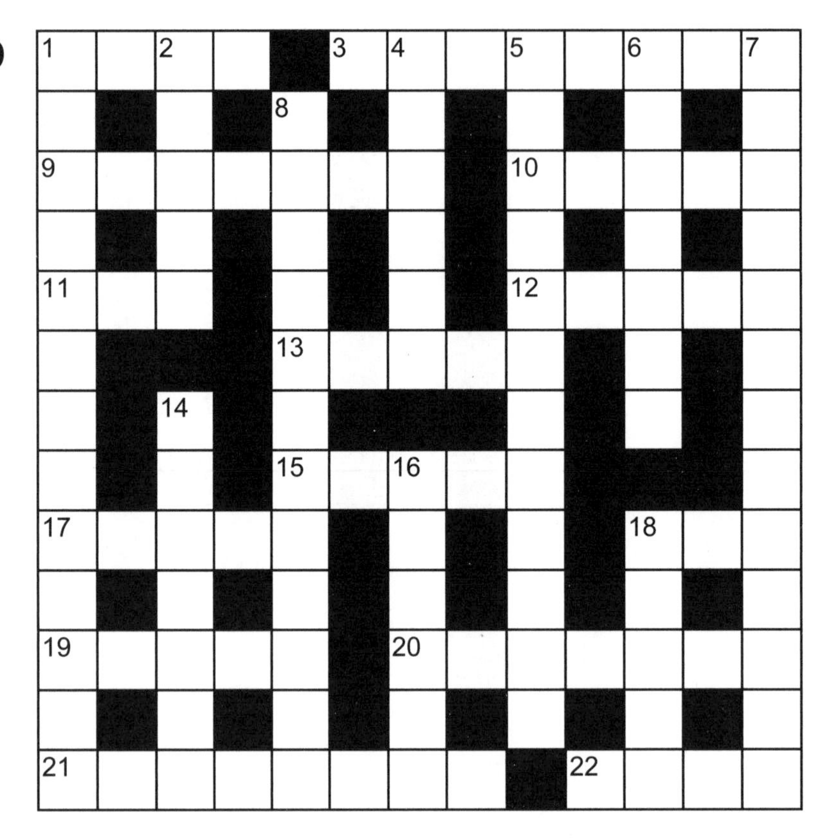

Across

1 After the beginning of (4)
3 Unusual (8)
9 Tool that is useful for the Arctic (3,4)
10 Throw forcefully (5)
11 Violate a law of God (3)
12 Robbery (5)
13 Scoundrel (5)
15 Temporary stop (5)
17 Rocky; harsh (5)
18 Short cylindrical piece of wood (3)
19 Invigorating medicine (5)
20 Eg Colin Jackson (7)
21 Hugging (8)
22 Push; poke (4)

Down

1 Peculiar or individual (13)
2 Connection; link (3-2)
4 Cooking in the oven (6)
5 Unofficially (3,3,6)
6 Posting (7)
7 Given to thievery (5-8)
8 Pertaining to a person's life (12)
14 Ignored; avoided (7)
16 Poorly dressed child (6)
18 Lighter (5)

Crossword

Puzzle 130

Across

1 Obnoxiously forward (5)
4 Ruin (5)
10 Accounts inspector (7)
11 Conical tent (5)
12 Bunch of threads (4)
13 Based on reason (8)
16 Small inflatable boat (6)
17 Striped animals (6)
20 Citing as evidence (8)
21 Heroic tale (4)
23 Insurgent (5)
25 Decorative framework (7)
26 Sandy wasteland (5)
27 Fader (anag) (5)

Down

2 Not clear or precise (9)
3 Despise (4)
5 Merchant (8)
6 Close-fitting hat (3)
7 Endured (6)
8 Very untypical (5)
9 In a good way (4)
14 Standardise (9)
15 Film starring Juliette Binoche (8)
18 Trembles (6)
19 Make law (5)
20 Breezy (4)
22 Killer whale (4)
24 Insect that can sting (3)

Puzzle 131

Across

1 Make-believe (8)
5 Cut with scissors (4)
8 Parasitic insect (5)
9 Puts into something else (7)
10 Curved upwards (7)
12 Type of computer (7)
14 Eg from Ethiopia (7)
16 Arranged neatly (7)
18 Split (7)
19 Well-known (5)
20 Puts down (4)
21 Appreciates (8)

Down

1 Get the opinions of people (4)
2 Rejoices (6)
3 Immunity (9)
4 Arm strengthening exercise (4-2)
6 Jitters (6)
7 Place (8)
11 Remorseful (9)
12 Terrible (8)
13 A dirty house (6)
14 Stick to (6)
15 Universe (6)
17 Lyric poems (4)

Puzzle 132

Across

1 Group of actors in a show (4)
3 Gloaming (8)
9 English county (7)
10 Variety or kind (5)
11 Deep fissure (5)
12 Chats (7)
13 Publicly (6)
15 Marble (anag) (6)
17 Triangle with three unequal sides (7)
18 Fortune-telling card (5)
20 Enlighten; educate morally (5)
21 ___ Bloom: English actor (7)
22 Split apart (8)
23 ___ of Man: where one finds Douglas (4)

Down

1 Awareness (13)
2 Country in the Middle East (5)
4 Rousing from sleep (6)
5 Lawfully (12)
6 Respectable; refined (7)
7 Hidden store of valuables (8,5)
8 Pungent gas used as a preservative (12)
14 Avoidance (7)
16 State of sleep (6)
19 Steps of a ladder (5)

Puzzle 133

1		2		■	3	4		5		6		7
	■		■	8	■		■		■		■	
9							■	10				
	■		■		■		■		■		■	
11			■		■		■	12				
	■	■	■	13					■		■	
	■	14	■		■	■	■		■		■	
	■		■	15		16			■	■	■	
17					■		■		■	18		
	■		■		■		■		■		■	
19					■	20						
	■		■		■		■		■		■	
21								■	22			

Across

1 Uproarious party; hit hard (4)
3 Pithy saying (8)
9 Film directed by Stephen Gaghan (7)
10 Recorded on video (5)
11 Take or steal something (3)
12 Concerning (5)
13 Feign (3,2)
15 Corpulent (5)
17 Injure (5)
18 Mineral spring (3)
19 Impersonator (5)
20 Country whose capital is Kiev (7)
21 In the adjacent residence (4,4)
22 Gradually deprive of milk (4)

Down

1 Female professional (13)
2 Small woody plant (5)
4 Untape (anag) (6)
5 Outsmart (12)
6 Get better (7)
7 Largest inland sea (13)
8 Made in bulk (4-8)
14 Confound (7)
16 Old Portuguese currency (6)
18 Desire to hurt someone (5)

Crossword

Puzzle 134

Across

1 Repugnance (8)
5 Put down gently (4)
8 Join together; merge (5)
9 Restrained (7)
10 Of great size (7)
12 Seed bid (anag) (7)
14 Foliage (7)
16 French dance (7)
18 Civil action brought to court (7)
19 Yellow citrus fruit (5)
20 Predatory canine mammal (4)
21 Comes into flower (8)

Down

1 So be it (4)
2 Amended (6)
3 Quickest (9)
4 Flattened at the poles (6)
6 Hurting (6)
7 Give entirely to a cause (8)
11 Three-sided figures (9)
12 House with one storey (8)
13 Assertion (6)
14 Legume (6)
15 With hands on the hips (6)
17 Tiny social insects (4)

Puzzle 135

1		2		3		■	4	5		6		7
	■		■		■	8	■		■		■	
9							■		■		■	
	■		■		■	10						
11					■		■		■	■	■	
	■		■	■	■		■	12		13		
■	■		■	14					■		■	■
15					■		■	■	■		■	16
	■	■	■		■		■	17				
18		19					■		■		■	
	■		■		■	20						
	■		■		■		■		■		■	
21						■	22					

Across

1 Fill up with petrol (6)
4 On fire (6)
9 Fanciful daydream (7)
10 Erase or remove (7)
11 Hugh ___ : actor (5)
12 Annoying insects (5)
14 Headdress worn by a bishop (5)
15 Russell ___ : Gladiator actor (5)
17 Freight (5)
18 Pasta pockets (7)
20 Necessary (7)
21 Seek to hurt (6)
22 Apprehend someone (6)

Down

1 Safe place (6)
2 Spanish dance (8)
3 Praise highly (5)
5 Musical instrument (7)
6 Long nerve fibre (4)
7 Forces out (6)
8 Attention-grabbing (3-8)
13 Derisive (8)
14 Tuneful (7)
15 Gaseous envelope of the sun (6)
16 US currency (6)
17 Doctrine; system of beliefs (5)
19 Undergarment (4)

Puzzle 136

Across

1 Relishes (6)
7 Opposite of eastward (8)
8 23rd Greek letter (3)
9 Device that detects a physical property (6)
10 Not any of (4)
11 Long pointed elephant teeth (5)
13 Gelatin products (7)
15 Stashed away (7)
17 Pointed projectile (5)
21 Aquatic vertebrate (4)
22 Vedic hymn (6)
23 Part of a pen (3)
24 Art of controversial discussion (8)
25 Special honour shown publicly (6)

Down

1 Send for sale overseas (6)
2 Wood beams (6)
3 Eg from Geneva (5)
4 Pursuer (anag) (7)
5 Fraudster (8)
6 Grime or dirt (6)
12 Square scarf worn over the head (8)
14 Mythical female sea creature (7)
16 Prayer (6)
18 Country in central Africa (6)
19 Sing in a trilling manner (6)
20 Grind together (5)

Puzzle 137

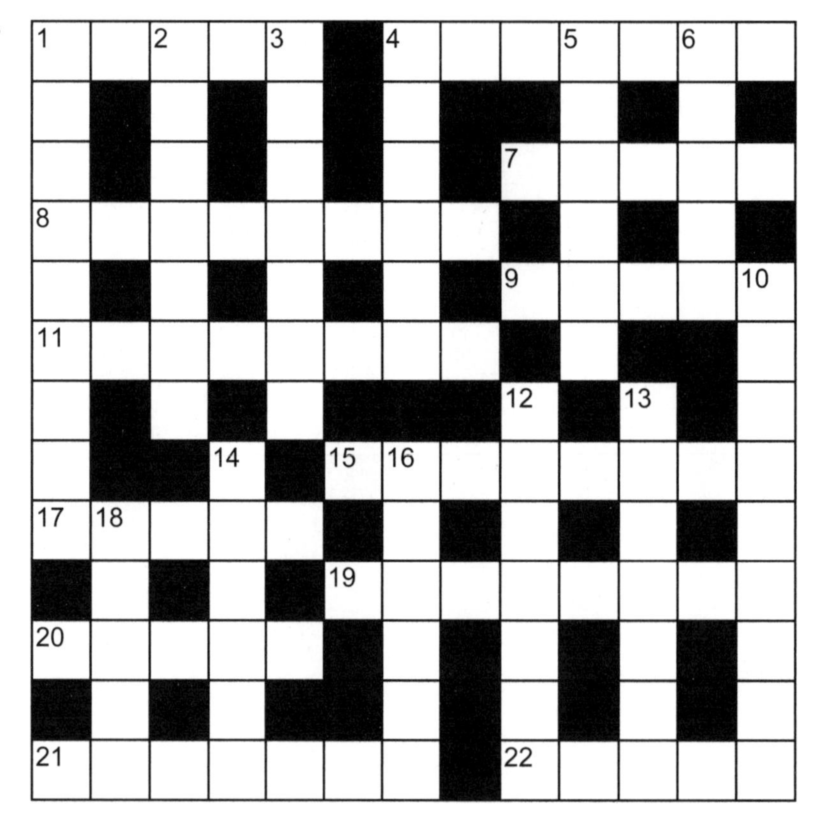

Across

1 Decorate (5)
4 Becomes less wide (7)
7 Smug smile (5)
8 Creature that eats both meat and plants (8)
9 Trap (5)
11 Usually (8)
15 Angelic (8)
17 Got to one's feet (5)
19 Excessive amount of something (8)
20 Apprehended with certainty (5)
21 Sceptic (7)
22 Avarice (5)

Down

1 Detachment (9)
2 Lead batsmen (cricket) (7)
3 Modern; up to date (7)
4 Pertaining to a nerve (6)
5 Cause to remember (6)
6 Electrician (5)
10 Very thin and bony (9)
12 Irritating (7)
13 Forgive (7)
14 What a spider spins (6)
16 Give a loud shout (6)
18 Ballroom dance (5)

Crossword

Puzzle 138

Across

1 Wilting; hanging limply (8)
5 Propel the body through water (4)
8 Escapade (5)
9 Old (7)
10 Imaginary line around the earth (7)
12 Warhead carried by a missile (7)
14 Shrine in France (7)
16 Martial art (2-5)
18 Enlist (7)
19 Frozen fruit juice on a stick (5)
20 Stage of twilight (4)
21 Promontory (8)

Down

1 Slender freshwater fish (4)
2 Fish-eating bird of prey (6)
3 Supreme (9)
4 Required (6)
6 Heat; affection (6)
7 Female head of a town (8)
11 Unflustered (9)
12 Lied under oath (8)
13 Expels (6)
14 Gentle sheen (6)
15 Plant of the daisy family (6)
17 Saw; observed (4)

Puzzle 139

Across

- **1** Floor covers (4)
- **3** Pepper plant (8)
- **9** Greek goddess of retribution (7)
- **10** Singing voice (5)
- **11** Entrance hallway (5)
- **12** Plant with starchy tuberous roots (7)
- **13** Scrape (anag) (6)
- **15** Compact group of mountains (6)
- **17** Four-stringed guitar (7)
- **18** Store of hoarded wealth (5)
- **20** Finished (5)
- **21** Error in printing or writing (7)
- **22** Showering with liquid (8)
- **23** Where one finds Tehran (4)

Down

- **1** Makers (13)
- **2** Stomach (informal) (5)
- **4** Region of France (6)
- **5** Adequate (12)
- **6** Solicit votes from (7)
- **7** American actor (6,7)
- **8** Intuitively designed (of a system) (4-8)
- **14** Pillage (7)
- **16** Lower someone's dignity (6)
- **19** External (5)

Crossword

Puzzle 140

Across

1 Greek goddess of wisdom (6)
7 Throaty (of a speech sound) (8)
8 Unit of resistance (3)
9 Pertaining to vinegar (6)
10 Domestic felines (4)
11 Submerged ridges of rock (5)
13 Eg a car (7)
15 Mediocre (7)
17 Small and elegant (5)
21 Open tart (4)
22 Margin of safety (6)
23 Dandy (3)
24 Tripped up (8)
25 ___ McCartney: fashion designer (6)

Down

1 Worshipper (6)
2 Showing compassion (6)
3 Ornamental stone (5)
4 Placed one on top of another (7)
5 Courgette (US) (8)
6 Claret (anag) (6)
12 Eg Daniel or Matthew (8)
14 In a nimble manner (7)
16 Personal attendants (6)
18 Full of happiness (6)
19 Ideally perfect state (6)
20 Transmits (5)

Puzzle 141

Across

1 Raise up (4)
3 Daydreamer (8)
9 Johannes ___ : Dutch painter (7)
10 Things to be done (5)
11 Style of piano-based blues (6-6)
13 Ronald ___ : former US President (6)
15 Beat as if with a flail (6)
17 Vagrancy (12)
20 Short letters (5)
21 Slope (7)
22 Overly concerned with detail (8)
23 Poses a question (4)

Down

1 Very small African parrot (8)
2 Refrain from (5)
4 Bad handwriting (6)
5 Branch of astronomy (12)
6 Stimulate a person (7)
7 ___ Daly: TV presenter (4)
8 Food shop (12)
12 Stiff cat hairs (8)
14 Formally approved (7)
16 Third sign of the zodiac (6)
18 Lives (anag) (5)
19 Break suddenly (4)

Puzzle 142

Across

1 Initiators (11)
9 Precise (5)
10 Vital plant juice (3)
11 Legend (5)
12 Pertaining to sound (5)
13 Intelligently (8)
16 Meddlesome person (8)
18 Bird claw (5)
21 Group of eight (5)
22 Sphere or globe (3)
23 Particle that holds quarks together (5)
24 Stargazers (11)

Down

2 One who eats a bit at a time (7)
3 Small loudspeaker (7)
4 Small stones (6)
5 ___ Andronicus: Shakespeare play (5)
6 Substance exuded by some trees (5)
7 Pretentious behaviour (11)
8 Prophetic of the end of the world (11)
14 Word having the same meaning as another (7)
15 Map line showing equal height (7)
17 Improvement (6)
19 Parts of the cerebrum (5)
20 African country whose capital is Niamey (5)

Puzzle 143

Across

1 Part of a pedestal (4)
3 Sign of approval (6-2)
9 Spend lavishly (7)
10 State of disgrace (5)
11 By chance (12)
14 Interdict (3)
16 Nasal passageway (5)
17 Draw (3)
18 Creator of film scripts (12)
21 Piece of code to automate a task (5)
22 Become airborne (4,3)
23 Estimating (8)
24 Hit hard (4)

Down

1 Upsets; agitates (8)
2 ___ & Gabbana: fashion house (5)
4 Weeding tool (3)
5 Coup (12)
6 Promising young actress (7)
7 Exclamation of relief (4)
8 Absurd (12)
12 Body of rules (5)
13 Modify with new parts (8)
15 Use again (7)
19 Ironic metaphor (5)
20 Type of air pollution (4)
22 Chemical element (3)

Crossword

Puzzle 144

Across

1 Too; in addition (4)
3 Deny (8)
9 Great ___ : island (7)
10 Titles (5)
11 Correct (5)
12 Round building (7)
13 Season after summer (6)
15 Capital of Canada (6)
17 Food pantries (7)
18 Fill with high spirits (5)
20 Unspecified object (5)
21 Fragrant gum or spice (7)
22 Landing and take-off area (8)
23 Opposite of an entrance (4)

Down

1 US actress (5,8)
2 Type of bandage (5)
4 Refuse to acknowledge (6)
5 Body of voters in a specified region (12)
6 Pungent gas (7)
7 Ineptitude in running a business (13)
8 Boxing class (12)
14 Small dog (7)
16 Birthplace of St Francis (6)
19 Attach to (5)

Puzzle 145

Across

1 Unspecified in number (4)
3 A large spar (8)
9 Backtrack (7)
10 Grins (anag) (5)
11 Understandably (12)
13 Dispute the truth of (6)
15 In the ___ : Elvis Presley song (6)
17 Gratitude (12)
20 Bring into a line (5)
21 Charlie ___ : early comic actor (7)
22 Examined in detail (8)
23 Female sheep (pl) (4)

Down

1 One who lives through affliction (8)
2 Short choral composition (5)
4 Set of clothes (6)
5 Immediately (12)
6 Lock of curly hair (7)
7 Throw a coin in the air (4)
8 Hostility (12)
12 These precede afternoons (8)
14 Powdered spice (7)
16 Frozen water spear (6)
18 Relation by marriage (2-3)
19 Spanish sparkling wine (4)

Crossword

Puzzle 146

Across

1 Taxis (4)
3 Small loudspeakers (8)
9 Receptacle for letters (7)
10 Fragile (5)
11 Fantastical creature (3)
12 Ancient object (5)
13 Not heavy (5)
15 Piece of furniture (5)
17 Cause to stop sleeping (5)
18 Pouch; enclosed space (3)
19 Form of identification (5)
20 US space probe to Jupiter (7)
21 Researched in detail (8)
22 Sight organs (4)

Down

1 Measurable by a common standard (13)
2 Short and sweet (5)
4 Appearing larger (of the moon) (6)
5 Easily (12)
6 Helped to happen (7)
7 Embarrassed (4-9)
8 Lowest possible temperature (8,4)
14 Summary of events (5-2)
16 ___ jumping: extreme sport (6)
18 Tarnish (5)

Puzzle 147

Across

1 Showy (6)
5 Witch (3)
7 Big and strong (5)
8 Break an agreement (7)
9 Clean spiritually (5)
10 Mathematical operation (8)
12 Ancient (3-3)
14 Chiefly (6)
17 Mocking (8)
18 Chris ___ : DJ and TV presenter (5)
20 Kitchen stoves (7)
21 Select group of people (5)
22 Increase in amount (3)
23 Plus points (6)

Down

2 Precipitating (7)
3 Scantily (8)
4 ___ feed: supply bit by bit (4)
5 Pipe from which water can be drawn (7)
6 Entrance (7)
7 Under (5)
11 Game that uses oblong pieces (8)
12 Deficiency of red blood cells (7)
13 Agreed or corresponded (7)
15 Young hare (7)
16 Therefore (5)
19 Comedy sketch (4)

Crossword

Puzzle 148

Across

1 Church instruments (6)
4 Astonished (6)
9 One who breaks the rules (7)
10 Last longer than others (of clothes) (7)
11 Freshwater fish (5)
12 Slopes (5)
14 Rapidity of movement (5)
15 Determine the quality of an ore (5)
17 Musical instrument (5)
18 Live in (7)
20 Eg flies and beetles (7)
21 Most recent (6)
22 Made a request to God (6)

Down

1 Happens (6)
2 Explosive shells (8)
3 Incision; indent (5)
5 Hot-tasting condiment (7)
6 Sector (4)
7 Scattered rubbish; brides (anag) (6)
8 Posing a difficulty (11)
13 Government by a king or queen (8)
14 Signs (7)
15 Type of living organism (6)
16 Flipped a coin (6)
17 Show-off (5)
19 Lift something heavy (4)

Puzzle 149

Across

1 Pierce with a horn (4)
3 Automata (8)
9 Distinguished (7)
10 Weatherproof coat (5)
11 Cleans (5)
12 Repository (7)
13 Stewed or boiled (6)
15 Organ in the mouth of a mammal (6)
17 Corneas (anag) (7)
18 Hinged barriers between rooms (5)
20 Show pleasure facially (5)
21 Horizontal underground stem (7)
22 Drink consumed before bed (8)
23 Appends (4)

Down

1 British actress who became an MP (6,7)
2 Remains of an old building (5)
4 Real (6)
5 Valetudinarianism (12)
6 Caring for (7)
7 Brazenness (13)
8 Re-evaluation (12)
14 Eating grass (of cattle) (7)
16 ___ Bocelli: Italian operatic singer (6)
19 Egg-shaped solid (5)

Crossword

Puzzle 150

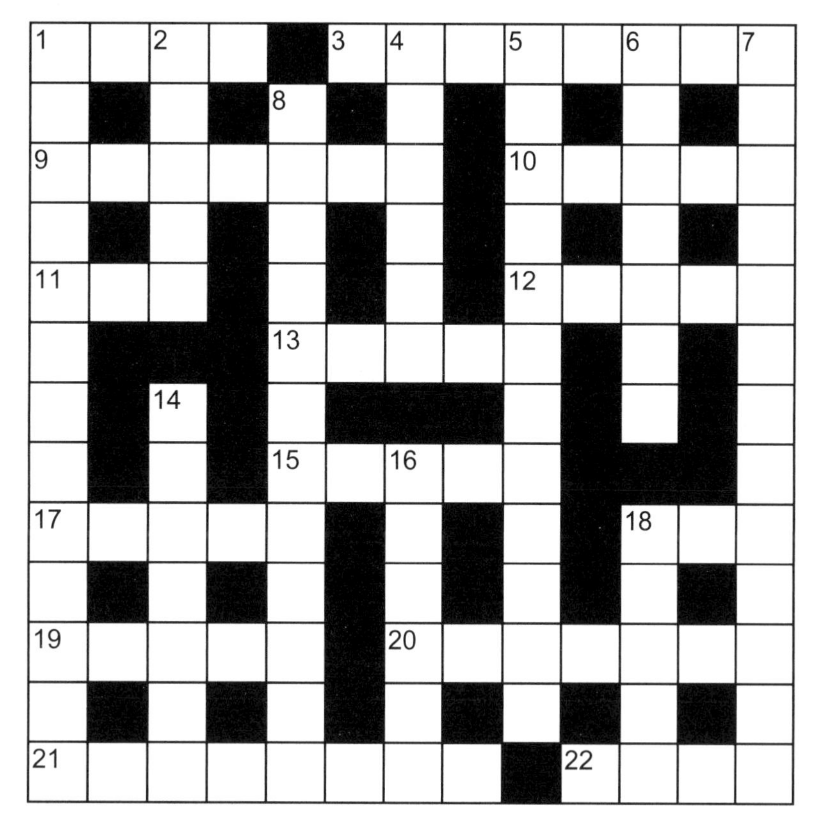

Across

1 ___ Major: the Great Bear (4)
3 Foretells (8)
9 Paul ___ : British magician (7)
10 From that time (5)
11 Cutting tool (3)
12 Draw or bring out (5)
13 Suppress (5)
15 ___ Agassi: former tennis star (5)
17 Coming after (5)
18 Turn upside down (3)
19 Shallow recess (5)
20 Relating to motion (7)
21 Kitchen sideboards (8)
22 True and actual (4)

Down

1 Lacking in control (13)
2 Tough fibrous tissue (5)
4 Leaser (anag) (6)
5 Doubting the truth of (12)
6 Pipe (7)
7 Lacking originality (13)
8 Main premises of a company (12)
14 Outer layer of a hair (7)
16 Labourer at a port (6)
18 Levy (5)

Puzzle 151

Across

1 Most pleasant (6)
5 Argument (3)
7 Expect; think that (5)
8 Diacritical marks (7)
9 Form of oxygen (5)
10 Very annoying (8)
12 Pleaded with; asked for money (6)
14 Brought about (6)
17 Printed version of data on a computer (4,4)
18 Entrance hall (5)
20 Sleeveless garment (7)
21 A score of two under par (golf) (5)
22 Evergreen coniferous tree (3)
23 Wrinkle in an item of clothing (6)

Down

2 Vast (7)
3 Bushy-tailed rodent (8)
4 Grain store (4)
5 Holiday locations (7)
6 Made less narrow (7)
7 Academy Award (5)
11 Horticulturist (8)
12 Sheriff's officer (7)
13 One who places bets (7)
15 Female ruler (7)
16 Not true (5)
19 ___ Berra: baseball player (4)

Crossword

Puzzle 152

Across

1 Trembled (8)
5 ___ Scholes: former England footballer (4)
8 More mature (5)
9 James Joyce novel (7)
10 Cut of beef (7)
12 Apiary (7)
14 Dressed in a vestment (7)
16 Accrued (7)
18 Protective helmet (4,3)
19 ___ Els: golfer (5)
20 Valley (4)
21 Musical wind instrument (8)

Down

1 Type of footwear (4)
2 One of the halogens (6)
3 Outstandingly bad (9)
4 Liken to; correspond (6)
6 Descend down a rock face (6)
7 Diminished (8)
11 Fossil fuel (9)
12 Inhaled (8)
13 Conduct reconnaissance (6)
14 The boss at a newspaper (6)
15 Mustang; wild horse (6)
17 ___ Campbell: actress (4)

Puzzle 153

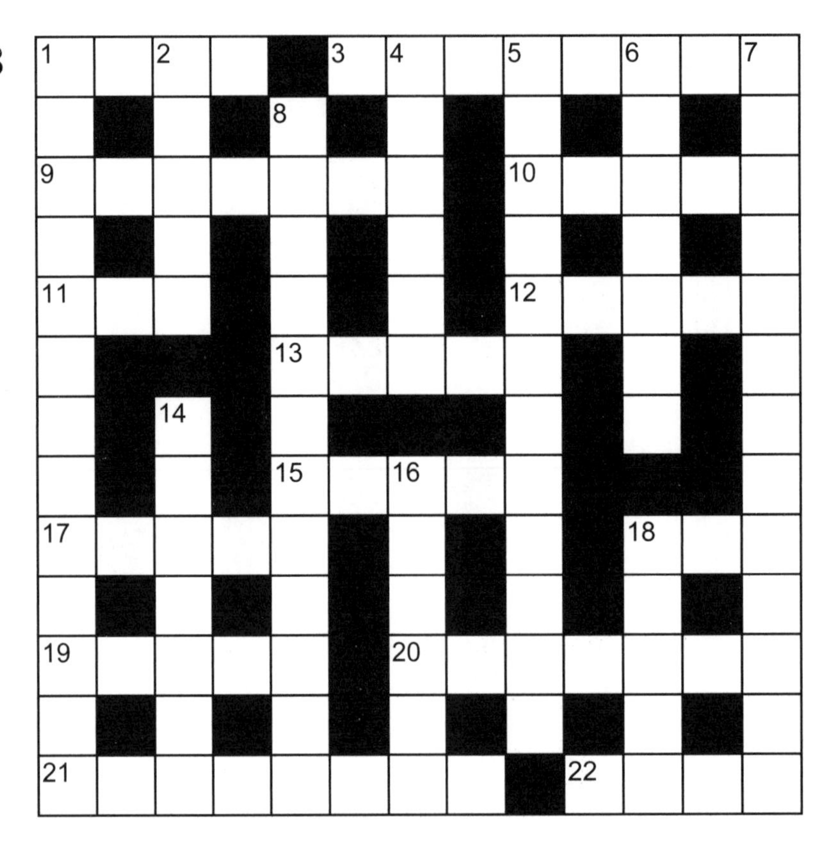

Across

1 Charged particles (4)
3 Word for word (8)
9 Inns (7)
10 Ring-shaped object (5)
11 Affirmative vote (3)
12 Meal (5)
13 Sheet (anag) (5)
15 Moderate and well-balanced (5)
17 Seize firmly (5)
18 ___ Rida: American rapper (3)
19 Loop with a running knot (5)
20 Having solidified from lava (of rock) (7)
21 Relating to critical explanation (8)
22 Donkey noise (4)

Down

1 Inflexibility (13)
2 Flaring stars (5)
4 Make certain of (6)
5 Place of conflict (12)
6 Cruel use of authority (7)
7 Naughtily (13)
8 Principal face of a building (12)
14 Edible mollusc (7)
16 Minimal bathing suit (6)
18 Fine powdery foodstuff (5)

Crossword

Puzzle 154

Across

1 Faith (8)
5 Depressions (4)
9 West Indian dance (5)
10 A central point (5)
11 Very loud (of a voice) (10)
14 Where one watches films (6)
15 Bear witness (6)
17 The people in a group (10)
20 Colour lightly (5)
21 Not with anybody (5)
22 Large stone (4)
23 Relating to an empire (8)

Down

1 Anger or irritate (4)
2 Compact mass (4)
3 Easy-going (4-8)
4 Elongated rectangle (6)
6 Financial statements (8)
7 Saltiness (8)
8 Teach to accept a belief uncritically (12)
12 Curved sword (8)
13 Assisting the memory (8)
16 Greatly respect (6)
18 Large desert in Asia (4)
19 Transaction (4)

Puzzle 155

Across

1 Units of electrical resistance (4)
3 Squander money (8)
9 Marmoset (7)
10 Lindsay ___ : US actress (5)
11 Not allowable (12)
14 Seventh Greek letter (3)
16 Game fish (5)
17 Hair colourant (3)
18 Intense (12)
21 A satellite of Uranus (5)
22 Stronghold (7)
23 Irritating (8)
24 Chief god of ancient Greece (4)

Down

1 Person not accepted by society (8)
2 Snake (5)
4 Charged particle (3)
5 Narcissism (4-8)
6 Breathed out (7)
7 Finished; complete (4)
8 Strikingly (12)
12 Exhibited (5)
13 Titles for newspaper articles (8)
15 ___ harp: instrument played by the wind (7)
19 Strong thread (5)
20 ___ Del Rey: singer (4)
22 Round bread roll (3)

Crossword

Puzzle 156

Across

1 Where darts players throw from (4)
3 Manufacturer (8)
9 Short trips on another's behalf (7)
10 Country in NE Africa (5)
11 Brusque and surly (12)
13 Change (6)
15 Infuriate (6)
17 Part of the mind (12)
20 Divide by two (5)
21 Slim (7)
22 Innate ability (8)
23 Burden (4)

Down

1 Defeated (8)
2 Employer (5)
4 Step down from a job (6)
5 Unplugged (12)
6 Mark written under a letter (7)
7 Ancient German letter (4)
8 Inadequate (12)
12 Sweet food courses (8)
14 Short close-fitting jacket (7)
16 In mint condition (6)
18 ___ days: the distant past (5)
19 Ostrichlike bird (4)

Puzzle 157

Across

- **1** Old toll road (8)
- **5** Hilltop (4)
- **9** Male bee (5)
- **10** Venomous snake (5)
- **11** Translucent (3-7)
- **14** Starting point (6)
- **15** Not awake (6)
- **17** At first sight (5,5)
- **20** Similar (5)
- **21** Plentiful (5)
- **22** Verge (4)
- **23** Fatherly (8)

Down

- **1** Clean up (4)
- **2** Violent disturbance (4)
- **3** Planned in advance (12)
- **4** Very difficult or complex (6)
- **6** Breaks (8)
- **7** Pays homage to (8)
- **8** Make a guess that is too high (12)
- **12** Heated surface used for cooking food (8)
- **13** Separating into parts (8)
- **16** Capital of Cuba (6)
- **18** Revolve around quickly (4)
- **19** Become healthy again (of a wound) (4)

Crossword

Puzzle 158

Across

1 Mixed up or confused (6)
4 Flourish (6)
9 Eg from Moscow (7)
10 Large bird of prey (7)
11 Walk with an affected gait (5)
12 Baking appliances (5)
14 Break the rules (5)
15 Receive a ball in one's hands (5)
17 Extreme (5)
18 Musical movements (7)
20 Countries (7)
21 Strongbox for valuables (6)
22 Opposite of open (6)

Down

1 Take into custody (6)
2 Cause deliberate damage to (8)
3 Authoritative proclamation (5)
5 Active part of a fire (7)
6 Small quantity (4)
7 Calls forth (6)
8 Contriving to bring about (11)
13 Feelings (8)
14 Stately hymn tune (7)
15 Of the universe (6)
16 Stopped temporarily (6)
17 Up to the time when (5)
19 One of two equal parts (4)

Puzzle 159

Across

1 Select from a large amount (4)
3 Obscures the light from a celestial body (8)
9 Agreement (7)
10 Hang with cloth (5)
11 Not catching fire easily (3-9)
14 Touch gently (3)
16 Tiger ___ : top golfer (5)
17 State of armed conflict (3)
18 Gossip (12)
21 Humped ruminant (5)
22 Big ___ : song sung by Shirley Bassey (7)
23 Rump (8)
24 Undergarments (4)

Down

1 Large hard-shelled oval nuts (8)
2 Cloth woven from flax (5)
4 Partly digested animal food (3)
5 Unseasonably warm period (6,6)
6 Lacking depth (7)
7 Takes to court (4)
8 Intense anxiety (12)
12 Type of large deer (5)
13 Places where fruit trees are grown (8)
15 Strong verbal attack (7)
19 Beneath (5)
20 Protective crust over a wound (4)
22 Sorrowful (3)

Crossword

Puzzle 160

Across

1 Packs of cards (5)
4 Belief that there is no God (7)
7 Express one's opinion (5)
8 Stayed in place (8)
9 Short-tempered; ardent (5)
11 Merciless (8)
15 Eg plaice (8)
17 Evade (5)
19 Newspaper reports (8)
20 A point in question (5)
21 Aids (7)
22 Symbol (5)

Down

1 Affected the flow of something (9)
2 Regular journey to and from work (7)
3 Airless (anag) (7)
4 Attendants upon God (6)
5 Impose or require (6)
6 Woodland spirit (5)
10 Sailors of light vessels (9)
12 Very eager to get something (7)
13 Small mound (7)
14 Long-legged rodent (6)
16 The words of a song (6)
18 Expels from a position (5)

Puzzle 161

Across

- **1** Money that is owed (4)
- **3** Central principle of a system (8)
- **9** Sets free or releases (7)
- **10** Unit of length (5)
- **11** Smallest quantity (5)
- **12** Melting (7)
- **13** Spiky; barbed (6)
- **15** Showing utter resignation (6)
- **17** Dishonourable (7)
- **18** Sweet-scented shrub (5)
- **20** ___ firma: dry land (5)
- **21** Fit in place (7)
- **22** Honourably (8)
- **23** Dairy product (4)

Down

- **1** Having unusually flexible joints (6-7)
- **2** Strong lightweight wood (5)
- **4** Not real or genuine (6)
- **5** Sleepwalking (12)
- **6** Last beyond (7)
- **7** Vigorously (13)
- **8** Disorganised person (12)
- **14** Non-specific (7)
- **16** Cordial (6)
- **19** Reluctant (5)

Puzzle 162

Across

1 Five lines on which music is written (5)
4 Cigarette ends (5)
10 French city (7)
11 Spiritual nourishment (5)
12 Hints (4)
13 In spite of the fact (8)
16 Had a strong and unpleasant smell (6)
17 Moves in a spiralling pattern (6)
20 The bones of the body (8)
21 Sound of a lion (4)
23 Bring down (5)
25 Masticating (7)
26 Hollow metal objects that ring (5)
27 Sediment (5)

Down

2 Part added to the end of a story (9)
3 Opening for air; outlet (4)
5 Light axe (8)
6 Rubbish container (3)
7 Light teasing repartee (6)
8 Small hill (5)
9 Whip (4)
14 Pulling out of the ground (9)
15 Postponement (8)
18 Small shoots (6)
19 Verbalise (5)
20 Sodium chloride (4)
22 Scorch (4)
24 Very small (3)

Puzzle 163

Across

1 Brought up; cared for (8)
5 Bloodsucking insect (4)
9 Wild dog of Australia (5)
10 Attractively stylish (5)
11 Expert on a subject (10)
14 Artefacts (6)
15 Raise up (6)
17 People in a novel (10)
20 Uproarious party or fight (5)
21 Country in SE Asia (5)
22 Catherine ___ : British comedienne (4)
23 Beaten (8)

Down

1 Moves the head to show agreement (4)
2 Sprints (4)
3 Informally (12)
4 Improve the quality of (6)
6 Fills with air (8)
7 Musical instrument (8)
8 Without equal (12)
12 Highly critical remark (8)
13 Agreeable (8)
16 Serving no functional purpose (6)
18 A Crown document (4)
19 Extol (4)

Crossword

Puzzle 164

Across

1 Jar (4)
3 Lays in wait for (8)
9 Having two sets of chromosomes (7)
10 ___ Mortensen: actor (5)
11 Fast food item (12)
14 High value playing card (3)
16 Drink copiously (5)
17 Snake-like fish (3)
18 Stretched out completely (12)
21 Expect to happen (5)
22 Release someone from duty (7)
23 Type of melon (8)
24 Protruding part of the lower jaw (4)

Down

1 Of a court of law (8)
2 Slight error of judgement (5)
4 Deranged (3)
5 Not capable of being checked (12)
6 Cleanliness (7)
7 Facial blemish (4)
8 As a result (12)
12 Facial hair (5)
13 Short heavy club (8)
15 Give reasons for (7)
19 Annelid worm with suckers (5)
20 Lesion (4)
22 Cereal grass (3)

Puzzle 165

Across

1 Cloth worn around the waist (4)
3 Comfy seat (8)
9 Selfishness (7)
10 Deprive of weapons (5)
11 Songbird (5)
12 Take out (7)
13 Approached (6)
15 One who judges a literary work (6)
17 Recover (7)
18 Burdened (5)
20 Not concealed (5)
21 Not as quiet (7)
22 Establish firmly (8)
23 Narrate (4)

Down

1 Any means of advancement (8,5)
2 Tread heavily (5)
4 Very crowded (of a place) (6)
5 Comical tuner (anag) (12)
6 Inflexible and unyielding (7)
7 Device for changing TV channel (6,7)
8 Chatter (6-6)
14 Illness (7)
16 Small fox with large pointed ears (6)
19 Propel forwards (5)

Crossword

Puzzle 166

Across

1 Pots (4)
3 Occasional (8)
9 Hits with the fist (7)
10 First Pope (5)
11 Home for a pig (3)
12 Gets less difficult (5)
13 British noblemen (5)
15 Make a sound expressing pain (5)
17 Wanderer (5)
18 Exclamation of surprise (3)
19 Drink noisily (5)
20 Outburst of anger (7)
21 Waterside area (8)
22 First man (4)

Down

1 Not heat-treated (of milk) (13)
2 Nursemaid (5)
4 Show-off (6)
5 Symbolising (12)
6 Hates (7)
7 Plant with bright flowers (13)
8 Art of planning a dance (12)
14 Temporary camp (7)
16 Public speaker (6)
18 Bitterly pungent (5)

Puzzle 167

Across

1 Highest point (11)
9 ___ Allan Poe: American writer (5)
10 Conciliatory gift (3)
11 Unexpected plot element (5)
12 Frenzied (5)
13 Comment at the bottom of a page (8)
16 Hard grains left after the milling of flour (8)
18 Male relation (5)
21 New ___ : Indian capital (5)
22 Pair of people (3)
23 Breed of dog (5)
24 Questioning a statement (11)

Down

2 20th letter of the Greek alphabet (7)
3 Assembly of people (7)
4 Gold lump (6)
5 Monotonous hum (5)
6 Ashley ___ : actress (5)
7 Beyond acceptability (3,2,6)
8 Conjecture (11)
14 Rendering invalid (7)
15 A thousand thousand (7)
17 Dish served at a formal dinner (6)
19 Fabric (5)
20 Do extremely well at (5)

Crossword

Puzzle 168

Across

1 Large sticks (6)
5 Container for a drink (3)
7 Fluffy and soft (5)
8 Open area of grassland (7)
9 Sound of any kind (5)
10 Make less complex (8)
12 Fussy (6)
14 Throat (6)
17 Branch of mathematics (8)
18 Become ready to eat (of fruit) (5)
20 The weather conditions in an area in general (7)
21 An easy task (5)
22 Small numbered cube (3)
23 Female monster (6)

Down

2 Sully (7)
3 Shapeless (8)
4 Clive ___ : British Sin City actor (4)
5 Distrustful of sincerity (7)
6 Weasel-like animal (7)
7 Make a god of (5)
11 Hitting with the fist (8)
12 Wooed (7)
13 Go faster than (7)
15 Agrees or corresponds (7)
16 Group (5)
19 One less than ten (4)

Puzzle 169

Across

1 Dreadful (4)
3 Wrestled (8)
9 Remove clothes (7)
10 Loose scrums (rugby) (5)
11 Rope with a running noose (5)
12 Restricted in use (7)
13 Table linen; woven fabric (6)
15 Frozen plain (6)
17 European country (7)
18 Detailed financial assessment (5)
20 Paint (anag) (5)
21 Arranging a piece of music (7)
22 Majesty (8)
23 Slide; lose grip (4)

Down

1 Deceitful behaviour (6-7)
2 Travels on a bicycle (5)
4 Steal livestock (6)
5 Pram (12)
6 Found (7)
7 Deprived (13)
8 Showed (12)
14 Eyelash cosmetic (7)
16 Capital of the Bahamas (6)
19 Imbibe (5)

Crossword

Puzzle 170

Across

1 Aromatic herb (8)
5 One of the continents (4)
8 Economise (5)
9 The exposure of bedrock (7)
10 Flower arrangement (7)
12 Modernised (7)
14 Eg using a straw (7)
16 Completely enveloping (7)
18 Talk in a rambling way (7)
19 Cancel (5)
20 Moral obligation (4)
21 Fragrant toiletries (8)

Down

1 Soft pulp; crush food (4)
2 Attacked at speed (6)
3 Well timed (9)
4 Exist in great numbers (6)
6 Shows indifference (6)
7 Putting into practice (8)
11 Wonder about (9)
12 Not injured (8)
13 Sudden (6)
14 Begins (6)
15 Symbolic (6)
17 With the addition of (4)

Puzzle 171

Across

1 Adjoin (4)
3 Bleak; stark (8)
9 Eg ape or human (7)
10 Aqualung (5)
11 Edward ___ : composer (5)
12 Decanting (7)
13 Make possible (6)
15 Aircraft housing (6)
17 Thin and bony (7)
18 Act of stealing (5)
20 Game of chance (5)
21 Married man (7)
22 Prayer service (8)
23 Openly refuse to obey an order (4)

Down

1 Capable of being understood (13)
2 Exploiting unfairly (5)
4 Free from a liability (6)
5 Obfuscation (12)
6 Funny (7)
7 In an inflated manner (13)
8 Blasphemous (12)
14 Place in order (7)
16 Large snake (6)
19 Rub out (5)

Crossword

Puzzle 172

Across

1 Pieces of tough fibrous tissue (6)
5 Month (3)
7 Brazilian dance (5)
8 Coward (7)
9 Showered with love (5)
10 Sharp heel (8)
12 Son of Daedalus in Greek mythology (6)
14 Law enforcers (6)
17 Mounted guns (8)
18 Gemstones (5)
20 Eroding (7)
21 Published false statement (5)
22 Not wet (3)
23 Continuously (6)

Down

2 Stupid (7)
3 Over the hill (6-2)
4 Among (4)
5 Cocktail with gin and vermouth (7)
6 Golfing measure of distance (7)
7 Notices (5)
11 Building used by local government (4,4)
12 Seize and take custody of (7)
13 Affably (7)
15 Native of the East End of London (7)
16 Fishing net (5)
19 Cries (4)

Puzzle 173

Across

1 Pristine (5-3)
5 Deserve (4)
9 Male monarchs (5)
10 The lion who rules over Narnia (5)
11 Lingering sensation of flavour (10)
14 Point in an orbit furthest from earth (6)
15 Ice homes (6)
17 Member of Parliament (10)
20 Shout of appreciation (5)
21 Dwelling (5)
22 At any time (4)
23 Thawed (8)

Down

1 Capital of Azerbaijan (4)
2 Spots (4)
3 State of dissatisfaction (12)
4 Desires what another has (6)
6 Indirect reference (8)
7 Gibberish (8)
8 Mapmaker (12)
12 Tangible (8)
13 Extremely compatible partner (8)
16 Something done (6)
18 Low humming sound (4)
19 Very long period of time (4)

Crossword

Puzzle 174

Across

1 Italian sausage (6)
7 Separated (8)
8 19th Greek letter (3)
9 Bad-tempered mythical creature (6)
10 Froth of soap and water (4)
11 Impudent; cheeky (5)
13 Insects found where you sleep (7)
15 Funnel-shaped river mouth (7)
17 On two occasions (5)
21 Alcoholic drink (4)
22 Unfurl (6)
23 ___ Botham: cricketer (3)
24 Soft-bodied beetle (4-4)
25 Larger (6)

Down

1 Stomach crunches (3-3)
2 Giggles (6)
3 Extremely happy period (5)
4 Streets (7)
5 Weapon (8)
6 Experienced sailor (3,3)
12 Closure of a system or factory (8)
14 Small piece of fried bread (7)
16 Animal carapaces (6)
18 Doing nothing (6)
19 One who has a salary (6)
20 Tiny piece of food (5)

Puzzle 175

Across

1 Study of the nature of God (8)
5 Upper front part of a boot (4)
8 Many times (5)
9 Alternative form (7)
10 Lift up (7)
12 Patella (7)
14 Sanction (7)
16 Have a positive impact on (7)
18 Structure resembling an ear (7)
19 People not ordained (5)
20 Freedom from difficulty (4)
21 Approximate (8)

Down

1 Walked or stepped (4)
2 Tempt (6)
3 Painting that depicts scenery (9)
4 Throw in the towel (4,2)
6 Graphical representation of a person (6)
7 Forbearance (8)
11 The masses (3,6)
12 Potentially self-destructive (8)
13 Musical dramas (6)
14 Judge (6)
15 Top aim (anag) (6)
17 Extravagant publicity (4)

Crossword

Puzzle 176

Across

1 Qualifications (8)
5 Cry of derision (4)
9 A woolly ruminant animal (5)
10 Individual things (5)
11 Failing to remember (10)
14 Accustoms to something (6)
15 Screen of metal bars (6)
17 Deficiency (10)
20 The body below the ribs and above the hips (5)
21 Upper part of the leg (5)
22 Unpleasant smell (4)
23 Buffers (8)

Down

1 Position adopted for a photo (4)
2 Unwrap (4)
3 Enhancements (12)
4 One's twilight years (3,3)
6 Qualified for entry (8)
7 Left one's job (8)
8 Type of sweet (12)
12 Conflict internal to a country (5,3)
13 Remedial (8)
16 Martial art (4,2)
18 Prefix denoting one thousand (4)
19 Reasons; explanations (4)

Puzzle 177

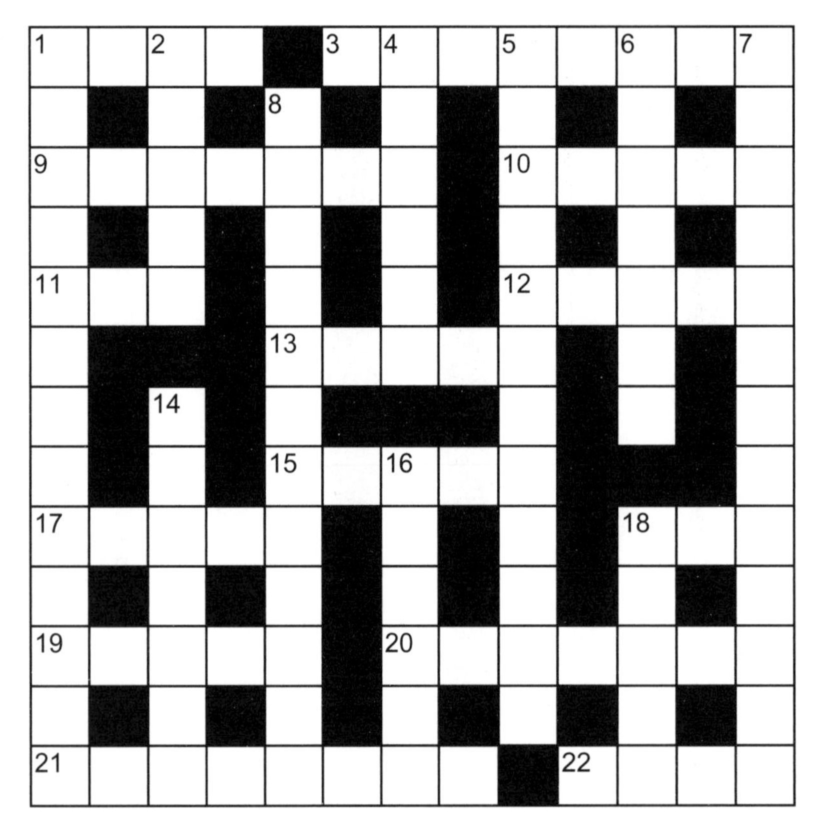

Across

1 Raise to the third power (4)
3 Eg London and Paris (8)
9 Quality of lacking transparency (7)
10 Wall painting (5)
11 Pronoun used to refer to a ship (3)
12 Savoury jelly (5)
13 Follows orders (5)
15 Teacher (5)
17 Litre (anag) (5)
18 Eg English Breakfast (3)
19 Bolt for fastening metal plates (5)
20 Discard from memory (7)
21 Guiding principle (8)
22 Heavy metal (4)

Down

1 Dealing with different societies (5-8)
2 Slow down (5)
4 A person in general (6)
5 Limitless (12)
6 Appropriate (7)
7 Complete in itself (of a thing) (4-9)
8 Type of cloud (12)
14 Friendless (7)
16 Emotional shock (6)
18 Follow the position of (5)

Crossword

Puzzle 178

Across

1 Light blast of wind (4)
3 Not genuine (8)
9 Act of going back in (2-5)
10 Natural elevation (5)
11 Antique; not modern (3-9)
13 Unkempt (of hair) (6)
15 Bivalve mollusc (6)
17 Absolute authority in any sphere (12)
20 Wrong (anag) (5)
21 Someone who provides food (7)
22 A magical quality (8)
23 Solely (4)

Down

1 Small whale with a blunt snout (8)
2 Evil spirit (5)
4 Soul; spirit (6)
5 Major type of food nutrient (12)
6 Something left over (7)
7 Prophet (4)
8 Uncurled (12)
12 Correctly (8)
14 US state (7)
16 Adheres to; fastens (6)
18 Wading bird (5)
19 Grows older (4)

Puzzle 179

Across

1 Doorway (8)
5 Jelly or culture medium (4)
8 Basic units of an element (5)
9 Envelops (7)
10 Alphabetical lists (7)
12 Designer of trendy clothes (7)
14 Feeling guilty (7)
16 Beg (7)
18 Garden flower (7)
19 ___ Nash: writer of light verse (5)
20 Helps (4)
21 Cosiness (8)

Down

1 Vivacity (4)
2 Causing distress or trouble (6)
3 Link (9)
4 Approval; recognition (6)
6 Massive system of stars (6)
7 Held out against (8)
11 Compound vowel character (9)
12 Flowering plant (5,3)
13 Specified (6)
14 Reach (6)
15 Confuse (6)
17 Ceases (4)

Crossword

Puzzle 180

Across

1 Son of one's brother or sister (6)
4 Eventual outcome (6)
9 Pig's foot (7)
10 Jealous (7)
11 Spacious (5)
12 Tall structure on a castle (5)
14 Blunder (5)
15 Senior figure in a tribe (5)
17 Customary practice (5)
18 Musical performance (7)
20 South American country (7)
21 Grates on (6)
22 Participant in a game (6)

Down

1 Innate character of a person (6)
2 Put forward an idea (8)
3 Act of going in (5)
5 Personal (7)
6 Ring of light around the head (4)
7 Type of muscle (6)
8 Dejected (11)
13 Great skill (8)
14 Please or delight (7)
15 Archimedes' famous cry (6)
16 Great fear (6)
17 Customary (5)
19 Blue-green colour (4)

Puzzle 181

Across

1 Average value; miserly (4)
3 Summary (8)
9 Peas and beans (7)
10 Portion (5)
11 Malediction (5)
12 ___ Crowe: Gladiator actor (7)
13 Be preoccupied with (6)
15 Book of accounts (6)
17 Data input device (7)
18 ___ Coogan: English comedian (5)
20 Show triumphant joy (5)
21 Newtlike salamander (7)
22 Flight of steps (8)
23 365 days (4)

Down

1 Spite (13)
2 Extreme displeasure (5)
4 Room attached to a church (6)
5 Act of reclamation (12)
6 Floating mass of frozen water (7)
7 Scheming person (7-6)
8 Imitator (12)
14 Shoulder blade (7)
16 Mistakes in printed matter (6)
19 Decay (5)

Crossword

Puzzle 182

Across

1 Fill a suitcase (4)
3 Complete loss of electrical power (8)
9 Mechanical keyboard (7)
10 Stylish (5)
11 Jail term without end (4,8)
13 State of mental strain (6)
15 Less fresh (of bread) (6)
17 Loving (12)
20 Isle of ___ : island near Southampton (5)
21 Closest (7)
22 Informal term for a feline pet (8)
23 Circular movement of water (4)

Down

1 Intended to appeal to ordinary people (8)
2 Finely cut straw (5)
4 Acquires a new skill (6)
5 In accordance with general custom (12)
6 Relating to sight (7)
7 Playthings (4)
8 Constantly; always (12)
12 Fervently (8)
14 Safe places (7)
16 Basic metrical unit in a poem (6)
18 Change (5)
19 Exchange (4)

Puzzle 183

Across

1 Burst or break (4)
3 Relating to education and scholarship (8)
9 Most unattractive (7)
10 Produce eggs (5)
11 Exclamation of contempt (3)
12 Smell (5)
13 Sailing vessel (5)
15 Jessica ___-Hill : British heptathlete (5)
17 Assumed proposition (5)
18 Twitch (3)
19 Become active (of a volcano) (5)
20 Make more sugary (7)
21 Paying out money (8)
22 Small pond (4)

Down

1 Copious abundance (13)
2 Flatten on impact (5)
4 ___ acid: lemon juice constituent (6)
5 Displeased (12)
6 Pastures (7)
7 Gradual healing (13)
8 Feeling depressed (5-7)
14 Calculate (7)
16 Liam ___ : Schindler's List actor (6)
18 Trite (anag) (5)

Crossword

Puzzle 184

Across

1 Move (8)
5 Absorbent pad (4)
9 Moved by air (5)
10 Ship frames (5)
11 Giving good value for money (10)
14 Continue to exist (6)
15 Pertaining to life (6)
17 Stifling (10)
20 ___-soprano: singing voice (5)
21 Door hanger (5)
22 Ones (anag) (4)
23 Machine used to surf the internet (8)

Down

1 Precious red gem (4)
2 Big cat (4)
3 Compulsory military service (12)
4 Child who skips school (6)
6 Exploratory oil wells (8)
7 Roman building (8)
8 Type of contest (12)
12 Male journalists (8)
13 Steal or misappropriate money (8)
16 Quickly (6)
18 Intertwined segment of rope (4)
19 Sweet juicy fruit (4)

Puzzle 185

Across

1 Sprints (6)
5 Type of music (3-3)
8 Opposite of short (4)
9 Complete (8)
10 Bob ___ : US singer (5)
11 Type of treatment for a disorder (7)
14 Power to give orders (13)
16 List one by one (7)
18 Tiny crustaceans (5)
20 Eg Rudolph (8)
22 US state (4)
23 Outlaw (6)
24 Bright patch of colour (6)

Down

2 Writer of an advice column (5,4)
3 Nonsense (7)
4 White aquatic bird (4)
5 Secret (4-4)
6 ___ bear: powerful mammal (5)
7 Widely cultivated cereal grass (3)
12 Announces officially (9)
13 Shape of the waxing moon (8)
15 Tumult (7)
17 Denim (anag) (5)
19 Weapons (4)
21 Large period of time (3)

Crossword

Puzzle 186

Across

1 Ate greedily (8)
5 Unit of liquid capacity (4)
9 Work tables (5)
10 Lover of Juliet (5)
11 Eg baptism and matrimony (10)
14 Involving direct confrontation (4-2)
15 Part of a motor (6)
17 Underwater vessels (10)
20 Ethical (5)
21 Not dead (5)
22 Close by (4)
23 Freshwater crustacean (8)

Down

1 Fathers (4)
2 Container for flowers (4)
3 Untimely (12)
4 Steers (anag) (6)
6 Exemption (8)
7 Clothing that covers the legs (8)
8 Therapeutic use of plant extracts (12)
12 Eg rooks and knights (8)
13 Capital of Australia (8)
16 Hot spice (6)
18 Very short skirt or dress (4)
19 Wire lattice (4)

Puzzle 187

Across

1 Listen to (4)
3 Commonplace (8)
9 Seriously (7)
10 Draw off liquid from (5)
11 Written in pictorial symbols (12)
13 Ratio of reflected to incident light (6)
15 Imaginary (6)
17 Disregarding the rules (5,3,4)
20 Musical toy (5)
21 Apparatus (7)
22 Overcame (8)
23 Wet with condensation (4)

Down

1 Large cask (8)
2 Unconditional love (5)
4 Casino ___ : James Bond film (6)
5 Freedom from control (12)
6 Greed (7)
7 Pull abruptly (4)
8 Without parallel (6,2,4)
12 In a carefree manner (8)
14 Zephyrs (7)
16 Hinder the progress of (6)
18 Expel from a country (5)
19 Read quickly (4)

Puzzle 188

Across

1 Upsetting (11)
9 Tears (anag) (5)
10 Large vessel (3)
11 The Hunter (constellation) (5)
12 Lump or bump (5)
13 A canine (3,5)
16 Design engraved into a material (8)
18 Name of a book (5)
21 Narrow roads (5)
22 Vitality (3)
23 Lift up (5)
24 Fraudulently (11)

Down

2 Asked to come along (7)
3 Wooden bar across a window (7)
4 Still existing (6)
5 Cleanse by rubbing (5)
6 Book (5)
7 Business run jointly by its members (11)
8 Energetically or vigorously (11)
14 Anarchic (7)
15 Soft woven fabric (7)
17 Concept (6)
19 Musical times (5)
20 Our planet (5)

Puzzle 189

Across

1 Get off (6)
5 Crux of a matter (3)
7 Derogatory in an indirect way (5)
8 Garden bird (7)
9 Pipes (5)
10 Until now (8)
12 Accepted (6)
14 Grinned (6)
17 Push button outside a house (8)
18 Extreme pain (5)
20 Large area of land (7)
21 Quoted (5)
22 Band who sang Shining Light (3)
23 Spiny-finned fish (6)

Down

2 Thinning out branches of a tree (7)
3 Protected; toughened (8)
4 Present (4)
5 Seven-a-side game (7)
6 Blighted (7)
7 Hits swiftly (5)
11 Not appropriate (8)
12 Capital of the US state of Georgia (7)
13 Enhance a photo (7)
15 Signs up (7)
16 Talked humorously (5)
19 Legendary creature (4)

Crossword

Puzzle 190

Across

1 Collide with (4)
3 Shields from (8)
9 Bodies of writing (7)
10 Form of expression (5)
11 Awe-inspiring (12)
13 Belonging to them (6)
15 Slender (6)
17 Evergreen shrub (12)
20 Major artery (5)
21 Serving no purpose (7)
22 Clip to keep something in place (8)
23 Large bodies of water (4)

Down

1 Say mean things about another (8)
2 ___ Simpson: cartoon character (5)
4 Cooks in the oven (6)
5 Insensitive to criticism (5-7)
6 Sophisticated hair style (7)
7 Japanese sport (4)
8 Person studying after a first degree (12)
12 Mesmerism (8)
14 Urges strongly (7)
16 Request earnestly (6)
18 Pass a rope through (5)
19 Young cow (4)

Puzzle 191

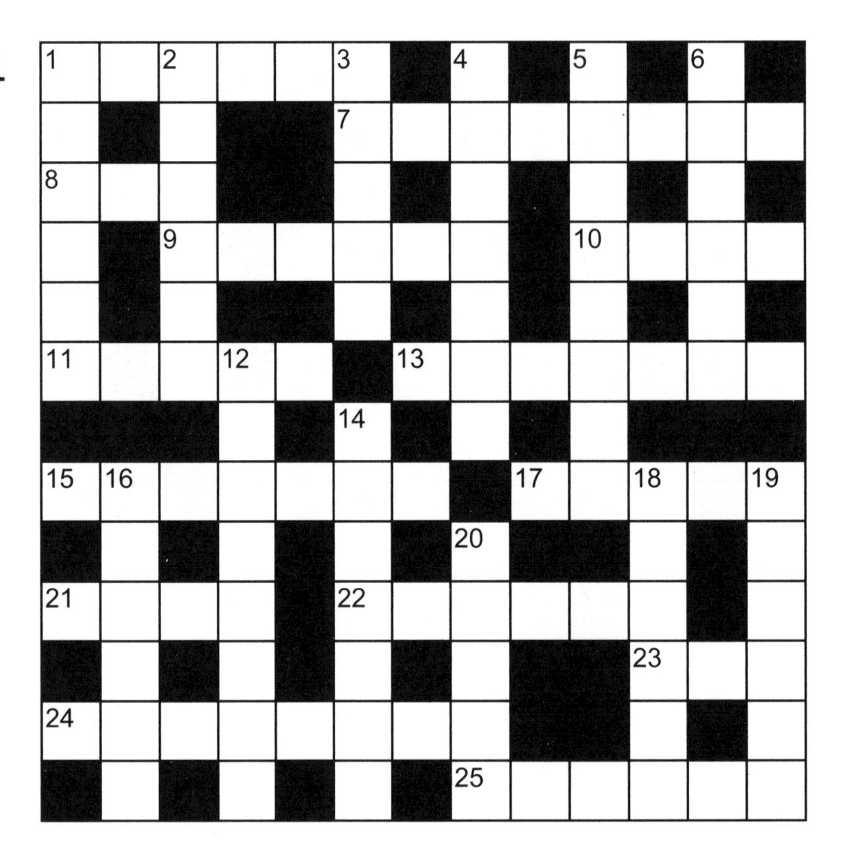

Across

1 ___ Fox: English actress (6)
7 Predict the future (8)
8 Unwell (3)
9 Self-evident truths (6)
10 Uncommon (4)
11 Supplementary component (3-2)
13 Written language for blind people (7)
15 Lack of (7)
17 Country in NE Africa (5)
21 Told an untruth (4)
22 Songbird (6)
23 Cheek (slang) (3)
24 Expression of gratitude (5,3)
25 Chase (6)

Down

1 Complex problem (6)
2 Eg Iceland (6)
3 Currently in progress (5)
4 These remove pencil marks (7)
5 Violently attacking (a building) (8)
6 Consisting of flowers (6)
12 Exaggerated (8)
14 Kind of abbreviation (7)
16 Happy; carefree (6)
18 Gives in (6)
19 Hairpiece (6)
20 Confusion (3-2)

Crossword

Puzzle 192

Across

1 Lacking humility (8)
5 Slightly open (4)
8 Pertaining to birth (5)
9 Travelling very quickly (7)
10 ___ oil: product of the flax plant (7)
12 Childbirth assistant (7)
14 Study of the past (7)
16 Deadlock (7)
18 Type of photographic shot (5-2)
19 Receded (5)
20 Look for (4)
21 Disperse (anag) (8)

Down

1 Public houses (4)
2 Tangled (of hair) (6)
3 Very tasty (9)
4 Crackle (6)
6 Linked (6)
7 Lack of flexibility (8)
11 Short films (9)
12 Curved surface of a liquid in a tube (8)
13 Argue against (6)
14 Aide (6)
15 Make a larger offer at auction (6)
17 Chances of winning (4)

Puzzle 193

Across

- **1** Bone of the forearm (4)
- **3** Unfit for consumption (of food) (8)
- **9** King Arthur's home (7)
- **10** Rigid (5)
- **11** Wet soil (3)
- **12** Keen (5)
- **13** Angry dispute (3-2)
- **15** Small room used as a steam bath (5)
- **17** Uniform jacket (5)
- **18** Dry (of wine) (3)
- **19** Subatomic particle such as a photon (5)
- **20** Eg anger or love (7)
- **21** Opposite of westerly (8)
- **22** Allot a punishment (4)

Down

- **1** Uneasy (13)
- **2** Wanderer (5)
- **4** Country (6)
- **5** Exemption from a rule (12)
- **6** Structures that span rivers (7)
- **7** Fizz (13)
- **8** Fence closure (anag) (12)
- **14** Nasal cavities (7)
- **16** Uncover (6)
- **18** Strike (5)

Crossword

Puzzle 194

Across

1 Increase in size (6)
4 From that place (6)
9 Artificial (3-4)
10 Contradicted; neutralised (7)
11 Slabs of peat for fuel (5)
12 Regulations (5)
14 Discharged a weapon (5)
15 Tropical fruit (5)
17 Additional (5)
18 Huge wave (7)
20 Concepts (7)
21 Selection (6)
22 Agreement or concord (6)

Down

1 Hostility (6)
2 All-round view (8)
3 Approaches (5)
5 Matthew ___ : former England cricketer (7)
6 Coming immediately after (4)
7 Discharges (6)
8 Perceptive; insightful (11)
13 Bright and glistening (8)
14 Extreme enthusiast (7)
15 Style of architecture (6)
16 Nigella ___ : English food writer (6)
17 Consumed (of food) (5)
19 Unravel (4)

Puzzle 195

Across

- **1** Doubtful (4)
- **3** Slower than sound (8)
- **9** Judicious (7)
- **10** Broadcast again (5)
- **11** Personnel at work (5)
- **12** Go back over (7)
- **13** Phrases that are not taken literally (6)
- **15** Upward slope (6)
- **17** Perfectly (7)
- **18** Despised (5)
- **20** Where one finds Rome (5)
- **21** Green vegetation (7)
- **22** Giving way under pressure (8)
- **23** Seek (anag) (4)

Down

- **1** Something that cannot be done (13)
- **2** Animal life of a region (5)
- **4** Speaks (6)
- **5** Atmospheric layer (12)
- **6** Tell a story (7)
- **7** Satisfaction (13)
- **8** Working for oneself (4-8)
- **14** Do repeatedly (7)
- **16** Punctuation mark (6)
- **19** Express gratitude (5)

Crossword

Puzzle 196

Across

1 Long green vegetable (8)
5 Familiar name for a potato (4)
9 Oarsman (5)
10 Ski run (5)
11 Machine with keys (10)
14 Destroy (6)
15 Wonder at (6)
17 Study of the essential nature of reality (10)
20 Physical strength; muscle (5)
21 Prevent access to something (5)
22 Compass point (4)
23 Aromatic plant used in cooking (8)

Down

1 Complain unreasonably (4)
2 Large loose hood (4)
3 Amusement park ride (5-2-5)
4 Large birds of prey (6)
6 Certain (8)
7 Gloomily (8)
8 Easy to converse with (12)
12 Deserving blame (8)
13 Opposite of departures (8)
16 Aureate (6)
18 Mischievous god in Norse mythology (4)
19 Gull-like bird (4)

Puzzle 197

Across

1 Neither good nor bad (2-2)
3 Put at risk (8)
9 Candid (7)
10 Joining together with cord (5)
11 Barely sufficient (5)
12 Substance used to remove heat (7)
13 Far from the intended target (6)
15 Lively Spanish dance (6)
17 Collate (7)
18 Individual things (5)
20 Clumsy (5)
21 Ignorant of something (7)
22 Protecting (8)
23 Deciduous trees (4)

Down

1 Deep consideration of oneself (4-9)
2 Capital of Bulgaria (5)
4 See (6)
5 Extremely large (12)
6 Facial expression showing disgust (7)
7 Virtuousness (13)
8 Showed not to be true (12)
14 Painting medium (7)
16 Yield or make (a profit) (6)
19 Electronic message (5)

Crossword

Puzzle 198

Across

1 Specialist in care for the feet (11)
9 Representative (5)
10 Trouble in mind or body (3)
11 Put a question to (5)
12 Harsh and grating in sound (5)
13 Happening every two years (8)
16 Coming out of (8)
18 Assembly (5)
21 Empty spaces (5)
22 Large body of water (3)
23 ___ Arabia: country (5)
24 Pairs of round brackets (11)

Down

2 Dogs that pull sledges (7)
3 Town in Berkshire (7)
4 Spanish rice dish (6)
5 Put off (5)
6 Breaks in two (5)
7 Astound (11)
8 Eg Queen of Hearts (7,4)
14 Narrow fissure (7)
15 Bishop's jurisdiction (7)
17 French dance (6)
19 Barack ___ : 44th US President (5)
20 Adhesive (5)

Puzzle 199

Across

1 German car manufacturer (4)
3 Beast with three heads (8)
9 Moderates; mitigates (7)
10 Command (5)
11 Aromatic herb of the mint family (5)
12 Statement of commemoration (7)
13 Being with organic and cybernetic parts (6)
15 Bubble violently (6)
17 Unpredictable (7)
18 Wound from a wasp (5)
20 Adult insect (5)
21 Exceeds; surpasses (7)
22 Liked sea (anag) (8)
23 ___ Giggs: former footballer (4)

Down

1 Destroying microorganisms (13)
2 Curbs; muffles (5)
4 Follows (6)
5 Variety of wildlife in an area (12)
6 Write again (7)
7 The Duchess of York (5,8)
8 Formal announcements (12)
14 Jeer noisily at (7)
16 Reverberated (6)
19 Creamy-white colour (5)

Crossword

Puzzle 200

Across

1 Millionth of a metre (6)
4 Slow to understand (6)
9 Stations where journeys end (7)
10 Stiff coarse hair (7)
11 Type of stopwatch (5)
12 Easy (of a job) (5)
14 Eg molar or incisor (5)
15 Purchaser (5)
17 Smell (5)
18 Capital of Kenya (7)
20 Simple song for a baby (7)
21 Church councils (6)
22 Confirmed or supported a decision (6)

Down

1 Short choral compositions (6)
2 Ritual (8)
3 Willow twig (5)
5 Charm; enchant (7)
6 An individual thing (4)
7 Restaurant (6)
8 Book lover (11)
13 Deliberately damage (8)
14 Marched (7)
15 Small drums (6)
16 Made a victim of (6)
17 Type of primula (5)
19 Graphic symbol (4)

Puzzle 201

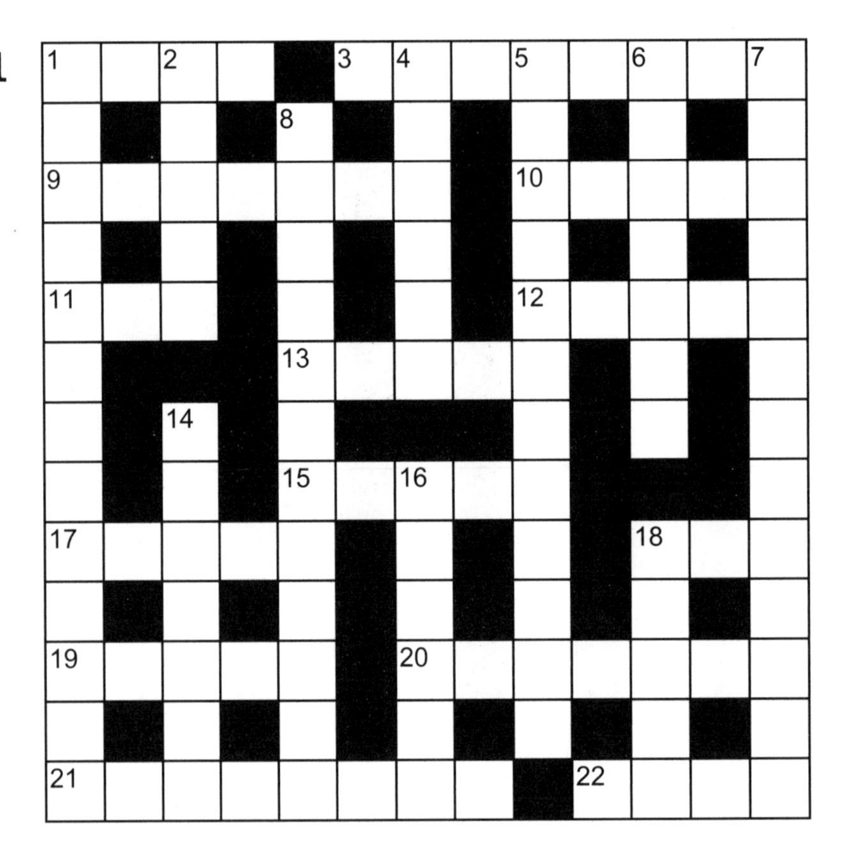

Across

1 Snug (4)
3 Partially hidden (8)
9 Long distance postal service (7)
10 Dry red wine (5)
11 Nay (anag) (3)
12 Supple (5)
13 Small house (5)
15 Competes in a speed contest (5)
17 Imitative of the past (5)
18 Ant and ___ : presenting duo (3)
19 Work spirit (5)
20 Small falcon (7)
21 Higher in rank (8)
22 Declare untrue (4)

Down

1 Dull and uninteresting (13)
2 Cover with liquid (5)
4 Simple song (6)
5 Failure to act with prudence (12)
6 Highest vantage point of a building (7)
7 Completely (opposed) (13)
8 Troublemaker (6-6)
14 Tomato sauce (7)
16 Harbinger of spring (6)
18 Mournful song (5)

Crossword

Puzzle 202

Across

1 Protrudes (8)
5 Mats (4)
9 Exclusive story (5)
10 Innate worth (5)
11 Beam anchored at only one end (10)
14 Middle Eastern language (6)
15 Attitude or body position (6)
17 Analogy (10)
20 Pinkish-red colour (5)
21 Confound (5)
22 Covers; tops (4)
23 Listen to again (4,4)

Down

1 Monetary unit of Mexico (4)
2 Woodwind instrument (4)
3 Vehemently (12)
4 Very reliable (6)
6 Not giving affection (8)
7 Fortified wines (8)
8 Developmental (12)
12 Absurd (8)
13 Battered (8)
16 Banish; eliminate (6)
18 Island of Indonesia (4)
19 Overly submissive (4)

Puzzle 203

Across

1 Put up with (8)
5 Short tail (4)
8 Sudden forward thrust (5)
9 Japanese flower arranging (7)
10 Set apart (7)
12 Percussion instrument (7)
14 Capable of being remedied (7)
16 Tragedy by Shakespeare (7)
18 Uncomplaining (7)
19 Printed insert supplied with a CD (5)
20 Elephant tooth (4)
21 Melanins (anag) (8)

Down

1 Narrated (4)
2 Hang around; remain (6)
3 Test again (2-7)
4 Irrelevant pieces of information (6)
6 Item of neckwear (6)
7 Journey across (8)
11 Having effect (9)
12 Central American monkey (8)
13 Thespians (6)
14 Hot pepper (6)
15 Extreme confusion (6)
17 Church song (4)

Crossword

Puzzle 204

Across

1 Not hot (4)
3 Most saccharine (8)
9 Took small bites out of (7)
10 Manages (5)
11 Appeal (5)
12 Ancestry (7)
13 Excitingly strange (6)
15 Where one finds Athens (6)
17 Mental process or idea (7)
18 Remedies (5)
20 General hatred (5)
21 Ardent (7)
22 Ominous (8)
23 Pass (anag) (4)

Down

1 Characterised by great care (13)
2 Seventh sign of the zodiac (5)
4 Walk like a duck (6)
5 Behavioural peculiarity (12)
6 Make amends (7)
7 Blandness (13)
8 International multi-sport event (7,5)
14 Relating to Oxford (7)
16 Walk with long steps (6)
19 Leases (5)

Puzzle 205

Across

1 Banner or flag (6)
4 Stretch prior to exercise (4-2)
9 Flat highland (7)
10 Make ineffective (7)
11 Nearby (5)
12 Surface upon which one walks (5)
14 Faith in another (5)
15 Breadth (5)
17 Arm of a body of water (5)
18 River in Africa (7)
20 Art of public speaking (7)
21 Sleepy (6)
22 Served (anag) (6)

Down

1 Anticipate (6)
2 Followed a person closely (8)
3 Church farmland (5)
5 Aerial rescue (7)
6 Bamako is the capital here (4)
7 Religious act of petition (6)
8 Eg full stops and commas (11)
13 Views (8)
14 Statements of intent to harm (7)
15 Magician (6)
16 Remained (6)
17 Visual representation (5)
19 Short note or reminder (4)

Crossword

Puzzle 206

Across

1 Obvious (8)
5 Eg an arm or leg (4)
9 Singing voices (5)
10 Sprites (5)
11 Decorative (10)
14 Not level (6)
15 Edits (6)
17 Scoring (10)
20 Dance club (5)
21 Become very hot (5)
22 Aromatic herb (4)
23 Pennant (8)

Down

1 Expression of regret (4)
2 A person's head (4)
3 Revival of something (12)
4 Sugary flower secretion (6)
6 Alluring (8)
7 Groundless (8)
8 Resolvable (12)
12 Became less intense (8)
13 Act of retaliation (8)
16 Economy; providence (6)
18 Move about aimlessly; wander (4)
19 Smudge (4)

Puzzle 207

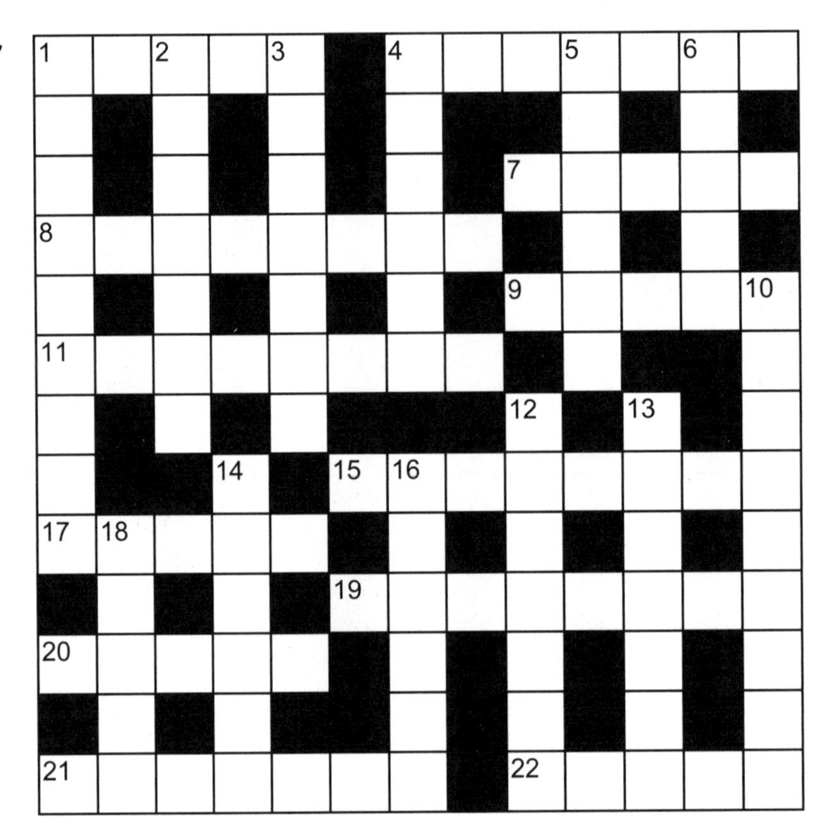

Across

1 Entrance barriers (5)
4 Dirtier (7)
7 Lean or thin (5)
8 Short film (8)
9 Lavish (5)
11 Story with a symbolic message (8)
15 Where one finds Glasgow (8)
17 Steer (5)
19 Squid (8)
20 Confess to be true (5)
21 Progress (7)
22 Appears (5)

Down

1 Domesticated cavy (6,3)
2 Gardening tools (7)
3 Electronic retention of data (7)
4 ___ shower: eg the Perseids (6)
5 Mottled marking (6)
6 Deserves (5)
10 Appears as the star of the show (9)
12 Large dark low cloud (7)
13 Aural pain (7)
14 ___ Currie: former politician (6)
16 Accuse; run at (6)
18 Reversed (5)

Crossword

Puzzle 208

Across

1 Finish (6)
4 Brushes (6)
9 Actually; in reality (2,5)
10 Bring up (7)
11 Music with a recurrent theme (5)
12 ___ John: Rocket Man singer (5)
14 Gets weary (5)
15 Mistake (5)
17 Plants of a region (5)
18 Symbols of disgrace (7)
20 Aptitude (7)
21 Colour of a lemon (6)
22 US state (6)

Down

1 Small shrubs with pithy stems (6)
2 Protector; guardian (8)
3 Tortilla topped with cheese (5)
5 Quayside areas (7)
6 Beige colour (4)
7 Partition that divides a room (6)
8 Neutral (11)
13 Hurling (8)
14 Wavering effect in a musical tone (7)
15 Without difficulty (6)
16 Grand ___ : steep-sided gorge (6)
17 ___ Tuck: friend of Robin Hood (5)
19 Image of a god (4)

Puzzle 209

Across

- **1** Pertaining to the arts (8)
- **5** Nocturnal insect (4)
- **8** Thick sweet liquid (5)
- **9** Gave way to pressure (7)
- **10** Single-horned creature (7)
- **12** Breastbone (7)
- **14** Chemical element with symbol Y (7)
- **16** Late (7)
- **18** Icy (7)
- **19** Venerate; worship (5)
- **20** Move like a wheel (4)
- **21** Additional book matter (8)

Down

- **1** Apex or peak (4)
- **2** Immature insects (6)
- **3** Unintentional (9)
- **4** Shelter (6)
- **6** Alumnus of a public school (3,3)
- **7** Pursuit of pleasure (8)
- **11** Bring about (9)
- **12** More powerful (8)
- **13** Nitty-gritty (6)
- **14** Shouted out (6)
- **15** An advance; progress (6)
- **17** Hold as an opinion (4)

Crossword

Puzzle 210

Across

1 Expel; drive out (4)
3 Protective garments (8)
9 Harden (7)
10 Push gently (5)
11 Inadequately manned (12)
13 Cover or conceal (6)
15 Follow-up drink (6)
17 Using both letters and numerals (12)
20 Sporting stadium (5)
21 Rank in the forces (7)
22 Distribute (8)
23 Critical examination (4)

Down

1 Sudden release of emotion (8)
2 Players who form a team (5)
4 Conceit (6)
5 Not special (3-2-3-4)
6 Items used for climbing up (7)
7 Appear to be (4)
8 Street (12)
12 Wristband (8)
14 Large waves (7)
16 Acquired skills (6)
18 Wash in water to remove soap or dirt (5)
19 Suffered the consequences (4)

Puzzle 211

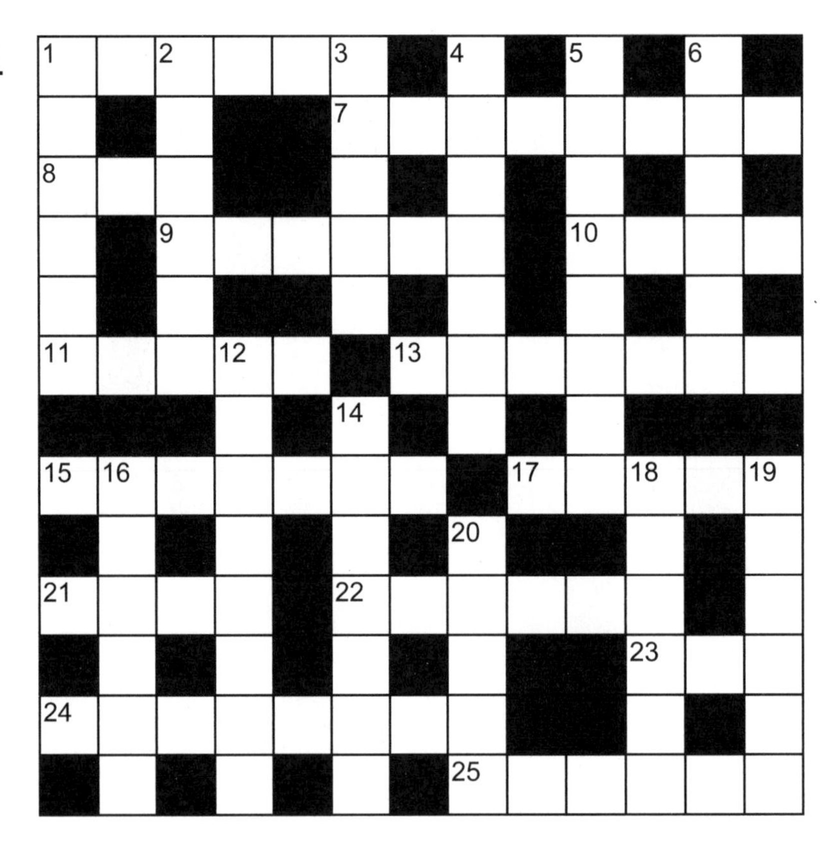

Across

1 Republic once ruled by Idi Amin (6)
7 Pestered constantly (8)
8 Nevertheless (3)
9 George ___ : composer (6)
10 Suggestion; thought (4)
11 Small heron (5)
13 Rearranged letters of a word (7)
15 Obedient (7)
17 Lure an animal into a trap (5)
21 Delude (4)
22 End a dispute (6)
23 Mixture of gases we breathe (3)
24 Range of colours (8)
25 At sixes and ___ : in disarray (6)

Down

1 Refined in manner (6)
2 Part of a stamen (6)
3 Live by (5)
4 Confusing (7)
5 Item of sweet food (8)
6 Former Spanish currency (6)
12 Proof of something (8)
14 People who manage college finances (7)
16 Takes the place of (6)
18 Make (6)
19 Hankers after (6)
20 Plant stalks (5)

Crossword

Puzzle 212

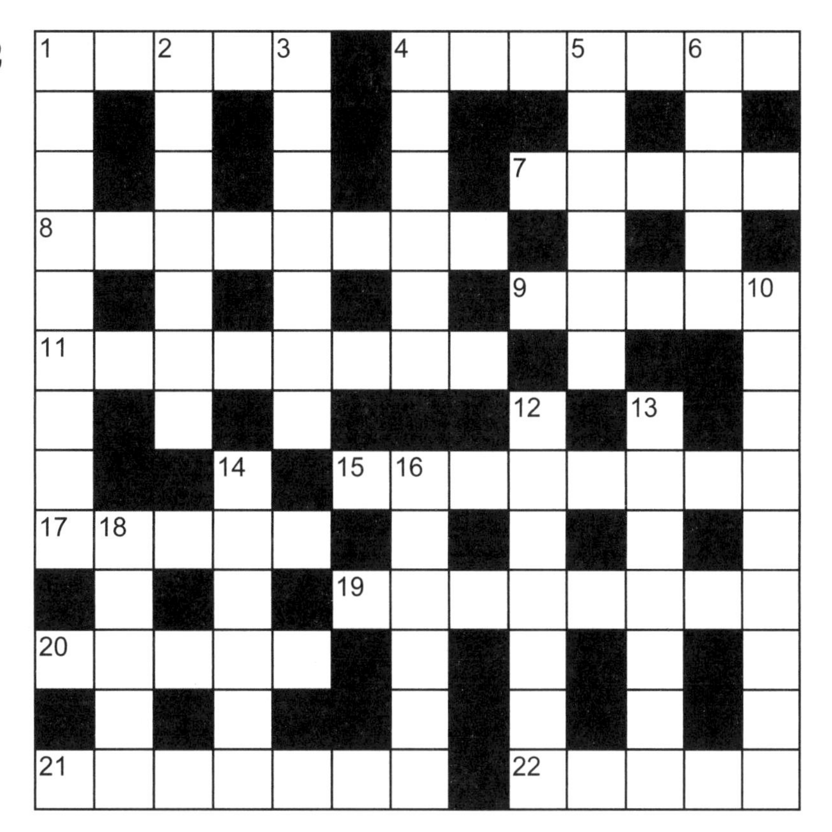

Across

1 ___ Bellamy: Welsh footballer (5)
4 Pestering constantly (7)
7 Dark wood (5)
8 Take to pieces to examine (8)
9 Takes part in a game (5)
11 Refuge (8)
15 Porch (8)
17 Microscopic fungus (5)
19 Car light (8)
20 Young sheep (5)
21 Diminish the worth of (7)
22 Latin American dance (5)

Down

1 Discordant mix of sounds (9)
2 So soon (7)
3 Deity (7)
4 Cloud of gas in space (6)
5 Eat hurriedly (6)
6 Character in the musical Oliver! (5)
10 Ongoing television serial (4,5)
12 Curbs (7)
13 Type of alcohol (7)
14 Line of equal pressure on a map (6)
16 Medium-sized feline (6)
18 Avoid (5)

Puzzle 213

Across

1 Unfortunately (5)
4 Damage the reputation of (5)
10 Let out (7)
11 Record on tape (5)
12 Ewers (4)
13 Cartographer (8)
16 Inclined one's head to show approval (6)
17 Whole (6)
20 Visible horizons (8)
21 Loud noise (4)
23 Long-handled spoon (5)
25 This starts on 1st January (3,4)
26 Makes a garment from wool (5)
27 Large wading bird (5)

Down

2 Supposedly (9)
3 Incline (4)
5 Division of a musical work (8)
6 Additionally (3)
7 Inhabitant of Troy (6)
8 Make good on a debt (5)
9 Guided journey (4)
14 Tailless Australian marsupial (5,4)
15 Send to a different place (8)
18 Large solitary cats (6)
19 Baked ___ : popular tinned food (5)
20 Ales (anag) (4)
22 Study assiduously (4)
24 University teacher (3)

Crossword

Puzzle 214

Across

1 A single time (4)
3 Fine form of leather (8)
9 Tried a new product (7)
10 Cavalry sword (5)
11 Ill-mannered (12)
14 Curved shape (3)
16 Entice to do something (5)
17 Place where one sees animals (3)
18 Nationally (12)
21 Obsession (5)
22 Friendly goodbye (7)
23 Bubbling sound of water flowing (8)
24 Narrow strip of land (4)

Down

1 Glass-like volcanic rock (8)
2 Temporary lodgings (5)
4 Help; assist (3)
5 Wearing glasses (12)
6 Communal settlement in Israel (7)
7 Christmas (4)
8 Unseen observer (3,2,3,4)
12 Send money (5)
13 Exterior of a motor vehicle (8)
15 Singer (7)
19 Big (5)
20 Complacent (4)
22 Argument against something (3)

Puzzle 215

Across

1 Become worse (11)
9 Lived (anag) (5)
10 Sense of self-esteem (3)
11 Strong ringing sound (5)
12 Rugby set piece (5)
13 Catastrophe (8)
16 Became visible (8)
18 Stomach exercise (3-2)
21 Passageway (5)
22 Large deer (3)
23 Push back (5)
24 Basically (11)

Down

2 To the same degree (7)
3 Final stage of an extended process (7)
4 Turn upside down (6)
5 Small streams (5)
6 Belonging to them (5)
7 Uninvited guest (11)
8 Divine rule (11)
14 Finery (7)
15 ___ ball: item used by clairvoyants (7)
17 Marionette (6)
19 Gains possession of (5)
20 Money container (5)

Crossword

Puzzle 216

Across

1 Free from danger (6)
4 Rhesus (anag) (6)
9 West Indian musical style (7)
10 ___ Monroe: famous actress (7)
11 Person who always puts in a lot of effort (5)
12 Mental impressions (5)
14 Showing a willingness to achieve results (3-2)
15 Trench (5)
17 Period of darkness (5)
18 Italian fast racing car (7)
20 Remove a difficulty (7)
21 Keep hold of (6)
22 Moves very slowly (6)

Down

1 Repeat from memory (6)
2 Most foolish (8)
3 Opposite of lower (5)
5 Sign of the zodiac (7)
6 British nobleman (4)
7 Gets to one's feet (6)
8 Deep regret (11)
13 Move to another country (8)
14 Dry red table wine of Italy (7)
15 Resisted (6)
16 Spirited horses (6)
17 At no time (5)
19 Smallest pig of the litter (4)

Puzzle 217

1		2		■	3	4		5		6		7
	■		■	8	■		■		■		■	
9							■	10				
	■		■		■	■	■		■		■	
11						12						■
	■	■	■		■		■		■		■	13
14		15	■	16					■	17		
	■		■		■		■		■	■	■	
■	18									19		
20	■		■		■	■	■		■		■	
21					■	22						
	■		■		■		■		■		■	
23								■	24			

Across

1 Mocks (4)
3 Ascot cat (anag) (8)
9 Capital of Ontario (7)
10 Bring together (5)
11 Careful management of the environment (12)
14 Louse egg (3)
16 Underground worker (5)
17 Flightless bird (3)
18 In a sparing manner (12)
21 Arose from slumber (5)
22 Worry (7)
23 Think deeply for a period of time (8)
24 Salver (4)

Down

1 Reserved; diffident (8)
2 Element with atomic number 5 (5)
4 One and one (3)
5 Compensate for (12)
6 Used for storing fat (of body tissue) (7)
7 Semi-precious agate (4)
8 Sporadic (12)
12 Snake toxin (5)
13 Ability to float (8)
15 Type of newspaper (7)
19 Guide a vehicle (5)
20 Injure (4)
22 Snip (3)

Crossword

Puzzle 218

1 2 3 4 5 6 7 8 9 10 11 12 13 14 15 16 17 18 19 20 21 22 23

Across

1 Gangs (4)
3 Animal that hunts (8)
9 Rider (7)
10 Type of lizard (5)
11 Uncertain (12)
13 Machine that creates motion (6)
15 Afternoon snooze in Spain (6)
17 The proprietor of an eating establishment (12)
20 Swiftness or speed (5)
21 Quick musical tempo (7)
22 Move out the way of (8)
23 Small particles of stone (4)

Down

1 Old World monkeys (8)
2 Game similar to bowls (5)
4 Sat an exam again (6)
5 Insistently (12)
6 Touches the skin of another lightly (7)
7 Area of a house (4)
8 Clarity (12)
12 Put into action (5,3)
14 Made a conjecture about (7)
16 Clergyman (6)
18 Gardening tool (5)
19 ___ Ifans: Welsh actor (4)

Puzzle 219

Across

1 Supporter of James II (8)
5 Protest march (abbrev) (4)
9 Cathedral (5)
10 Sets of six balls (cricket) (5)
11 Greet formally (5,5)
14 Leads a discussion (6)
15 Contort (6)
17 Process of dying out (10)
20 About (5)
21 Move effortlessly through air (5)
22 Soft drink (US) (4)
23 Process of sticking to a surface (8)

Down

1 Hard green gem (4)
2 Dove sounds (4)
3 Relation by marriage (7-2-3)
4 Crafty (6)
6 Infinite time (8)
7 Thinks about something continually (8)
8 First language (6,6)
12 Eg physics and biology (8)
13 Started to lose strength (8)
16 Put on a production (6)
18 Flightless bird (4)
19 Adolescent (abbrev) (4)

Crossword

Puzzle 220

Across

1 Type of palm tree (6)
7 Forgave (8)
8 Not me (3)
9 Socially awkward (6)
10 Young children (4)
11 Act slowly (5)
13 Performing a task again (7)
15 Factory for casting metal (7)
17 Broom composed of twigs (5)
21 Temporary outside shelter (4)
22 Spectator (6)
23 Roe (anag) (3)
24 Eloquently (8)
25 Portable computer (6)

Down

1 Had corresponding sounds (6)
2 Avoiding waste; thrifty (6)
3 With speed (5)
4 Not crying (3-4)
5 Small window on a ship (8)
6 Isaac ___ : physicist (6)
12 Grow longer (8)
14 Briefness (7)
16 Excessively (6)
18 Begin to grow (6)
19 Fictional (4,2)
20 Precious stone (5)

Puzzle 221

Across

1 Changeable (8)
5 Freezes over (4)
8 Fissures (5)
9 ___ power: energy source (7)
10 Opposite of morning (7)
12 Clinging shellfish (7)
14 Surpassed (7)
16 Combined metals (7)
18 Intrusions (7)
19 Opposite of outer (5)
20 Yellow part of an egg (4)
21 Opposites (8)

Down

1 Action word (4)
2 Make changes to improve something (6)
3 Certainly (9)
4 Wildcats (6)
6 Religious leader (6)
7 Strive (8)
11 Of times past (9)
12 Lawfulness (8)
13 Not singular (6)
14 More likely than not (4-2)
15 States as one's opinion (6)
17 Large periods of time (4)

Crossword

Puzzle 222

Across

1 Young lions (4)
3 Appetising drink (8)
9 Person proposed for office (7)
10 Less moist (5)
11 Smooth textile fibre (5)
12 Item of clerical clothing (7)
13 Cavalry swords (6)
15 Wall painting; mural (6)
17 Occidental (7)
18 Type of bread roll (5)
20 Worthiness (5)
21 Expressed audibly (7)
22 In these times (8)
23 Venerable ___ : English monk (4)

Down

1 Female politician in the US (13)
2 Uneven (of a surface) (5)
4 Penetrate (6)
5 Reallocate (12)
6 Camera stands (7)
7 Prescience (13)
8 Indifferent to (12)
14 Cover or partly cover (7)
16 Physical wound (6)
19 Ravine (5)

Puzzle 223

Across

1 Something easy or certain (8)
5 Whirring sound; prickly seed case (4)
9 Doctor (5)
10 Strong desires (5)
11 Section of an orchestra (10)
14 Recapture (6)
15 Stringed instrument (6)
17 Component part (10)
20 Alert (5)
21 Apart from (5)
22 Skirt worn by ballerinas (4)
23 Easy victory (8)

Down

1 Arrived (4)
2 African antelope (4)
3 Specialist cricketing position (12)
4 Propel with force (6)
6 Awkward (8)
7 Sonorous (8)
8 The ? symbol (8,4)
12 Source of annoyance (8)
13 Having no current (of a body of water) (8)
16 Public square in Italy (6)
18 Capital of the Ukraine (4)
19 Read (anag) (4)

Puzzle 224

1		2		■	3	4		5		6		7
	■		■	8	■		■		■		■	
9							■	10				
	■		■		■		■		■		■	
11												■
	■	■	■		■		■		■		■	12
13		14				■	15					
	■		■		■	16	■		■	■	■	
■	17									18		
19	■		■		■		■		■		■	
20					■	21						
	■		■		■		■		■		■	
22								■	23			

Across

1 Dutch cheese (4)
3 Lists (8)
9 Mathematical rule (7)
10 Haggard (5)
11 Despicable (12)
13 Very milky (6)
15 Next after seventh (6)
17 Separation; alienation (12)
20 Consent to (5)
21 Due to the fact that (7)
22 Aided (8)
23 Belonging to a woman (4)

Down

1 Measure of effectiveness (8)
2 Protective garment (5)
4 Walks heavily and firmly (6)
5 Grandeur (12)
6 Make a sucking sound (7)
7 Takes an exam (4)
8 Large grocery stores (12)
12 Breaks into pieces (8)
14 Guarantees (7)
16 Nebula (anag) (6)
18 Display freely (5)
19 Tibetan Buddhist monk (4)

Puzzle 225

Across

1 Napping (8)
5 Nothing (4)
9 Public announcement officer (5)
10 Common edible fruit (5)
11 Very noisy (10)
14 ___ Reed: English actor (6)
15 Regard with approval (6)
17 Result of a bang on the head (10)
20 Iron alloy (5)
21 Go about stealthily (5)
22 Overly curious (4)
23 Experiencing great hunger (8)

Down

1 Of like kind (4)
2 Release; give out (4)
3 Resolutely (12)
4 Papal representative (6)
6 Extremely happy (8)
7 Supervisor (8)
8 Person who listens into conversations (12)
12 Soft leather shoe (8)
13 The first people to do something (8)
16 Bodyguard (6)
18 ___ Amos: US singer-songwriter (4)
19 Beat with a whip (4)

Puzzle 226

Across

1 Strongbox (4)
3 Narrow street or passage (8)
9 Raises dough (using yeast) (7)
10 Thermosetting resin (5)
11 Regardless of (12)
13 Pay attention to (6)
15 Long mountain chain (6)
17 Joblessness (12)
20 Oak tree nut (5)
21 Payments in addition to wages (7)
22 Re-evaluate (8)
23 Bovine animals (4)

Down

1 Military people (8)
2 Talent; ability (5)
4 Heed (6)
5 Very exciting (12)
6 Anybody (7)
7 Spool-like toy (2-2)
8 Calculations of dimensions (12)
12 Devoted to a cause (8)
14 Venetian boat (7)
16 Spherical objects (6)
18 County of SE England (5)
19 Equitable (4)

Puzzle 227

Across

1 Measure of heat (11)
9 Word of farewell (5)
10 Came across (3)
11 Relating to vision (5)
12 Small drum (5)
13 An unspecified person (8)
16 Monstrous creature (8)
18 Concealing garments (5)
21 Fish-eating mammal (5)
22 Word expressing negation (3)
23 Angered; irritated (5)
24 Mark an event (11)

Down

2 Perfect example of a quality (7)
3 Inactive pill (7)
4 Destroyed (6)
5 Pollex (5)
6 Manor (anag) (5)
7 Inattentive (11)
8 Creating an evocative mood (11)
14 Deciphering machine (7)
15 Warmest (7)
17 Symbol or representation (6)
19 Prologue (abbrev) (5)
20 Play a guitar (5)

Crossword

Puzzle 228

Across

1 Enclosed (5)
4 Suggest (7)
7 Halle ___ : actress (5)
8 Game of chance (8)
9 Country in the Arabian peninsula (5)
11 Making ineffective (8)
15 Work surface (8)
17 Screams (5)
19 Pink wading bird (8)
20 ___ Lavigne: Canadian singer (5)
21 Vital content (7)
22 Type of herring (5)

Down

1 At this time (9)
2 Flog; whip (7)
3 Arid areas (7)
4 Positively charged atomic particle (6)
5 Kitchen tool to remove vegetable skin (6)
6 Small loose stones (5)
10 Type of organisation (3-6)
12 Mountain in N Greece (7)
13 Sharp painful blow (7)
14 Relating to high mountains (6)
16 Refer to indirectly (6)
18 ___ Presley: US singer (5)

Puzzle 229

Across

1 These shine in the night sky (5)
4 Closes (5)
10 Two lines of verse (7)
11 Pointed weapon (5)
12 A large amount (4)
13 Insincere praise (8)
16 Person authorised to draw up contracts (6)
17 Wesley ___ : US actor (6)
20 Guests; callers (8)
21 Delighted (4)
23 Smash into another vehicle (5)
25 Source of aluminium (7)
26 Conflict (5)
27 Woollen fabric (5)

Down

2 Cuts off (9)
3 Small stream (4)
5 Suffering from indecision (8)
6 Foot extremity (3)
7 Keen insight (6)
8 Main plant stem (5)
9 Military unit (4)
14 Kicking out of school (9)
15 Sticks used as supports (8)
18 Abrupt (6)
19 Babies' beds (5)
20 Bad habit (4)
22 Dominion (4)
24 Tool for making holes in leather (3)

Crossword

Puzzle 230

Across

1 Insincere and dishonest (3-5)
5 Change (4)
9 Powerful forward movement (5)
10 Jump over (5)
11 Responsible to an authority (10)
14 Moon of the planet Jupiter (6)
15 Hydrocarbon with formula C8H18 (6)
17 Overseer (10)
20 Pertaining to bees (5)
21 Ringo ___ : one of the Beatles (5)
22 Therefore (Latin) (4)
23 Person of varied learning (8)

Down

1 Mission (4)
2 Unpleasant giant (4)
3 Astonishing; amazing (3-9)
4 Nudges out of the way (6)
6 Percussion sound (8)
7 Walked unsteadily (8)
8 In a greedy manner (12)
12 Convince (8)
13 Ensnaring (8)
16 Ludicrous failure (6)
18 Molten matter (4)
19 Curved shape (4)

Puzzle 231

Across

1 Cleansed thoroughly (8)
5 Soup (anag) (4)
8 Papal court (5)
9 Suit makers (7)
10 Started an essay again (7)
12 Knife attached to a rifle (7)
14 Insurance calculator (7)
16 Irritated (7)
18 Accommodation (7)
19 Form of humour (5)
20 Depend on (4)
21 Trade (8)

Down

1 Unwell (4)
2 Scarcity (6)
3 Obviously (9)
4 Obtain by coercion (6)
6 Quantum of electromagnetic radiation (6)
7 Sororal (8)
11 Joke (9)
12 Short respite (8)
13 Unfold (6)
14 In a slow tempo (6)
15 Shady garden alcove (6)
17 Sort; variety (4)

Crossword

Puzzle 232

Across

1 Fully (6)
4 Utterly senseless (6)
9 Type of polish (7)
10 Additions to a document (7)
11 People who are greatly admired (5)
12 Remains somewhere (5)
14 Brushed clean (5)
15 Large waterbirds (5)
17 Verse (5)
18 Enclosed fortification (7)
20 Encode (7)
21 Scottish landowners (6)
22 Person making an auction offer (6)

Down

1 ___ Williams: singer (6)
2 ___ rose: climbing Chinese rose (8)
3 Areas of mown grass (5)
5 Sum of money owed that cannot be recovered (3,4)
6 On top of (4)
7 Decomposes (6)
8 Overstated (11)
13 Naive or sentimental (4-4)
14 Rescued (anag) (7)
15 Small pet rodent (6)
16 Experienced adviser; business coach (6)
17 Christina ___ : actress (5)
19 ___ Moore: Hollywood actress (4)

Puzzle 233

1		2		■	3	4		5		6		7
	■		■	8	■		■		■		■	
9							■	10				
	■		■		■	■	■		■		■	
11						12						■
	■	■	■		■		■		■		■	13
14		15	■	16					■	17		
	■		■		■		■		■	■	■	
■	18									19		
20	■		■		■	■	■		■		■	
21					■	22						
	■		■		■		■		■		■	
23								■	24			

Across

1 Gear wheels (4)
3 Dress clothes (4,4)
9 Beautified (7)
10 ___ Cooper: US rocker (5)
11 Corresponding; proportionate (12)
14 Strong drink (3)
16 Device used to connect to the internet (5)
17 Hurried (3)
18 Heavy long-handled tool (12)
21 Plantain lily (5)
22 Ruled (7)
23 At all; of any kind (8)
24 Inheritor (4)

Down

1 Office attached to an embassy (8)
2 Marrying man (5)
4 Was in first place (3)
5 Graphical (12)
6 Pilot (7)
7 Turn or slide violently (of a vehicle) (4)
8 Coming between two things in time (12)
12 Move sideways (5)
13 An unwelcome person; invader (8)
15 ___ Joan Hart: American actress (7)
19 ___ Carlo: area of Monaco (5)
20 Melt (4)
22 Fish eggs (3)

Crossword

Puzzle 234

Across

1 Country gentleman (6)
7 Breakfast food (8)
8 Female sheep (3)
9 Groups of birds (6)
10 Dull colour (4)
11 ___ DeGeneres: US comedienne (5)
13 Interminable (7)
15 Egg white (7)
17 Killer whales (5)
21 Vertical spar on a ship (4)
22 Emotionally dependent (6)
23 Not on (3)
24 Study of animal behaviour (8)
25 Vivacious (6)

Down

1 Snow vehicle with runners (6)
2 Of practical benefit (6)
3 The beginning of an era (5)
4 Deleting (7)
5 Remarkable (8)
6 Leave a place (6)
12 Explosion (8)
14 Nuclear ___ : device that generates energy (7)
16 Temporary shelter (4-2)
18 Wolflike wild dog (6)
19 Poorly ventilated (6)
20 Type of plastic; record (5)

Puzzle 235

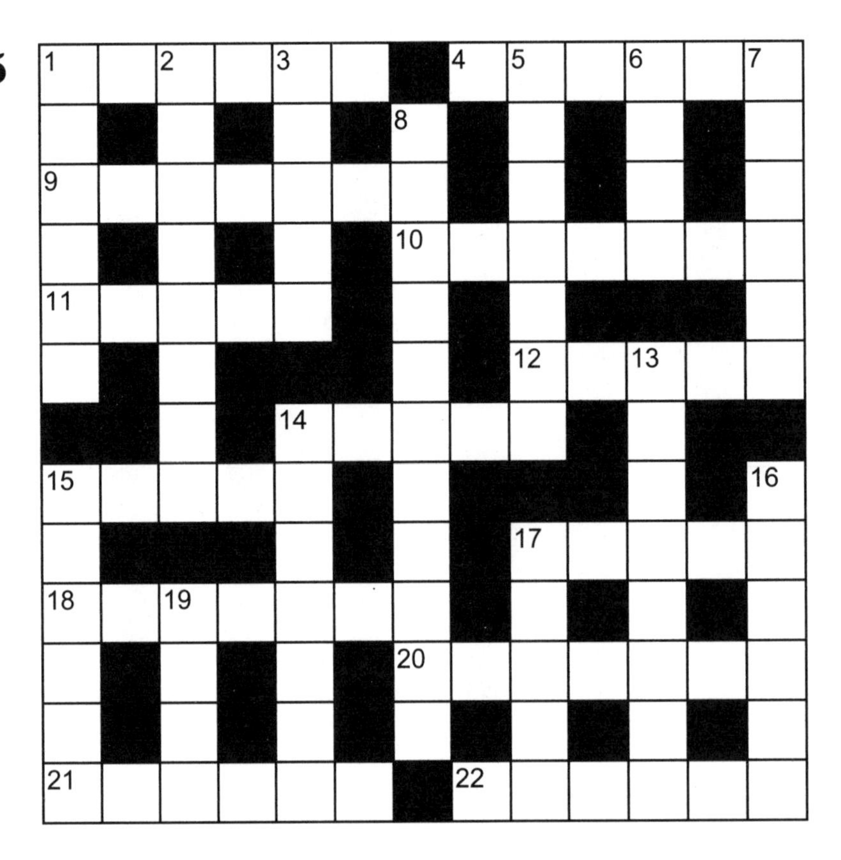

Across

1 Springy (6)
4 Raise in relief (6)
9 Japanese art of paper folding (7)
10 Reptiles (7)
11 Stratum (5)
12 Overcooked (5)
14 Get by begging (5)
15 Tortoise carapace (5)
17 Consumer (5)
18 Guilty person (7)
20 Point of view (7)
21 Holds up (6)
22 African fly that transmits sleeping sickness (6)

Down

1 Umbrella (informal) (6)
2 Vehicle with one wheel (8)
3 Seat (5)
5 Bacterium (7)
6 By word of mouth (4)
7 Coloured evening sky (6)
8 Shaman (5,6)
13 Confine (8)
14 Explain more clearly (7)
15 Dismissed from a job (6)
16 Copper and tin alloy (6)
17 Imposing poems (5)
19 Hang loosely; droop (4)

Crossword

Puzzle 236

Across

1 Identical; unchanged (4)
3 Belongings (8)
9 Of the stomach (7)
10 Implant (5)
11 Scornful (12)
13 Oppressively hot (6)
15 Arachnid (6)
17 Donation (12)
20 Ascend (5)
21 Brass wind instrument (7)
22 Made less bright (8)
23 Computer memory unit (4)

Down

1 Wisdom (8)
2 Craftsman who uses stone (5)
4 List of ingredients for a dish (6)
5 Excessively forward (12)
6 Ricochet (7)
7 Jedi Master in Star Wars films (4)
8 Overwhelmingly compelling (12)
12 Having dark hair (8)
14 More spacious (7)
16 Walk very quietly (6)
18 State indirectly (5)
19 Decorated a cake (4)

Puzzle 237

Across

1 ___ Ryder: actress (6)
7 Wanderer (8)
8 Make imperfect (3)
9 Expedition to see animals (6)
10 Subsequently (4)
11 Edits (anag) (5)
13 Revoke (7)
15 Personal belongings (7)
17 Slender plants of the grass family (5)
21 Home for a bird (4)
22 Freshest (6)
23 Bristle-like appendage (3)
24 Looking up to (8)
25 Representation of a concept; diagram (6)

Down

1 Burrowing marsupial (6)
2 Cared for (6)
3 Pertaining to birds (5)
4 Catches fire (7)
5 Something in the way (8)
6 Confine as a prisoner (6)
12 Vivid and brilliant (of a colour) (8)
14 Template (7)
16 Wicked people (6)
18 Large property with land; holding (6)
19 Yellowish-brown pigment (6)
20 Small branches (5)

Crossword

Puzzle 238

Across

1 Mischievous fairies (4)
3 Confused mixture (8)
9 Starting up (of software) (7)
10 Country in the Himalayas (5)
11 Reception room in a large house (5)
12 Adolescent (7)
13 Turn down (6)
15 Letters like 'a' and 'e' (6)
17 Passenger vehicle (7)
18 Inferior to (5)
20 Church instrument (5)
21 Standing erect (7)
22 Showed a TV show (8)
23 Speak indistinctly (4)

Down

1 Pictures (13)
2 Jewel from an oyster shell (5)
4 Blocks of metal (6)
5 From this time on (12)
6 Satisfy; conciliate (7)
7 Fairground ride (6-7)
8 Importance (12)
14 Very boastful person (7)
16 Group of touring entertainers (6)
19 Royal (5)

Puzzle 239

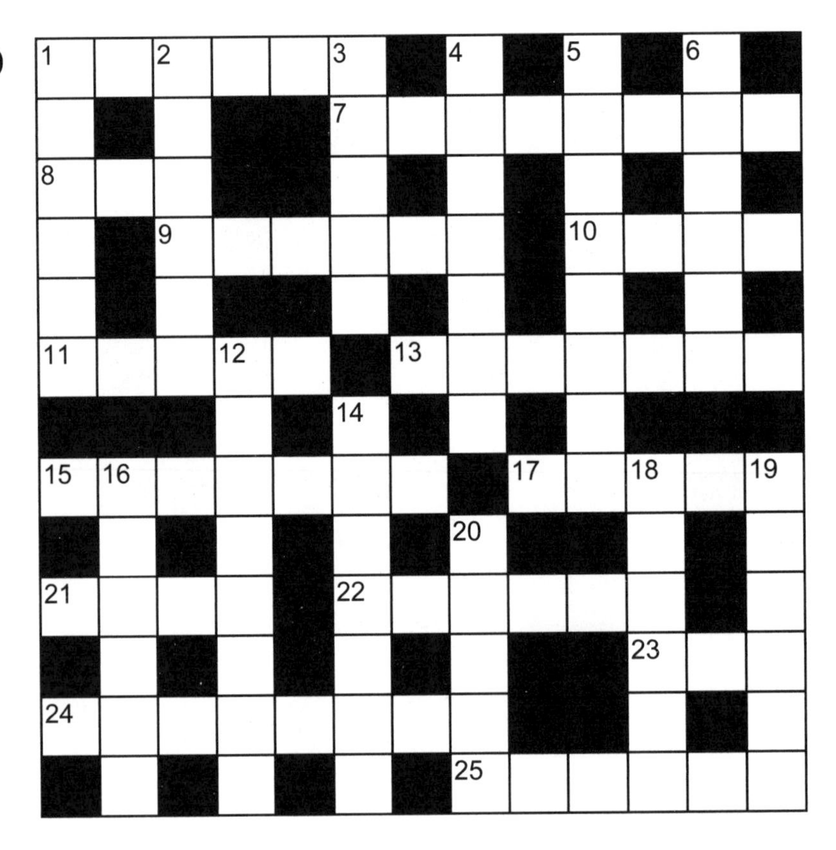

Across

1 Domesticated llama (6)
7 Opposite of Northern (8)
8 Bitumen (3)
9 Long thin line or band (6)
10 Raised edges (4)
11 Silk dress fabric (5)
13 Temporary stay (7)
15 Upstart; one who has recently gained wealth (7)
17 ___ Hayes: US soul and funk singer (5)
21 Greenish-blue colour (4)
22 Stinging plant (6)
23 Decay (3)
24 Permits to do something (8)
25 Remains in one place in the air (6)

Down

1 Towards the rear (6)
2 Clergyman (6)
3 Anaemic-looking (5)
4 Birds of the family Cuculidae (7)
5 Cigars (8)
6 Slight earthquake (6)
12 Done away with (8)
14 Unity (7)
16 Clear from a charge (6)
18 Strongly opposed (6)
19 Boxes (6)
20 Store in a secret place (5)

Crossword

Puzzle 240

Across

1 Canines (4)
3 British soldiers (historical) (8)
9 Expressed disapproval facially (7)
10 Random number game (5)
11 ___ Willis: daughter of Demi Moore (5)
12 Urgent (7)
13 ___ Coyle: Girls Aloud singer (6)
15 Rut (6)
17 Visual symbolism (7)
18 Appear suddenly (3,2)
20 Metric unit of capacity (5)
21 Alfresco (4-3)
22 Boating (8)
23 Unwanted wild plant (4)

Down

1 In a servile manner (13)
2 Darkness (5)
4 Small whirlpools (6)
5 Someone skilled in penmanship (12)
6 Cordate (anag) (3,4)
7 Easily angered (5-8)
8 Action of breaking a law (12)
14 Severe (7)
16 Wealthy person in business (6)
19 Stage (5)

Puzzle 241

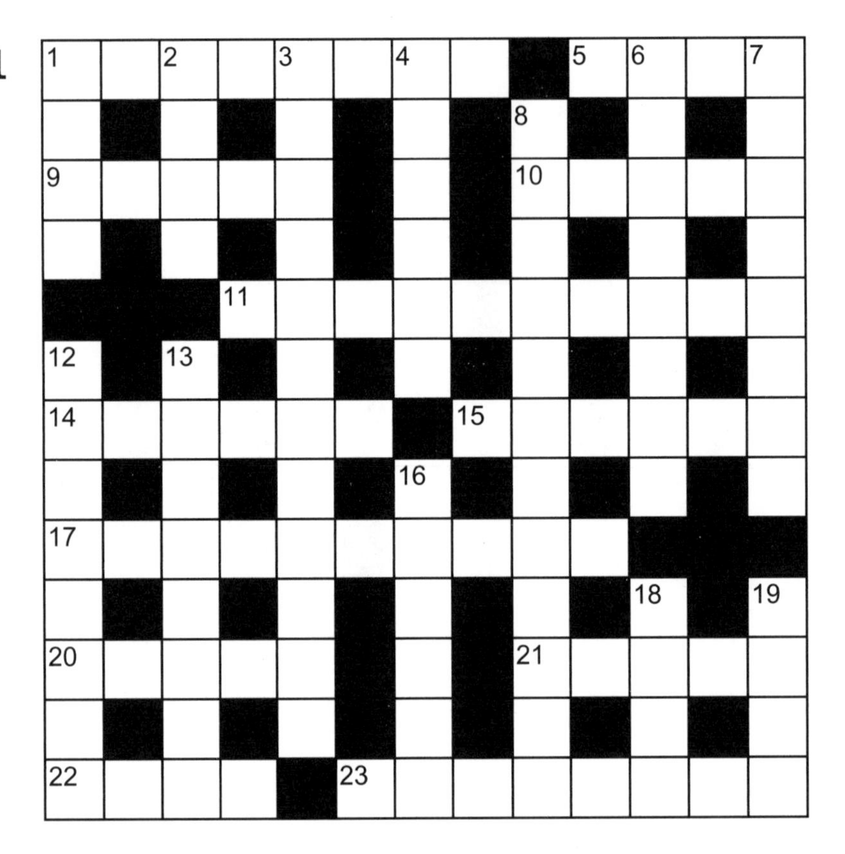

Across

1 Appointed member of the House of Lords (4,4)
5 Soothing remedy (4)
9 Major African river (5)
10 Heavy noble gas (5)
11 Heavy burden (4,6)
14 Enjoy greatly (6)
15 Small (6)
17 One who studies the stars (10)
20 A Fish Called ___ : film (5)
21 Tease or pester (5)
22 Sweet potatoes (4)
23 Progeny (8)

Down

1 Fine open fabric (4)
2 Typeface (4)
3 Opposite of amateur (12)
4 Encrypt (6)
6 Renounce or reject (8)
7 Medieval musician (8)
8 Based on untested ideas (12)
12 Large open road (8)
13 Precious metallic element (8)
16 Potassium compound (6)
18 Cat sound (4)
19 English public school (4)

Crossword

Puzzle 242

Across

1 Animal enclosure (4)
3 Admitted (8)
9 Look something over closely (7)
10 Ben ___ : Scottish mountain (5)
11 Firework display (12)
14 Add together (3)
16 Cuts slightly (5)
17 One more than five (3)
18 Not discernible (12)
21 Underground railway (5)
22 Violent troublemakers (7)
23 Electrical component (8)
24 Makes damp (4)

Down

1 Least expensive (8)
2 Germaine ___ : Australian author (5)
4 Eg Hedwig in Harry Potter (3)
5 Declaration of sainthood (12)
6 Gadgets (7)
7 Shallow food container (4)
8 Quarrelsome and uncooperative (12)
12 Ride a bike (5)
13 Overabundances (8)
15 Periods of 60 seconds (7)
19 Musical note (5)
20 Mire (anag) (4)
22 ___ de Janeiro: Brazilian city (3)

Puzzle 243

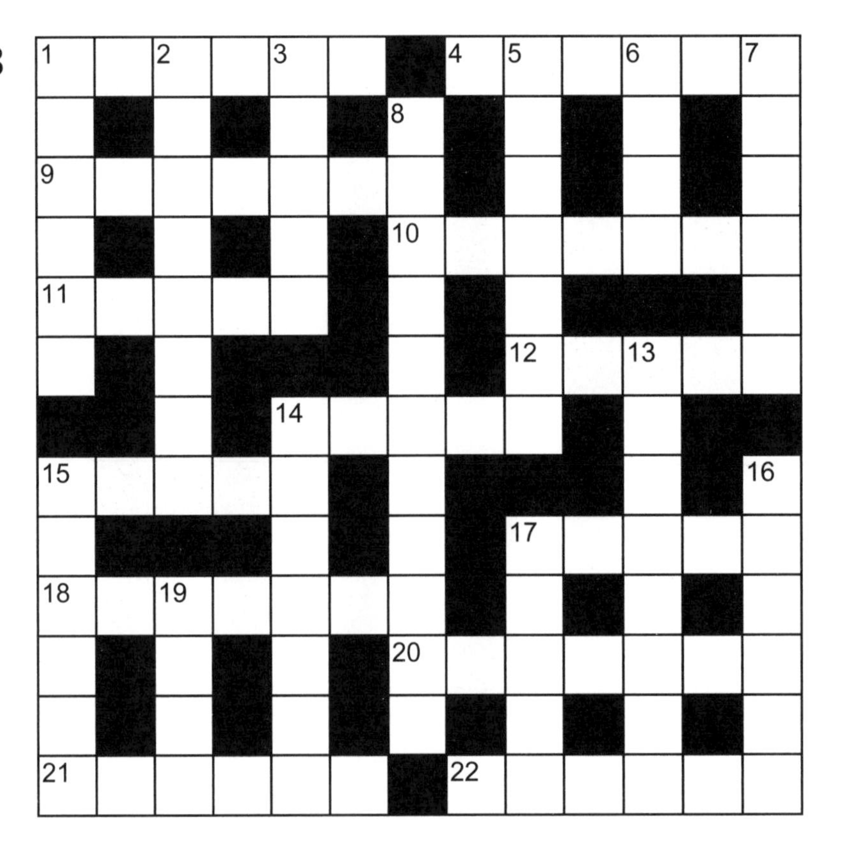

Across

1 Fame (6)
4 Worldwide (6)
9 One who settles a dispute (7)
10 Well-behaved (7)
11 Mournful poem (5)
12 Sharp blade (5)
14 Unwanted plants (5)
15 Small group ruling a country (5)
17 Prohibited by social custom (5)
18 Film about a magical board game (7)
20 Tenth month of the year (7)
21 Force; vigour (6)
22 Straighten out (6)

Down

1 Machine that harvests a crop (6)
2 Peer (8)
3 Humorous (5)
5 Front runners (7)
6 Endure (4)
7 Solicitor (6)
8 Movement towards a destination (11)
13 African country (8)
14 Alerting to danger (7)
15 Naive and superficial (6)
16 Decanted (6)
17 Colossus (5)
19 Microscopic arachnid (4)

Crossword

Puzzle 244

Across

1 Roald ___ : author (4)
3 Judges; evaluates (8)
9 Dissimilar (7)
10 Traditional English breakfast (3-2)
11 Faithful (5)
12 Spouse (7)
13 Rough and uneven (of a cliff) (6)
15 Small carnivorous mammal (6)
17 Competitor (7)
18 Cotton twill fabric (5)
20 Strikes with the foot (5)
21 Plants that live a year or less (7)
22 Salad sauce (8)
23 Extremely (4)

Down

1 Verified again (6-7)
2 Of great weight (5)
4 Slumbers (6)
5 Bubbling (12)
6 Maxims (7)
7 In a manner that exceeds what is necessary (13)
8 Binoculars (5,7)
14 Prompting device (7)
16 Make an unusually great effort (6)
19 Angry (5)

Puzzle 245

Across

1 Separate and distinct (8)
5 Group of countries in an alliance (4)
8 Representative; messenger (5)
9 Biting (7)
10 Raising (7)
12 Caribbean dance (7)
14 Diplomatic building (7)
16 These aid sight (7)
18 Device that records the movements of someone (7)
19 Short and stout (5)
20 Less than average tide (4)
21 Decade from 1920 - 1929 (8)

Down

1 Profound (4)
2 Rescuing (6)
3 Monarchists (9)
4 Topple (6)
6 Introduction (4-2)
7 Class of things (8)
11 Not allowed (9)
12 Make more light (8)
13 Capital of Bahrain (6)
14 Cowers (anag) (6)
15 Norway lobsters (6)
17 Exercise venues (4)

Puzzle 246

Across

1 Naturally associated (11)
9 Not telling the truth (5)
10 Small green vegetable (3)
11 Magical incantation (5)
12 Regal (5)
13 Vacations (8)
16 Learned people (8)
18 Naves (anag) (5)
21 Bring to the conscious mind (5)
22 Midge ___ : Scottish musician (3)
23 Recommended strongly (5)
24 Character; nature (11)

Down

2 Trying experiences (7)
3 Crash together (7)
4 Small portion or share (6)
5 Big cat (5)
6 Crisp; pleasantly cold (5)
7 Harmful and sneaky (11)
8 Insensitivity (11)
14 Tedium (7)
15 Fatty substance (7)
17 Puma (6)
19 Female relation (5)
20 Remnant of a fallen tree (5)

Puzzle 247

Across

1 Brawny (8)
5 Roman poet (4)
9 Very clear (5)
10 Shapes (5)
11 Existing from the beginning (10)
14 Smells (6)
15 Passionate (6)
17 Official inspection (10)
20 Bird (5)
21 Dwarfish creature (5)
22 Flat and smooth (4)
23 Versions of a book (8)

Down

1 Shopping centre (US) (4)
2 Garment for the foot (4)
3 Insuring (12)
4 Take as being true (6)
6 Upright (8)
7 Shows (8)
8 Malice ___ : intention to harm (12)
12 Talk with (8)
13 Capable of happening (8)
16 Made amends for (6)
18 Benicio del ___ : actor (4)
19 Part of a camera (4)

Crossword

Puzzle 248

Across

1 Opposite of least (4)
3 Similarity (8)
9 Travel somewhere (7)
10 Machine; automaton (5)
11 Invigoratingly (12)
14 First on the list (3)
16 Commerce (5)
17 Beer (3)
18 Deceiver (6-6)
21 Russian spirit (5)
22 Large household water container (7)
23 People with auburn hair (8)
24 Leg joint (4)

Down

1 The greater part (8)
2 Mark or wear thin (5)
4 ___ Winehouse: singer (3)
5 Agreements; plans (12)
6 Garden flower (7)
7 Stringed instrument (4)
8 Animal lacking a backbone (12)
12 Lift with effort (5)
13 Awful (8)
15 Poked (7)
19 Bedfordshire town (5)
20 Finished; complete (4)
22 Auction offer (3)

Puzzle 249

Across

1 Causing great damage (11)
9 Crime of setting something on fire (5)
10 Snow runner (3)
11 Earlier (5)
12 Japanese food (5)
13 Well-meaning but interfering person (2-6)
16 Famished (8)
18 Ice home (5)
21 Service colour of the army (5)
22 Born (3)
23 Sense experience (5)
24 Affiliation (11)

Down

2 Final parts of stories (7)
3 Small restaurant or cafe (7)
4 Uncertain (6)
5 Holding or grasping device (5)
6 Close-fitting garments (5)
7 Journeys of exploration (11)
8 Becoming less (11)
14 Most feeble (7)
15 Cigarette constituent (7)
17 Andre ___ : former US tennis player (6)
19 Vegetables related to onions (5)
20 Exceed; perform better than (5)

Puzzle 250

Across

1 Circuits of a racetrack (4)
3 Mood (8)
9 Comfort (7)
10 Go to see (5)
11 Every (3)
12 Give a solemn oath (5)
13 Impair (5)
15 Opposite of old (5)
17 Spread by scattering (5)
18 Light brown colour (3)
19 Assert that something is the case (5)
20 Assistant (7)
21 Popular fizzy beverage (8)
22 Warm up (4)

Down

1 Lazy (13)
2 Dashboard (5)
4 Breakfast food (6)
5 Detective (12)
6 Beginning to exist (7)
7 Amusement (13)
8 Female fellow national (12)
14 Prepare beforehand (7)
16 Towards a higher place (6)
18 Herb (5)

Puzzle 251

Across

1 Urge (6)
7 Fee paid to use someone's services when required (8)
8 Tack (3)
9 Ball-shaped object (6)
10 Mite (anag) (4)
11 Thin roofing slabs (5)
13 Attack (7)
15 Stinging plants (7)
17 The furnishings in a room (5)
21 Engage in argument (4)
22 Respiratory condition (6)
23 Eg pecan or cashew (3)
24 Vehicle (8)
25 Eg Sir and Dame (6)

Down

1 Liveliness (6)
2 ___ and Gretel: fairy tale (6)
3 Put in considerable effort (5)
4 Non-believer in God (7)
5 Take legal action (8)
6 Breakfast food (6)
12 Coming from outside (8)
14 Corrupt (7)
16 Give a job to (6)
18 French fashion designer (6)
19 Paths (6)
20 Begin (5)

Crossword

Puzzle 252

Across

1 Visage (4)
3 Supported with money (8)
9 Reintegrate (7)
10 Extinguish (a fire) (5)
11 Act of influencing someone deviously (12)
14 Become firm (3)
16 Christmas show (abbrev) (5)
17 Feather scarf (3)
18 Sound of quick light steps (6-6)
21 Musical note (5)
22 Effective; having a striking effect (7)
23 Wearisome (8)
24 Repast (4)

Down

1 First in importance (8)
2 Stir milk (5)
4 Very cold (3)
5 And also (12)
6 SI unit of electric charge (7)
7 Song by two people (4)
8 Thick-skinned herbivorous animal (12)
12 Passenger ship (5)
13 Song for several voices (8)
15 Narrower (7)
19 In a ___ : very quickly (5)
20 Flake of soot (4)
22 ___ Thumb: folklore character (3)

Puzzle 253

1		2		■	3	4		5		6		7
	■		■	8	■		■		■		■	
9							■	10				
	■		■		■		■		■		■	
11			■		■		■	12				
	■	■	■	13					■		■	
	■	14	■		■	■	■		■		■	
	■		■	15		16			■	■	■	
17					■		■		■	18		
	■		■		■		■		■		■	
19					■	20						
	■		■		■		■		■		■	
21								■	22			

Across

1 Baby beds (4)
3 Tiny amount (8)
9 Very young infant (7)
10 Harsh and serious in manner (5)
11 Beam of light (3)
12 Avoid; garment (5)
13 Unabridged (5)
15 Fight (3-2)
17 Bird sound (5)
18 Performed an action (3)
19 Seeped (5)
20 One thousand million (7)
21 Female students' society (8)
22 Ancient harp (4)

Down

1 Things that are given (13)
2 ___ owl: common Eurasian owl (5)
4 Lunatic (6)
5 Ruinously (12)
6 Mournful poems (7)
7 Failure to be present at (13)
8 Spanish adventurer (12)
14 Very low temperature fridge (7)
16 European flatfish (6)
18 Common garden flower (5)

Crossword

Puzzle 254

Across

1 Ability to act as one wishes (4,4)
5 Jar lids (4)
8 Large mast (5)
9 Kitchen appliance (7)
10 Not anything (7)
12 Depict in a particular way (7)
14 Something showing a general rule (7)
16 Blocked up (7)
18 Poisonous metallic element (7)
19 Coldly (5)
20 The south of France (4)
21 Amaze (8)

Down

1 Dandies (4)
2 Cream pastry (6)
3 Roaming (9)
4 Form of church prayer (6)
6 Soup flavour (6)
7 Spread out untidily (8)
11 Quentin ___ : Kill Bill director (9)
12 Announce publicly (8)
13 Extinguished (6)
14 Proclamations (6)
15 Type of sandwich (6)
17 Legendary story (4)

Puzzle 255

Across

1 Team (4)
3 Coldly detached (8)
9 Leguminous plant also called lucerne (7)
10 Extent or limit (5)
11 Regather tins (anag) (12)
13 Workplace (6)
15 Incidental activity (6)
17 Firm rebuke (12)
20 Compass point (5)
21 Device that measures electric current (7)
22 Fence of stakes (8)
23 ___ Fitzgerald: famous jazz singer (4)

Down

1 Metrical analysis of verse (8)
2 Postpone (5)
4 Hate (6)
5 Short tale told to children (7,5)
6 Hide (7)
7 Look slyly (4)
8 Ordinary dress (5,7)
12 Exaggerated emotion (8)
14 Favouring centralised government (7)
16 Molecule that binds to another (6)
18 Praise enthusiastically (5)
19 Summit of a small hill (4)

Crossword

Puzzle 256

Across

1 Struggled against (6)
4 Modify (6)
9 Japanese dish of raw fish (7)
10 European deer (7)
11 Happening (5)
12 Shyly (5)
14 Requiring much mastication (5)
15 Roadside area (3-2)
17 Grip tightly; steal (5)
18 John ___ : tennis player (7)
20 Tidies (7)
21 Shove (6)
22 Joins together (6)

Down

1 Caught seafood (6)
2 Not proper (of behaviour) (8)
3 Raise up (5)
5 Propriety and modesty (7)
6 Official language of Pakistan (4)
7 Bird eaten at Christmas (6)
8 Greenish (11)
13 Least old (8)
14 Evergreen conifer (7)
15 Bewail (6)
16 Deep fissures (6)
17 Clear and apparent; obvious (5)
19 Pitcher (4)

Puzzle 257

Across

- **1** Large leaves of ferns (6)
- **5** Sort; kind (3)
- **7** Looking tired (5)
- **8** Elusive (7)
- **9** Be alive; be real (5)
- **10** Icing (8)
- **12** Enquiring (6)
- **14** Worshipped (6)
- **17** Person on the run (8)
- **18** Turns over and over (5)
- **20** Green gemstone (7)
- **21** Requirements (5)
- **22** Label (3)
- **23** Get away from (6)

Down

- **2** Returns to a former state (7)
- **3** Moving aimlessly (8)
- **4** Spice made from nutmeg (4)
- **5** Sharp tooth (7)
- **6** Made a garment by intertwining threads (7)
- **7** Danes (anag) (5)
- **11** Fans (8)
- **12** Person devoted to love (7)
- **13** Rudyard ___ : novelist (7)
- **15** Surround entirely (7)
- **16** Mounds of loose sand (5)
- **19** Plant stalk (4)

Crossword

Puzzle 258

Across

1 Sea rescue vessel (8)
5 Plant used for flavouring (4)
9 Poisonous (5)
10 Removes the lid (5)
11 Device for making coffee (10)
14 Novice (6)
15 On a ship or train (6)
17 Act of making known (10)
20 Loud metallic sound (5)
21 Domestic cat (5)
22 Tune (4)
23 Dishes that begin a meal (8)

Down

1 Thin strip of wood (4)
2 Cunning (4)
3 Study of microorganisms (12)
4 Join or fasten (6)
6 Final (8)
7 Straddle (8)
8 Fellow plotter (12)
12 Manufactures (8)
13 One who steers a boat (8)
16 Agreement (6)
18 Having inherent ability (4)
19 Extras (cricket) (4)

Puzzle 259

Across

1 Ways or tracks (5)
4 Carried out incompetently (7)
7 Lessen (5)
8 Bitterness (8)
9 Detected a sound (5)
11 Overly anxious and sensitive (8)
15 Individually crafted by a person (8)
17 Violent weather (5)
19 Fierce (8)
20 Hymn of thanksgiving (5)
21 Reaches (7)
22 Strange and mysterious (5)

Down

1 Containing toxins (9)
2 Insubstantial (7)
3 Underwriter (7)
4 Art of growing dwarfed trees (6)
5 Cup (6)
6 Come in (5)
10 Pronouncement (9)
12 Preventing success; unfavourable (7)
13 Ditherer (7)
14 Fleet of ships (6)
16 Prevents (6)
18 Browned bread (5)

Crossword

Puzzle 260

Across

- **1** Persuade gently (4)
- **3** Albert ___ : famous physicist (8)
- **9** Blushes (7)
- **10** Coral reef (5)
- **11** Utilise (3)
- **12** Camera image (abbrev) (5)
- **13** Steer (anag) (5)
- **15** Spike used by a climber (5)
- **17** Valuable thing (5)
- **18** Adult males (3)
- **19** Brief appearance in a film by someone famous (5)
- **20** Foot pedal (7)
- **21** Small stall at an exhibition (8)
- **22** Simple non-flowering plant (4)

Down

- **1** The facts surrounding an event (13)
- **2** Mix up (5)
- **4** Topics for debate (6)
- **5** Having an acrid wit (5-7)
- **6** Efficiency (7)
- **7** Former President of South Africa (6,7)
- **8** Detailed reports (12)
- **14** Started again (7)
- **16** Stain skin with indelible colour (6)
- **18** Gold ___ : award for coming first (5)

Puzzle 261

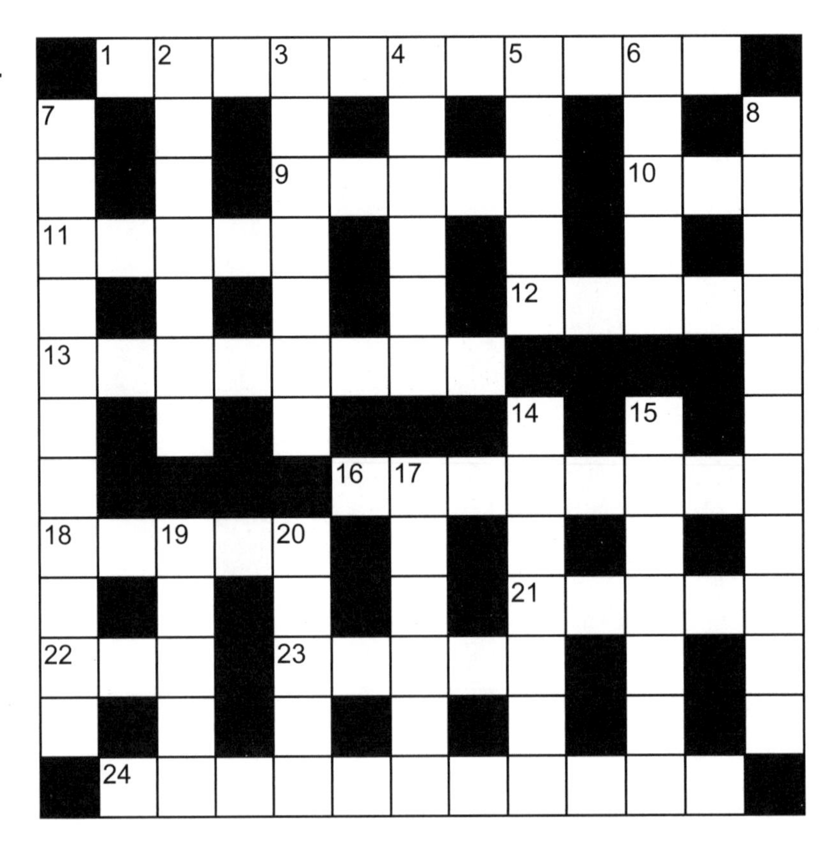

Across

1 Participation (11)
9 Mike ___ : US boxer (5)
10 Sound of a cow (3)
11 Secreting organ (5)
12 Opposite one of two (5)
13 Apportioned (8)
16 Material used as a colourant (8)
18 Involuntary muscle contraction (5)
21 Worthy principle or aim (5)
22 Much ___ About Nothing: play (3)
23 Happen again (5)
24 Eternity (11)

Down

2 Newsworthy (7)
3 Make obsolete (7)
4 Countenance (6)
5 Juicy fruit (5)
6 Insect larva (5)
7 Where one finds Kabul (11)
8 Scary movies (6,5)
14 Drug that relieves pain (7)
15 Repositories of antiques (7)
17 Woody-stemmed plants (6)
19 With a forward motion (5)
20 ___ Streep: Mamma Mia! actress (5)

Crossword

Puzzle 262

Across

1 Part of the eye (6)
7 Went before (8)
8 Metric unit of measurement (historical) (3)
9 Abandon a plan (6)
10 ___ Blyton: writer (4)
11 Beastly (5)
13 Hat with a wide brim (7)
15 Equality of political rights (7)
17 ___ Izzard: English stand-up comedian (5)
21 US pop star who sang I Got You Babe (4)
22 Restore honour (6)
23 Hip (anag) (3)
24 Composer of a sacred song (8)
25 Spiritual meeting (6)

Down

1 Explanation (6)
2 Long essay or dissertation (6)
3 Put into use (5)
4 Film starring Guy Pearce (7)
5 Low-spirited (8)
6 Sheep known for its wool (6)
12 Slender coiling leaves (8)
14 Involve in conflict (7)
16 Metamorphic rock (6)
18 Inhibit (6)
19 Fur of a stoat (6)
20 Modifies (5)

Puzzle 263

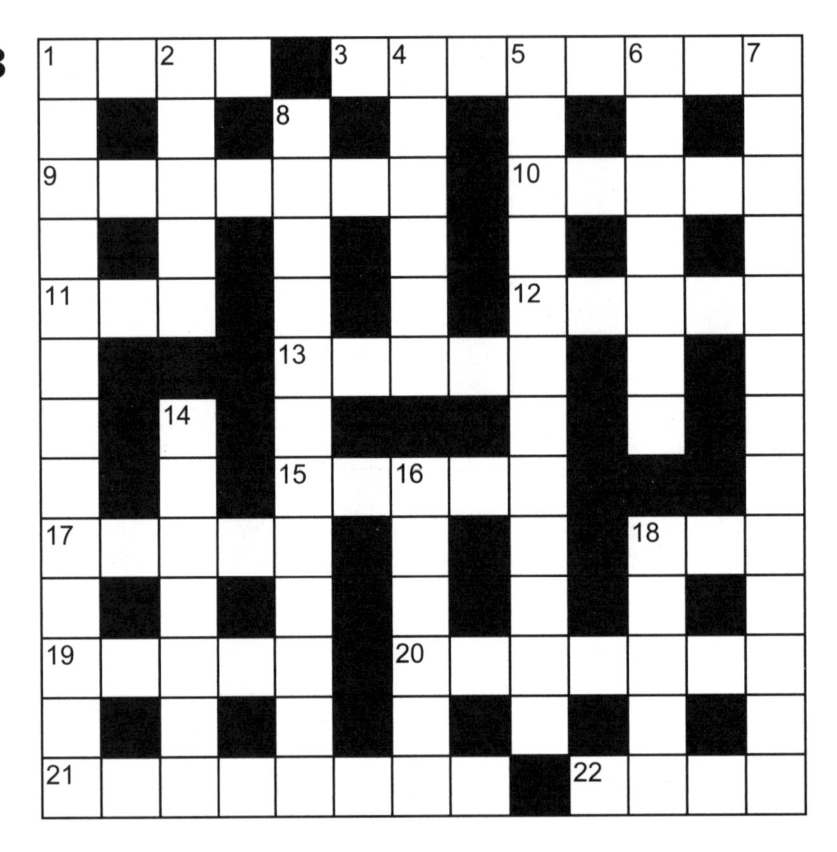

Across

1 Black ___ : Colombian bird (4)
3 Complying with orders (8)
9 Barrel makers (7)
10 Acer tree (5)
11 Flee (3)
12 More pleasant (5)
13 Thaws (5)
15 Sweet substance (5)
17 Special reward (5)
18 Intentionally so written (3)
19 Moisten meat (5)
20 Useful (7)
21 Publicity (8)
22 Make a request to God (4)

Down

1 Forever honest (13)
2 Headgear of a monarch (5)
4 Imperial capacity measure (6)
5 Clearly evident (12)
6 Regards as likely to happen (7)
7 Conceptually (13)
8 Female school boss (12)
14 Exercise for building arm muscles (5-2)
16 Assemble (6)
18 More secure (5)

Crossword

Puzzle 264

Across

1 ___ Williams: tennis star (6)
7 Tin gifts (anag) (8)
8 Female chicken (3)
9 Nerve cell (6)
10 Bitter-tasting substance (4)
11 Jollity (5)
13 Trace (7)
15 Inventor (7)
17 Walk heavily and firmly (5)
21 Primates (4)
22 Solemn promise (6)
23 Short sleep (3)
24 Eg a spider or scorpion (8)
25 Series of eight notes (6)

Down

1 Division of a group (6)
2 ___ bean: vegetable (6)
3 Burning (5)
4 Rendered senseless (7)
5 Catastrophe (8)
6 Getting older (6)
12 Conduct business (8)
14 Circling around (7)
16 ___ Everett: English actor (6)
18 Programme; timetable (6)
19 Colour between blue and red (6)
20 Japanese form of fencing (5)

Puzzle 265

Across

1 Johann Sebastian ___ : German composer (4)
3 Hideousness (8)
9 Underwater projectile (7)
10 Waggish (5)
11 Measure of length (3)
12 Barrier (5)
13 Spore (anag) (5)
15 Linear measures of three feet (5)
17 Metal spikes (5)
18 Steal (3)
19 Set of moral principles (5)
20 Large bag (7)
21 Small telescope (8)
22 Inflammation of an eyelid (4)

Down

1 Someone who drops things regularly (13)
2 Christmas song (5)
4 Small cave (6)
5 Not capable of justification (12)
6 Enunciate (7)
7 25th anniversary celebration (6,7)
8 Highly abstract (12)
14 Capricious (7)
16 Legal entitlements (6)
18 Cook meat in the oven (5)

Crossword

Puzzle 266

Across

1 Get beaten (4)
3 Things we are not familiar with (8)
9 Coal miner (7)
10 Anxious (5)
11 Preternatural (12)
13 Mould (6)
15 More needy (6)
17 Person who receives office visitors (12)
20 Red cosmetic powder (5)
21 Speak very quietly (7)
22 Moderately rich (4-2-2)
23 Tiny parasite (4)

Down

1 Field game (8)
2 Spirit of the air (5)
4 Limited in scope (6)
5 Not intoxicating (of a drink) (12)
6 Small songbird (7)
7 Leguminous plant (4)
8 Give a false account of (12)
12 Standards (8)
14 Not level (7)
16 Cooked slowly in liquid (6)
18 Urge into action (5)
19 ___ Barrymore: Hollywood actress (4)

Puzzle 267

Across

1 Troop leader (11)
9 Lacking meaning (5)
10 Cause friction (3)
11 Nearby (5)
12 Secret rendezvous (5)
13 Groups of similar things (8)
16 Cyan tail (anag) (8)
18 Locomotive (5)
21 Civilian dress (5)
22 Floor mat (3)
23 Belief in a creator (5)
24 Hostile and aggressive (11)

Down

2 Element needed by the body (7)
3 Usefulness (7)
4 Complainer (6)
5 Snow and rain mix (5)
6 Ahead of time (5)
7 Aircraft (pl) (11)
8 State of preoccupation (11)
14 Prison (informal) (7)
15 Become more rigid (7)
17 Christening (6)
19 Standpoint (5)
20 Rafael ___ : Spanish tennis star (5)

Crossword

Puzzle 268

Across

1 International exhibition (4)
3 Friendly (8)
9 Hit with the fist (7)
10 Gena Lee ___ : Baywatch actress (5)
11 Act of slowing down (12)
13 Irritable (6)
15 Part of a belt (6)
17 Swimming technique (12)
20 George ___ : Middlemarch writer (5)
21 Competitors in a sprint (7)
22 City in NE Scotland (8)
23 Audacity (4)

Down

1 Speed up (8)
2 Sudden fear (5)
4 Contemporary (6)
5 Building (12)
6 Young ox (7)
7 Volcano in Sicily (4)
8 Showing total commitment (12)
12 About-face (8)
14 Elevate (7)
16 Deprive of food (6)
18 Eg Mozart's Don Giovanni (5)
19 Second Greek letter (4)

Puzzle 269

Across

1 Face (anag) (4)
3 Component parts (8)
9 Contest (7)
10 Eighth Greek letter (5)
11 Brass instrument (5)
12 Originality (7)
13 Representatives (6)
15 Heavy food (6)
17 Inquisitive (7)
18 Outstanding (of a debt) (5)
20 Gives out (5)
21 Slanted letters (7)
22 Delaying (8)
23 Paradise garden (4)

Down

1 Lord of the Rings actress (4,9)
2 Hurled (5)
4 Putting down carefully (6)
5 Inspiring action (12)
6 Provoked or teased (7)
7 Black Eyed Peas star (5,8)
8 Contagiously (12)
14 Prior (7)
16 Allocate a duty (6)
19 Epic poem ascribed to Homer (5)

Crossword

Puzzle 270

Across

1 Not difficult (4)
3 Photograph (8)
9 Increase the duration of (7)
10 Made a mistake (5)
11 Quality of being genuine (12)
13 Closer (6)
15 Hit a snooker ball incorrectly (6)
17 Fully extended (12)
20 Shrub fence (5)
21 Aquatic mollusc (7)
22 Bogs or marshes (8)
23 Subject to debate (4)

Down

1 Outlines in detail (8)
2 Cry out loudly (5)
4 Invalidate; nullify (6)
5 Dictatorial (12)
6 Nonconformist (7)
7 Periodic movement of the sea (4)
8 Despair (12)
12 Support at the top of a seat (8)
14 Into parts (7)
16 Fit for cultivation (of land) (6)
18 Golden ___ : payment received on joining a company (5)
19 Friend (informal) (4)

Puzzle 271

Across

1 Pygmy chimpanzee (6)
5 Limb (3)
7 Chubby (5)
8 Green vegetation (7)
9 Makhaya ___ : South African cricketer (5)
10 Tooth (8)
12 Deduces from evidence (6)
14 Part of a dress (6)
17 Trifling (8)
18 Accustom to something (5)
20 Searched clumsily (7)
21 Trunk of the body (5)
22 24-hour period (3)
23 Loves dearly (6)

Down

2 Conquer by force (7)
3 Bedrooms (8)
4 Destroy (4)
5 Relating to knowledge based on deduction (1,6)
6 Settle a dispute (7)
7 Floral leaf (5)
11 Bewilder (8)
12 Provoked; encouraged (7)
13 Ostentatious (7)
15 Gather (7)
16 Foreign language (slang) (5)
19 Makes a mistake (4)

Crossword

Puzzle 272

Across

1 High-pitched flute (4)
3 Not genuine (8)
9 Area of land (7)
10 Move slowly (5)
11 Sewn edge (3)
12 Lively Bohemian dance (5)
13 Comic dramatic work (5)
15 Punctuation mark (5)
17 Vital organ (5)
18 Golf peg (3)
19 Male parent (5)
20 Form of an element (7)
21 Many (8)
22 Noes (anag) (4)

Down

1 A transient occurrence (5,2,3,3)
2 Public meeting for open discussion (5)
4 Like better (6)
5 Convalescence (12)
6 Prophets (7)
7 Conscious knowledge of oneself (4-9)
8 Maker (12)
14 ___ of the Opera: musical (7)
16 One's environment (6)
18 Plant spike (5)

Puzzle 273

Across

1 Scoundrel (6)
4 Attack (6)
9 Fish tanks (7)
10 Totals up (7)
11 Encounters (5)
12 Pungent edible bulb (5)
14 Softly radiant (5)
15 Palpitate (5)
17 Small antelope (5)
18 Religious sacrament (7)
20 Install; establish (7)
21 Inclined at an angle (6)
22 Scattered about untidily (6)

Down

1 Domains (6)
2 Memento (8)
3 Large amounts of land (5)
5 Swift-flying songbird (7)
6 Not in favour (4)
7 Make less tight (6)
8 Causing sudden upheaval (11)
13 Closely acquainted (8)
14 Shorten (7)
15 Plaque (6)
16 Common bird with a cooing voice (6)
17 Beginning of something (5)
19 Haul (4)

Crossword

Puzzle 274

Across

1 Well-known sentence (11)
9 Promotional wording (5)
10 Expected at a certain time (3)
11 Small firework (5)
12 At that place; not here (5)
13 Grow in number (8)
16 Out of date (8)
18 Admirable (5)
21 Ranked (5)
22 ___ Ivanovic: tennis player (3)
23 Unwarranted (5)
24 Condition in an agreement (11)

Down

2 Additional and supplementary part (7)
3 Small stones (7)
4 Hits repeatedly (6)
5 Refute by evidence (5)
6 Grasslike marsh plant (5)
7 Letter of recommendation (11)
8 Calm and sensible (5-6)
14 Strong stream of water (7)
15 Fear of heights (7)
17 Relating to a wedding (6)
19 Wild animal (5)
20 Furnish or supply (5)

Puzzle 275

Across

1 Eg Bertrand Russell (8)
5 Capital of Norway (4)
9 Group of witches (5)
10 Make right (5)
11 Make weak and infirm (10)
14 Constructs (6)
15 Tiny bag (6)
17 Suppression of objectionable material (10)
20 Roger ___ : English actor (5)
21 Make fun of someone (5)
22 ___ Hour: movie starring Jackie Chan (4)
23 Arriving at a destination (8)

Down

1 Pass the tongue over (4)
2 Donated (4)
3 Someone who makes sweets (12)
4 Scared (6)
6 Puts up with (8)
7 Small-scale musical drama (8)
8 Favouring private ownership (12)
12 Recent arrival (8)
13 Social gatherings for old friends (8)
16 Guarantee (6)
18 The wise men (4)
19 Mass of floating ice (4)

Crossword

Puzzle 276

Across

1 Argues (4)
3 Grassy clumps (8)
9 No pears (anag) (7)
10 Make inoperative (5)
11 Explanatory (12)
14 Small truck (3)
16 Colour of grass (5)
17 Long and narrow inlet (3)
18 Made poor (12)
21 Breathing organs (5)
22 Moved round an axis (7)
23 Extravagant fuss (8)
24 Participate in a game (4)

Down

1 Respite (8)
2 Opposite of best (5)
4 ___ Thurman: actress (3)
5 Strengthen; confirm (12)
6 Large knife (7)
7 Japanese beverage (4)
8 Bravely (12)
12 ___ Witherspoon: actress (5)
13 Frankly (8)
15 Existing solely in name (7)
19 Place providing accommodation (5)
20 Reveal indiscreetly (4)
22 17th Greek letter (3)

Puzzle 277

Across

1 Planetary bodies (6)
4 Machines for shaping wood (6)
9 Qualification attached to a statement (7)
10 Disentangle (7)
11 Observed (5)
12 Speak (5)
14 Make less miserable (5)
15 Not clearly stated (5)
17 Low value US coins (5)
18 Print anew (7)
20 A sudden impulse or desire (7)
21 Alarms (6)
22 Customary practices (6)

Down

1 Rubbing clean (6)
2 Settling for rest (of birds) (8)
3 Removed water (5)
5 Non-professional (7)
6 High fidelity (abbrev) (2-2)
7 Person gliding on ice (6)
8 Verify again (6-5)
13 Provoking; teasing (8)
14 The giving up of rights (7)
15 As compared to (6)
16 Willow twigs (6)
17 Sleeveless cloaks (5)
19 ___ Novello: Welsh composer and actor (4)

Crossword

Puzzle 278

Across

1 Singing voice (4)
3 Unmarried woman (8)
9 Insignificant (7)
10 Spin (5)
11 Lubricated (5)
12 Aseptic (7)
13 Damage (6)
15 Relating to cultural and national origins (6)
17 Old-fashioned (7)
18 Eg radio and television (5)
20 Data entered into a system (5)
21 This evening (7)
22 Stretched out (8)
23 Agitate (4)

Down

1 Self-confident and commanding (13)
2 Fabric with parallel ribs (5)
4 Burnish (6)
5 Second part of the Bible (3,9)
6 Instruction (7)
7 Amusement park ride (6,7)
8 School for young children (12)
14 Top prize (7)
16 Hay-cutting tool (6)
19 A finger or toe (5)

Puzzle 279

Across

1 Advocate of representative government (8)
5 Quartzlike gem (4)
9 Walks through water (5)
10 Very loud (5)
11 At right angles to the vertical (10)
14 River in South America (6)
15 Exhausts (6)
17 Eg Europe and Asia (10)
20 Bamboo-eating animal (5)
21 Certain to end in failure (2-3)
22 Kate ___ : British singer (4)
23 Substance causing a reaction (8)

Down

1 Weds (anag) (4)
2 Created (4)
3 Well travelled (12)
4 Although (6)
6 Publishing (8)
7 Person who remains true to the government (8)
8 Ineptness (12)
12 Cooking pot (8)
13 Wages (8)
16 Aromatic plant of the parsley family (6)
18 Slender woody shoot (4)
19 Soon; shortly (4)

Crossword

Puzzle 280

Across

1 Petty (5-6)
9 Less narrow (5)
10 Climbing shrub (3)
11 Detection technology (5)
12 Antelope (5)
13 Blue toys (anag) (8)
16 Large Spanish estate (8)
18 Theme for a discussion (5)
21 Spore-producing organisms (5)
22 Lubricate (3)
23 Stringed instrument (5)
24 Insects with brightly coloured wings (11)

Down

2 Official instruction (7)
3 Having few storeys (of a building) (3-4)
4 Positioned in the middle (6)
5 Courage; boldness (5)
6 Andrew Lloyd Webber musical (5)
7 Company (11)
8 Act of publishing content in several places (11)
14 Trap for the unwary (7)
15 Entrap (7)
17 Burning passion (6)
19 Rice dish (5)
20 Crave; desire (5)

Puzzle 281

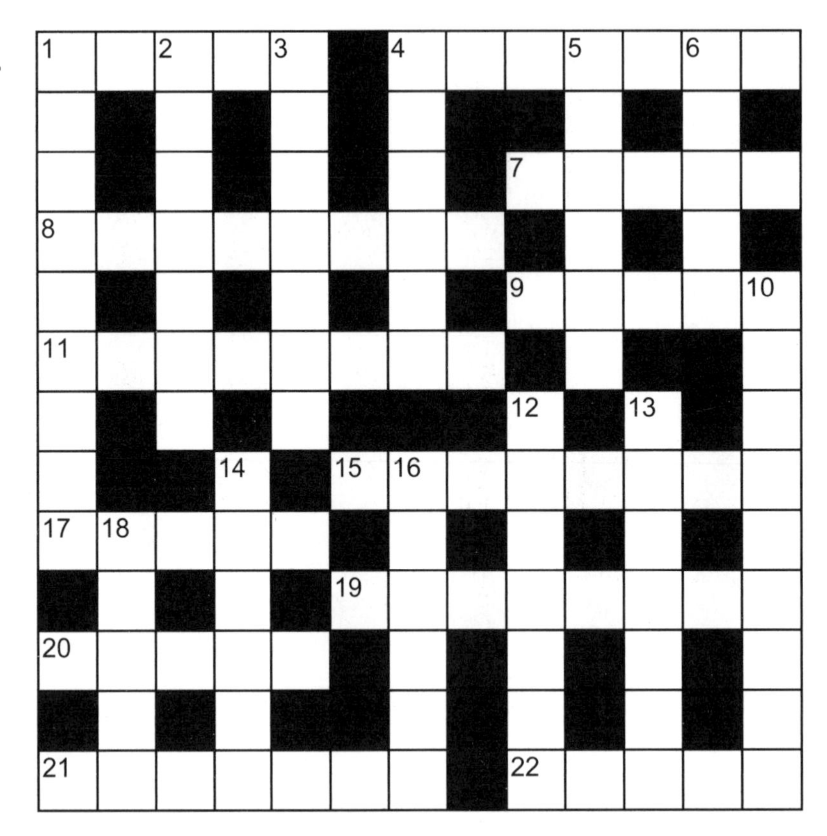

Across

1 Stinky (5)
4 Locking lips (7)
7 Abominable snowmen (5)
8 ___ Verdi: composer (8)
9 Cleanse the body (5)
11 Hand-woven pictorial design (8)
15 Personal magnetism (8)
17 Incites (5)
19 Type of pasta (8)
20 Double-reed instruments (5)
21 Stored away (7)
22 Vertical part of a step (5)

Down

1 Moving restlessly (9)
2 Victory (7)
3 Illness (7)
4 Guardian (6)
5 Playground structure (6)
6 Horse's cry (5)
10 Goal that levels a football match (9)
12 Heavy sea wave (7)
13 Diffusion of molecules through a membrane (7)
14 Venomous snakes (6)
16 Lifted with effort (6)
18 Circle a planet (5)

Crossword

Puzzle 282

Across

1 Particles around a comet (4)
3 Wine container (8)
9 Purplish red colour (7)
10 Kingdom (5)
11 Frighten; warning sound (5)
12 A child beginning to walk (7)
13 Provoke (6)
15 False (6)
17 Collection of sheets of paper (7)
18 Join together as one (5)
20 Sandy fawn colour (5)
21 Mischievous children (7)
22 Raised (8)
23 Feeling of resentment or jealousy (4)

Down

1 Friendly (13)
2 Molten rock (5)
4 Plays out (6)
5 Physics of movement through air (12)
6 Fishing boat (7)
7 Pitilessly (13)
8 Use of words that mimic sounds (12)
14 Resembling a feline (3-4)
16 Advance evidence for (6)
19 Rule (5)

Puzzle 283

Across

1 ___ together: assembled from parts (6)
5 At the present time (3)
7 Shadow (5)
8 Seems (7)
9 Period between childhood and adulthood (5)
10 Beneficial (8)
12 Metal shackles (6)
14 Stanzas (6)
17 Formal curse by a pope (8)
18 Cry of excitement (5)
20 Eg from Ankara (7)
21 Got up (5)
22 Snare or trap; alcoholic spirit (3)
23 Positioned (6)

Down

2 Bring an accusation against (7)
3 Making big demands on something (8)
4 Comply with an order (4)
5 Saunter (anag) (7)
6 Shrivels up (7)
7 Take illegally (5)
11 Pertaining to the chest (8)
12 Boasting (7)
13 Distant runner-up (4-3)
15 All together (2,5)
16 Join together (5)
19 Short hollow thud (4)

Crossword

Puzzle 284

Across

1 ___ Lendl: former tennis star (4)
3 Morally compel (8)
9 Stablemen (7)
10 Inner circle (5)
11 Formal notice (12)
13 Written document (6)
15 One overly concerned with minor details (6)
17 A grouping of states (12)
20 Negative ion (5)
21 Insanitary (7)
22 Go beyond a limit (8)
23 State of confusion (4)

Down

1 Great adulation (8)
2 ___ du Beke: ballroom dancer (5)
4 Divide into two parts (6)
5 Ineptness (12)
6 European country (7)
7 Jellied ___ : English dish (4)
8 Demands or needs (12)
12 Engravings (8)
14 Outline; silhouette (7)
16 Bring about (6)
18 Feudal vassal (5)
19 Burkina ___ : African country (4)

Puzzle 285

Across

1 Keep hold of (6)
4 Unit of astronomical length (6)
9 Obstruction (7)
10 Baltic country (7)
11 ___ Halfpenny: Welsh rugby player (5)
12 Moves back and forth (5)
14 Pale brownish-yellow colour (5)
15 Repeat something once more (5)
17 Brilliant (5)
18 Pairs (7)
20 Put in someone's care (7)
21 Eccentricity (6)
22 Eg adder and python (6)

Down

1 Debris (6)
2 Fantastic (8)
3 Nationality of Louis Walsh (5)
5 Severely simple (7)
6 ___ Penn: actor (4)
7 Washes (6)
8 Glass buildings (11)
13 Burrowing ground squirrel (8)
14 Affluent (7)
15 Style of art or architecture (6)
16 Jots down (6)
17 Silk fabric (5)
19 Second-hand (4)

Crossword

Puzzle 286

Across

1 Talk wildly (4)
3 Gathers in crops (8)
9 Unit of heat energy (7)
10 Trite (5)
11 Not familiar with or used to (12)
13 Implant deeply (6)
15 Wood used for cricket bats (6)
17 Person's physical state (12)
20 Run away with a lover (5)
21 Forbidden by law (7)
22 Completely preoccupied with (8)
23 Football boot grip (4)

Down

1 Hermits (8)
2 Roman country house (5)
4 Images (anag) (6)
5 Triumphantly (12)
6 Bizarre (7)
7 Utters (4)
8 Courtesy (12)
12 Sparkled (8)
14 Rowdy (7)
16 Separate into pieces (6)
18 Gold block (5)
19 Block a decision (4)

Puzzle 287

Across

1 Highest point (4)
3 Goods for sale (8)
9 Remittance (7)
10 Effluent system (5)
11 Shockingly (12)
14 Haul (3)
16 Assumed appearance (5)
17 Collection of many sheets of paper (3)
18 Making no money (12)
21 Thorax (5)
22 Move in an exaggerated manner (7)
23 Making certain of (8)
24 Take ___ : band (4)

Down

1 Of striking appropriateness (8)
2 District council head (5)
4 Long deep track (3)
5 Destruction of bacteria (12)
6 European primula (7)
7 Forefather (4)
8 Cooling device in the kitchen (12)
12 Breathe in audibly (5)
13 Person who supports a cause (8)
15 Twiners (anag) (7)
19 Cluster (5)
20 Throb; dull pain (4)
22 Cooling tool (3)

Solutions

1.

2.

P L G
CONFIGURE
L T A V
WOK HORSE
A N E D R
GOODS SLY
E L O I
ROLEMODEL
S E N

3.

4.

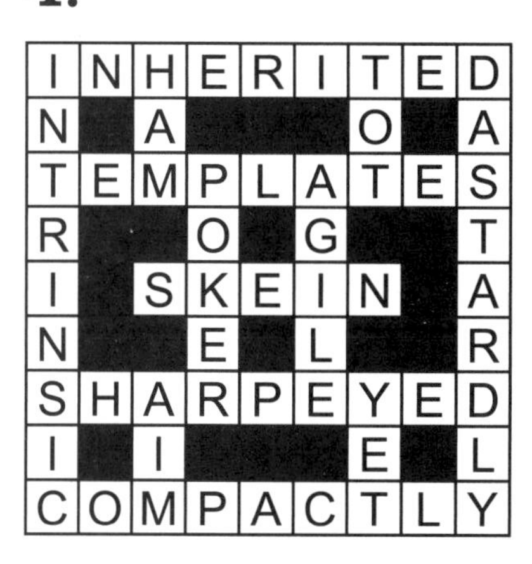

5.

6.

7.

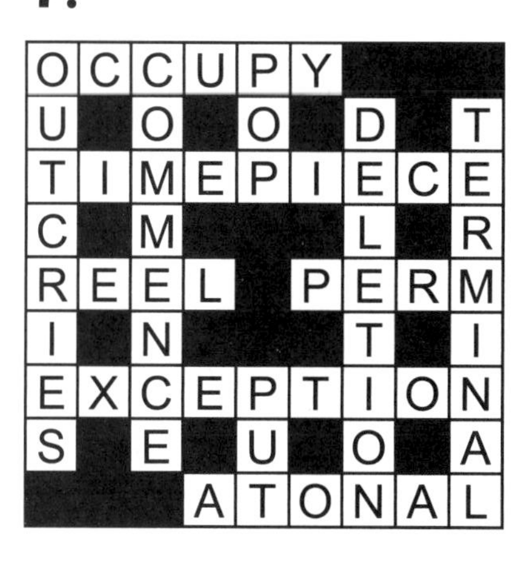

8.

9.

10.

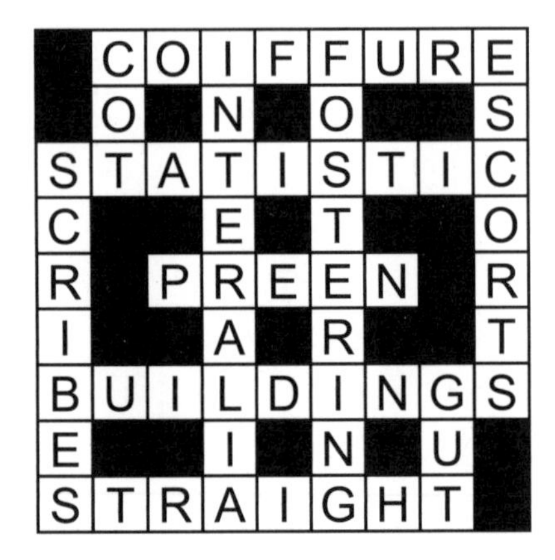

11.

12.

13.

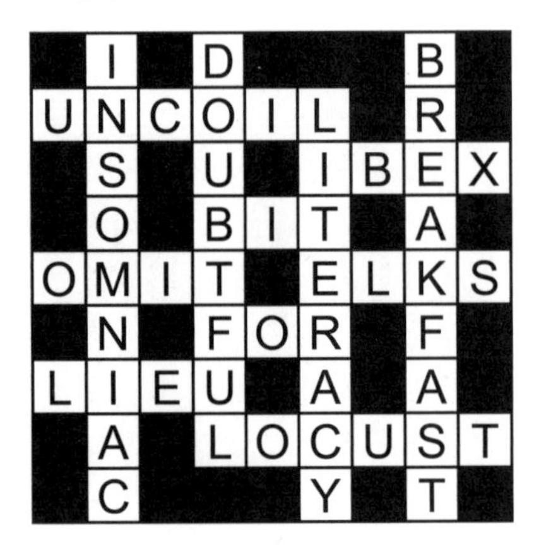

14.

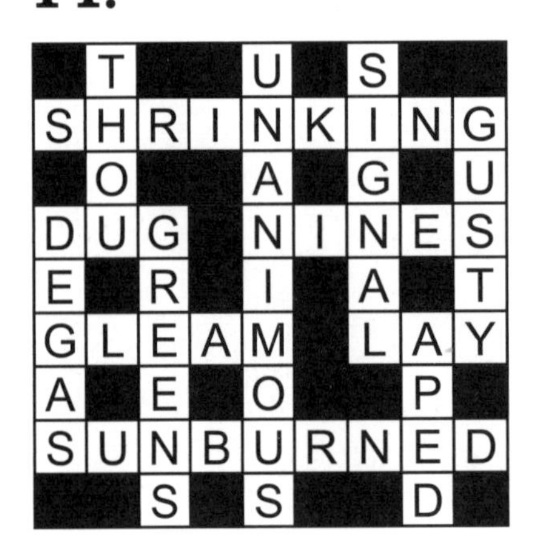

15.

16.

17.

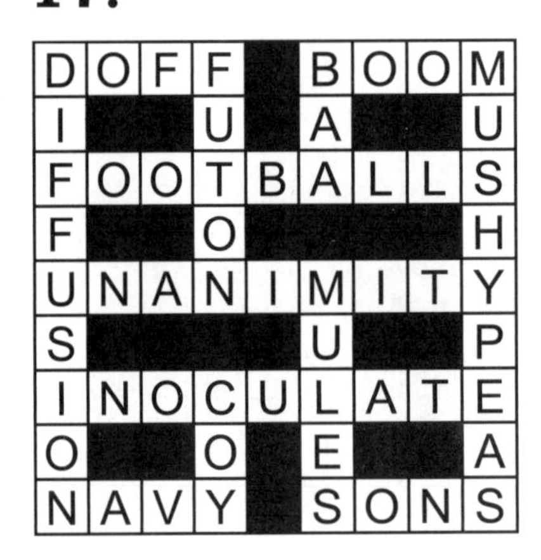

18.

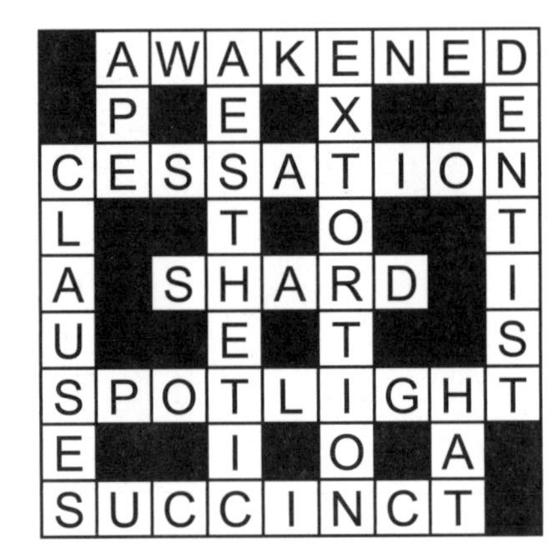

Solutions

19.

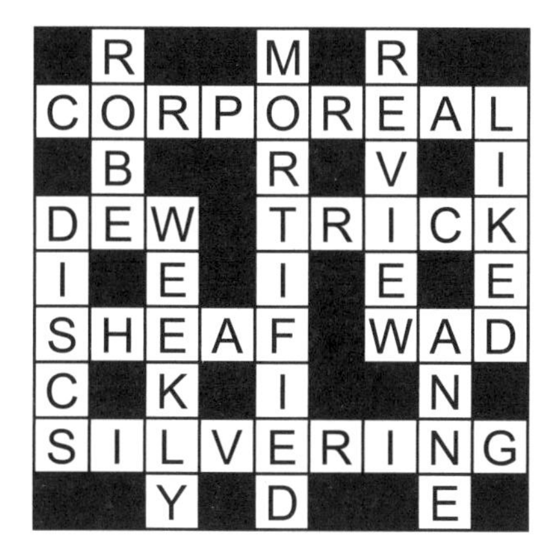

20.

I	N	C	E	■	C	I	A	O
R	■	■	L	■	O	■	■	C
R	E	P	E	L	L	E	N	T
I	■	■	C	■	■	■	■	A
T	O	T	T	E	R	I	N	G
A	■	■	■	■	O	■	■	O
B	A	T	T	A	L	I	O	N
L	■	■	H	■	E	■	■	A
E	P	E	E	■	S	O	I	L

21.

22.

23.

24.

25.

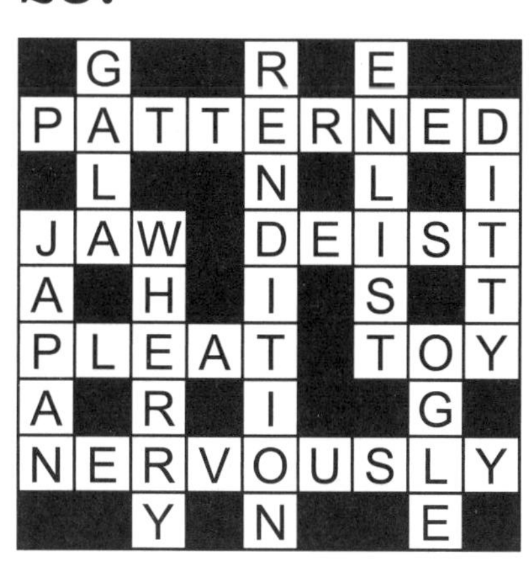

26.

27.

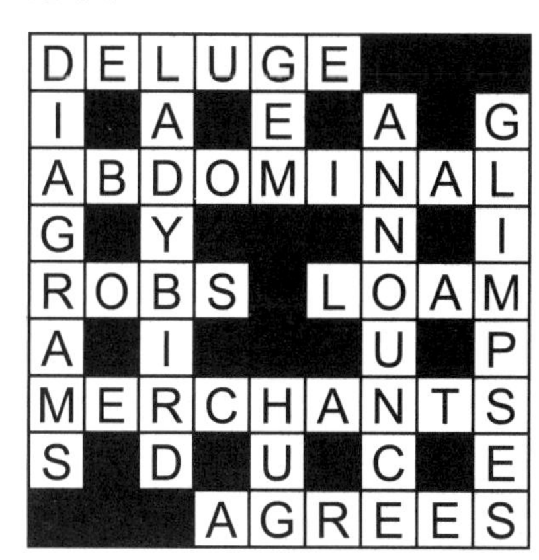

Solutions

28.

	B	O	A	R	D	I	N	G
	Y		C		I			R
S	E	A	C	H	A	N	G	E
T			O		L			M
A		F	R	E	E	S		L
N			D		C			I
D	E	V	I	A	T	I	O	N
U			O		I		D	
P	I	N	N	A	C	L	E	

29.

C	O	R	K	S	C	R	E	W
A		O				E		E
F	A	D		W		A		A
E		S	H	E	A	R	E	R
T				I				I
E	M	B	A	R	G	O		S
R		I		D		W	H	O
I		N				N		M
A	D	D	R	E	S	S	E	E

30.

S	W	A	L	L	O	W	E	D
T		F				O		I
R	E	T	A	I	L	E	R	S
E			W		A			C
T		W	A	R	P	S		R
C			S		A			E
H	A	P	H	A	Z	A	R	D
E		L				R		I
S	K	Y	R	O	C	K	E	T

31.

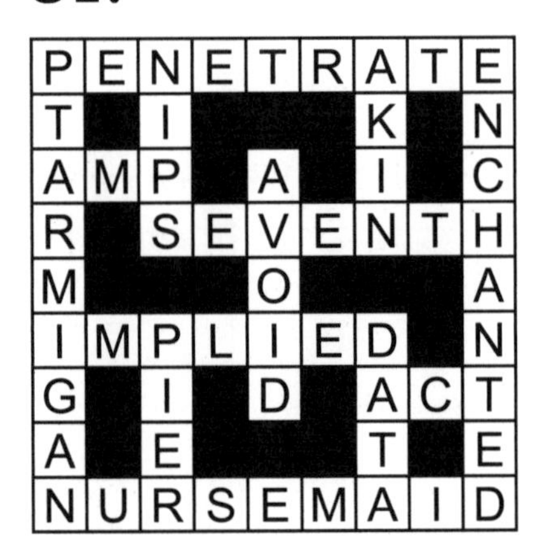

P	E	N	E	T	R	A	T	E
T		I				K		N
A	M	P		A		I		C
R		S	E	V	E	N	T	H
M				O				A
I	M	P	L	I	E	D		N
G		I		D		A	C	T
A		E				T		E
N	U	R	S	E	M	A	I	D

32.

F	A	R	O	F	F			
O		E		I		N		E
R	I	G	H	T	N	E	S	S
E		U				U		T
B	A	L	L		S	T	A	R
O		A				R		A
D	E	T	E	C	T	I	O	N
E		E		O		N		G
			E	X	P	O	S	E

33.

S		G		S		R	A	P
C	A	E	S	U	R	A		O
H		N		B		C		S
O	V	E	R	J	O	Y		T
O				U				E
L		F	I	D	D	L	E	R
I		R		I		O		I
N		A	C	C	O	U	N	T
G	U	Y		E		D		Y

34.

	M		F				I	
P	A	N	A	M	A		R	
	R		M		L	E	A	P
	S		O	P	T		S	
L	U	L	U		I	T	C	H
	P		S	I	T		I	
H	I	L	L		U		B	
	A		Y	O	D	E	L	S
	L				E		E	

35.

A	G	G	R	I	E	V	E	D
N		A				E		E
A	P	P	A	R	A	T	U	S
L			X		U			C
G		S	I	E	G	E		E
E			O		U			N
S	U	B	M	E	R	G	E	D
I		A				I		E
A	C	T	S	O	F	G	O	D

36.

B	R	E	A	K	D	O	W	N
I		Z				A		E
O	U	R		C		R		W
S		A	R	R	E	S	T	S
P				E				P
H	A	P	P	E	N	S		A
E		A		D		H	I	P
R		C				I		E
E	Y	E	O	P	E	N	E	R

Solutions

37.

■	B	■	E	■	A	■	C	■	S	■	B	■
C	O	N	F	I	G	U	R	A	T	I	O	N
■	D	■	F	■	A	■	A	■	A	■	O	■
C	Y	N	I	C	I	S	M	■	B	A	K	E
■	■	■	G	■	N	■	S	■	L	■	C	■
C	O	P	Y	I	S	T	■	R	E	L	A	Y
■	U	■	■	■	T	■	C	■	■	■	S	■
S	T	R	A	Y	■	T	R	O	T	T	E	D
■	S	■	S	■	A	■	A	■	W	■	■	■
S	T	O	P	■	M	I	D	N	I	G	H	T
■	R	■	I	■	U	■	L	■	S	■	O	■
D	I	S	R	E	S	P	E	C	T	F	U	L
■	P	■	E	■	E	■	D	■	S	■	R	■

38.

39.

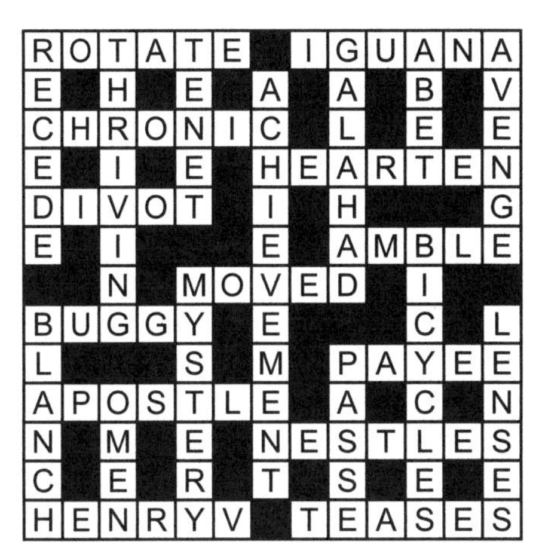

40.

■	C	H	A	I	R	P	E	R	S	O	N	■
A	■	E	■	N	■	L	■	U	■	W	■	A
M	■	A	■	K	N	E	L	L	■	N	E	T
E	N	D	O	W	■	A	■	E	■	E	■	R
L	■	S	■	E	■	T	■	R	A	D	I	O
I	D	E	A	L	I	S	M	■	■	■	■	C
O	■	T	■	L	■	■	■	T	■	F	■	I
R	■	■	■	■	P	A	L	O	M	I	N	O
A	C	T	E	D	■	D	■	O	■	R	■	U
T	■	E	■	O	■	V	■	L	E	E	R	S
E	R	R	■	G	R	E	E	K	■	M	■	L
S	■	S	■	M	■	N	■	I	■	E	■	Y
■	D	E	V	A	S	T	A	T	I	N	G	■

41.

42.

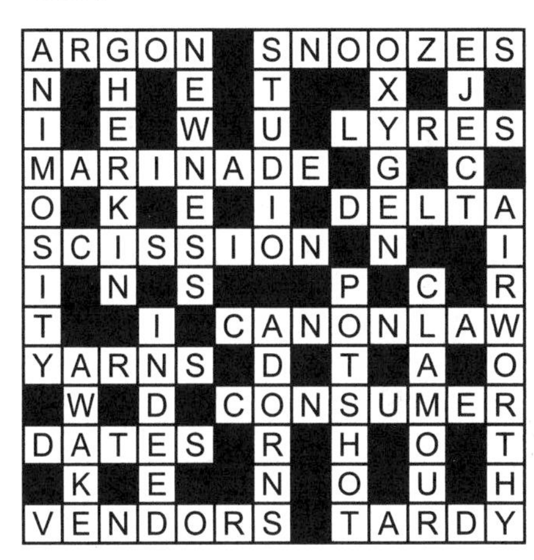

43.

44.

45.

Solutions

46.

R	E	P	A	I	D		F		E		F	
E		R			R	E	A	B	S	O	R	B
V	I	E			I		N		P		E	
E		F	R	O	L	I	C		O	M	A	R
R		I			L		I		U		K	
T	E	X	T	S		P	E	R	S	I	S	T
			H		F		R		A			
P	U	E	R	I	L	E		B	L	A	N	K
	R		A		U		G			V		I
R	A	M	S		V	I	R	A	G	O		N
	N		H		I		I			W	E	D
N	U	M	E	R	A	T	E			E		L
	S		D		L		F	O	N	D	L	Y

47.

D	I	L	L		P	R	E	F	E	C	T	S
I		I		A		E		O		H		T
N	E	S	T	L	E	D		R	O	U	T	E
O		Z		L				T		C		W
S	I	T	T	I	N	G	D	U	C	K	S	
A				M		I		I		L		G
U	R	N		P	I	V	O	T		E	A	U
R		O		O		E		O				I
	O	V	E	R	I	N	D	U	L	G	E	D
A		E		T				S		A		A
C	I	L	I	A		S	O	L	O	M	O	N
R		L		N		U		Y		M		C
E	X	A	L	T	I	N	G		F	A	D	E

48.

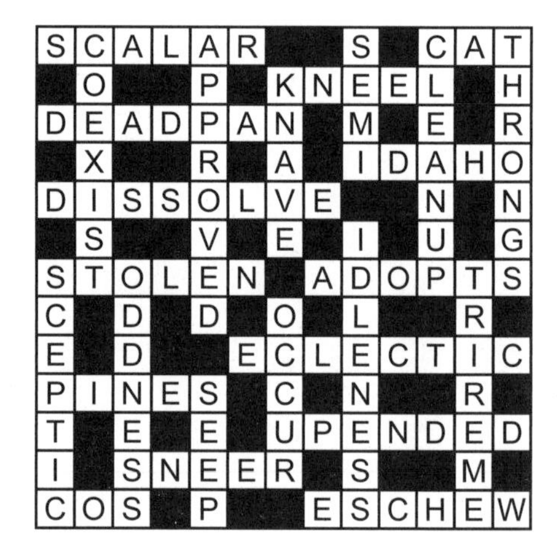

49.

L	A	K	E		J	E	T	T	I	S	O	N
I		O		C		A		R		P		I
F	L	A	V	O	U	R		I	C	I	N	G
E		L		M		T		G		D		H
S	H	A	R	P	S	H	O	O	T	E	R	
P				L		Y		N		R		P
A	M	B	L	E	D		M	O	R	S	E	L
N		R		T		S		M				A
	N	E	V	E	R	T	H	E	L	E	S	S
B		A		N		A		T		T		T
A	N	K	L	E		M	A	R	Q	U	E	E
U		U		S		E		Y		D		R
D	E	P	O	S	I	N	G		N	E	T	S

50.

51.

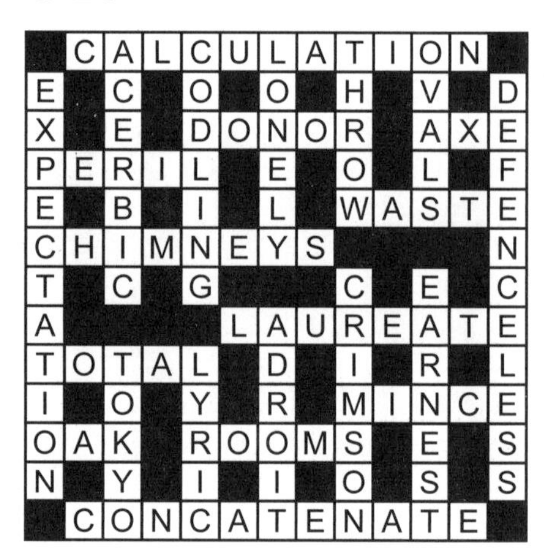

52.

53.

54.

E	V	E	R	Y	D	A	Y		A	G	O	G
T		N		A		B				R		E
C	O	M	I	C		B	A	H	R	A	I	N
H		E		H		E				N		E
		S		T		Y	O	U	N	G	E	R
S	C	H	I	S	M	S		P		E		O
P				M				G				U
I		S		A		H	O	R	R	O	R	S
R	O	M	A	N	I	A		A		S		
I		O				W		D		T		E
T	O	C	C	A	T	A		I	D	L	E	D
E		K				I		N		E		G
D	A	S	H		G	I	N	G	E	R	L	Y

Solutions

55.

C	L	A	P		T	R	O	P	I	C	A	L
U		L		D		A		A		A		I
B	O	B	B	I	N	G		R	A	D	O	N
I		U		S				S		E		T
C	O	M	B	I	N	A	T	I	O	N	S	
L				N		T		M		Z		L
E	V	E		F	O	L	I	O		A	G	A
S		N		E		A		N				N
	N	A	R	C	I	S	S	I	S	T	I	C
G		M		T				O		E		E
A	L	O	H	A		D	I	U	R	N	A	L
R		U		N		I		S		O		O
B	A	R	I	T	O	N	E		G	N	A	T

56.

T	U	B	A		S	T	A	D	I	U	M	S
H		L		C		H		I		N		E
E	P	I	S	O	D	E		V	O	W	E	L
S		N		M		L		E		O		F
I	N	K		M		M		R	E	U	S	E
X				E	X	A	M	S		N		V
T		S		N				I		D		I
H		O		C	A	N	T	O				D
S	O	L	V	E		O		N		S	E	E
E		I		M		O		A		H		N
N	A	C	R	E		D	A	R	K	E	S	T
S		I		N		L		Y		A		L
E	N	T	I	T	L	E	D		P	R	E	Y

57.

P	S	E	U	D	O			S		A	G	O
	C			R		C	A	K	E	S		V
D	E	S	P	A	I	R		Y		P		E
	P			U		A		E	S	H	E	R
S	T	A	R	G	A	Z	E			A		P
	R			H		Y		D		L		A
R	E	L	A	T	E		S	E	N	T	R	Y
A		I		S		M		T			E	
R		Q			S	I	D	E	K	I	C	K
E	Q	U	A	L		S		C			E	
B		E		O		E	X	T	E	N	D	S
I		U	M	B	E	R		E			E	
T	O	R		E			O	D	E	S	S	A

58.

F	O	R	E	W	O	R	D		A	T	O	M
I		O		E		U		U		S		A
R	A	V	E	L		C		N	O	U	N	S
E		E		T		K		D		N		S
			R	E	M	U	N	E	R	A	T	E
W		P		R		S		R		M		U
A	L	L	O	W	S		U	G	L	I	E	R
T		A		E		S		A		S		S
C	E	N	T	I	M	E	T	R	E			
H		T		G		E		M		S		D
F	A	I	T	H		I		E	M	P	T	Y
U		N		T		N		N		A		E
L	O	G	O		A	G	I	T	A	T	E	D

59.

R	O	P	E		S	C	R	I	B	B	L	E
E		U		Q		U		N		L		A
P	E	R	T	U	R	B		T	R	A	C	T
U		R		I		I		E		N		S
B	U	S	I	N	E	S	S	L	I	K	E	
L				T		T		L		E		P
I	M	A	G	E	S		B	I	S	T	R	O
C		N		S		J		G				N
	U	N	A	S	S	U	M	I	N	G	L	Y
A		U		E		M		B		E		T
C	O	L	O	N		B	E	L	I	N	D	A
T		A		C		L		E		I		I
S	O	R	C	E	R	E	R		H	E	E	L

60.

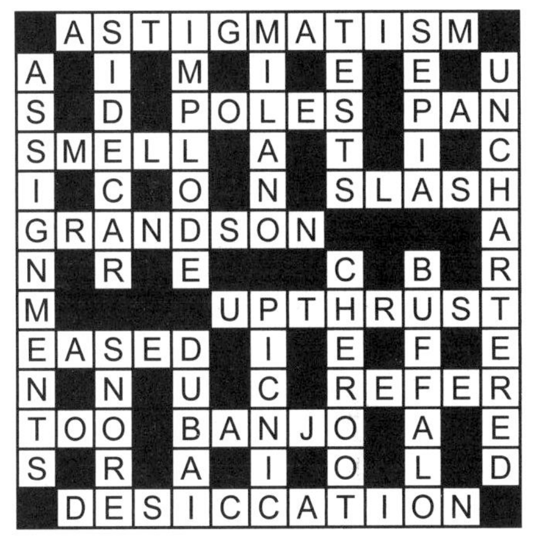

61.

C	O	D	E		B	E	R	I	B	E	R	I
O		A		E		A		N		N		N
N	O	Z	Z	L	E	S		C	I	V	I	C
T		E		E		I		O		Y		R
E	N	D		C		E		N	A	I	V	E
M				T	A	R	T	S		N		D
P		A		R				I		G		U
L		C		O	G	L	E	S				L
A	P	R	I	L		E		T		C	O	O
T		Y		Y		N		E		E		U
I	D	L	E	S		N	O	N	P	L	U	S
V		I		I		O		T		L		L
E	X	C	U	S	I	N	G		P	O	N	Y

62.

63.

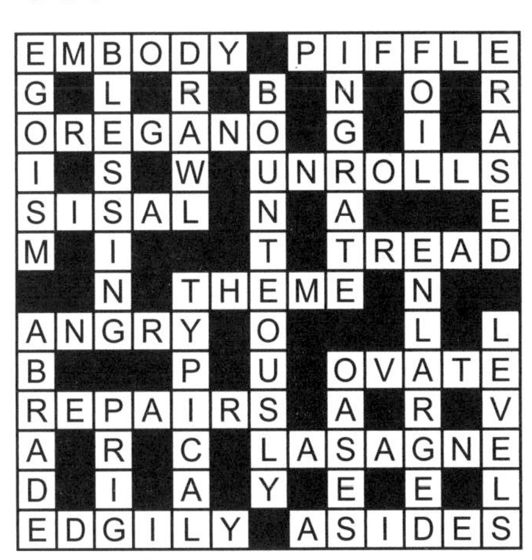

64.

E	T	H	E	R		P	A	N	A	C	H	E
P		A		E		O			C		I	
H		L		V		N		A	C	U	T	E
E	M	I	N	E	N	C	E		R		C	
M		B		R		H		B	U	S	H	Y
E	M	U	L	S	I	O	N		E			E
R		T		E				B		S		A
A			D		A	T	T	A	C	K	E	R
L	E	V	E	L		A		R		I		B
	N		L		F	L	A	M	E	N	C	O
A	S	H	E	S		E		A		N		O
	U		T			N		I		E		K
R	E	C	E	I	P	T		D	O	D	O	S

65.

	S	H	A	D	Y		S	C	A	L	D	
A		I		O		F		O		O		A
M	I	S	R	U	L	E		M	O	G	U	L
I		T		R		W		P				P
D	H	O	W		N	E	G	L	E	C	T	S
S		R		O		R		A		O		
T	R	I	C	K	S		M	I	N	N	O	W
		A		L		D		N		Q		I
T	A	N	Z	A	N	I	A		R	U	E	D
A				H		V		S		E		E
C	A	C	A	O		E	X	P	I	R	E	S
T		A		M		R		U		O		T
	K	N	E	A	D		S	N	A	R	L	

66.

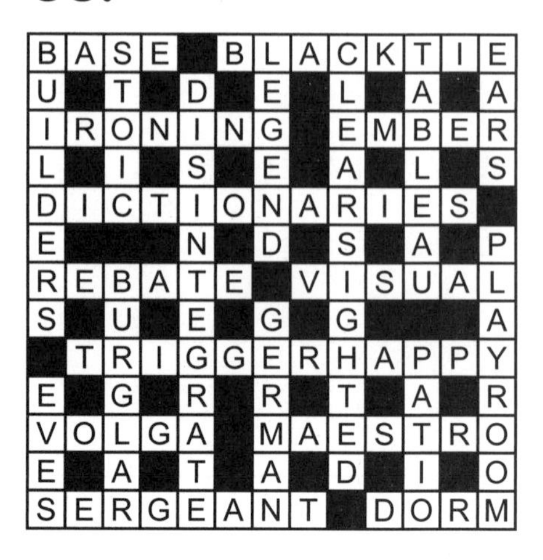

67.

D	A	B	S		A	V	O	I	D	I	N	G
I		A		A		A		N		N		U
R	E	S	T	F	U	L		T	A	S	T	Y
E		I		T				E		U		S
C	O	N	T	E	M	P	O	R	A	R	Y	
T				R		O		M		E		A
L	E	A		T	R	U	C	E		D	I	P
Y		M		H		R		D				P
	R	E	C	O	N	S	T	I	T	U	T	E
E		R		U				A		N		N
B	R	I	N	G		W	O	R	R	I	E	D
B		C		H		O		Y		T		I
S	L	A	N	T	I	N	G		L	Y	N	X

68.

69.

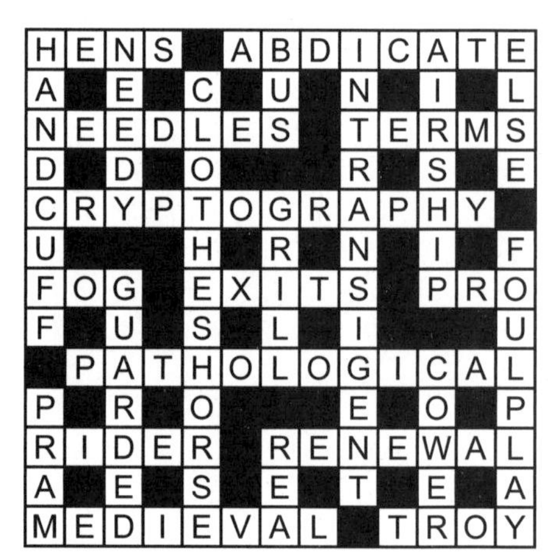

70.

71.

72.

D	E	B	I	L	I	T	Y		Z	I	N	C
I		L		I		I				C		R
S	W	A	R	M		N	A	I	V	E	L	Y
C		R		I		N				B		S
		E		T		E	N	D	M	O	S	T
P	A	D	D	L	E	D		I		X		A
R				E				S				L
E		B		S		O	Y	S	T	E	R	S
C	R	U	I	S	E	R		I		T		
I		F				D		P		H		T
O	F	F	S	I	D	E		A	B	A	S	H
U		E				A		T		N		U
S	E	T	T		C	L	U	E	L	E	S	S

Solutions

73.

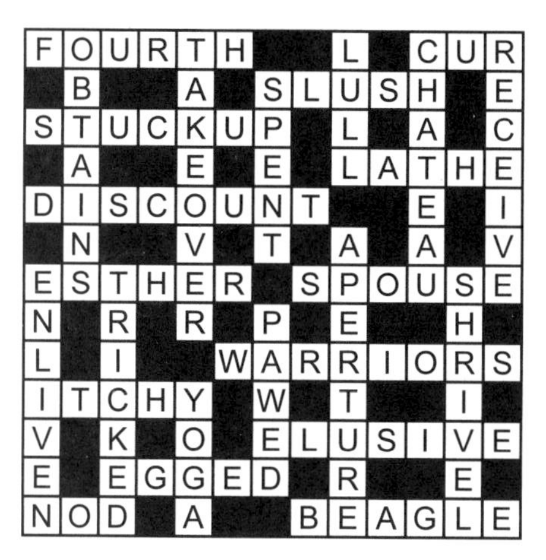

74.

	D	A	C	H	A		S	M	E	L	T	
G		M		O		R		A		A		K
A	M	P	H	O	R	A		G	A	B	L	E
L		L		T		I		E				G
L	O	I	N		A	N	A	L	Y	S	I	S
I		T		C		S		L		A		
C	R	U	S	O	E		D	A	N	C	E	R
		D		L		R		N		C		A
C	L	E	M	A	T	I	S		S	H	O	P
A				N		N		K		A		I
L	I	P	I	D		K	I	N	D	R	E	D
L		A		E		S		O		I		S
	S	W	O	R	D		S	W	A	N	K	

75.

76.

77.

78.

79.

80.

81.

Solutions

82.

A	R	G	O		M	I	L	I	T	A	R	Y
N		L		A		N		N		N		O
T	H	E	R	M	O	S		C	I	G	A	R
E		A		B		E		O		E		K
C	O	N	V	I	N	C	I	N	G	L	Y	
E				D		T		S		U		P
D	I	P	P	E	D		T	E	A	S	E	L
E		A		X		L		Q				A
	D	I	S	T	R	I	B	U	T	I	O	N
A		N		R		M		E		O		T
R	A	T	I	O		B	O	N	A	N	Z	A
I		E		U		E		T		I		I
D	E	R	I	S	O	R	Y		S	C	A	N

83.

U	T	A	H		B	R	U	S	H	O	F	F
N		N		A		U		E		R		E
I	N	V	E	R	S	E		L	I	B	Y	A
M		I		I		F		F		I		T
P	A	L		T		U		L	A	T	C	H
E				H	A	L	L	E		A		E
A		F		M				S		L		R
C		O		E	A	V	E	S				W
H	I	R	S	T		I		N		P	I	E
A		E		I		O		E		R		I
B	A	S	I	C		L	A	S	H	I	N	G
L		E		A		A		S		S		H
E	Y	E	G	L	A	S	S		S	E	N	T

84.

85.

R	E	S	E	N	T		S		H		A	
O		T			O	U	T	W	E	I	G	H
L	O	A			U		I		G		E	
L		T	E	A	C	U	P		E	R	N	E
E		I			H		E		M		C	
R	A	C	E	R		A	N	T	O	N	Y	M
			X		R		D		N			
S	W	E	E	T	E	R		X	Y	L	E	M
	E		G		V		M			A		I
C	E	D	E		E	P	O	N	Y	M		D
	V		S		N		W			B	O	W
R	I	D	I	C	U	L	E			D		A
	L		S		E		R	O	S	A	R	Y

86.

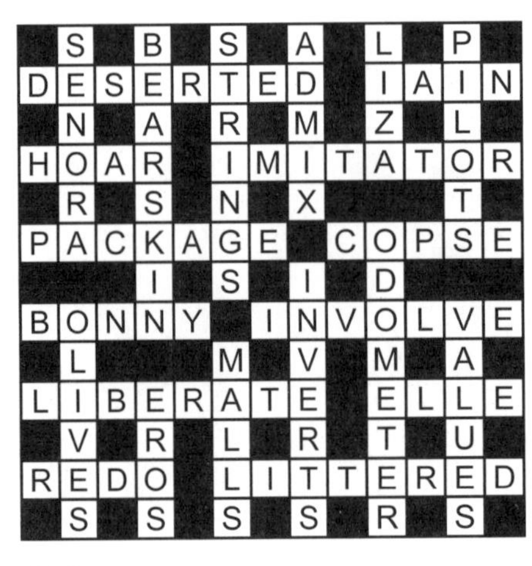

87.

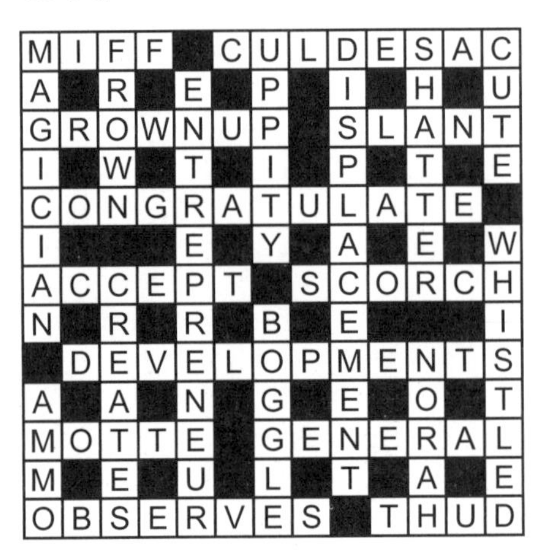

88.

89.

90.

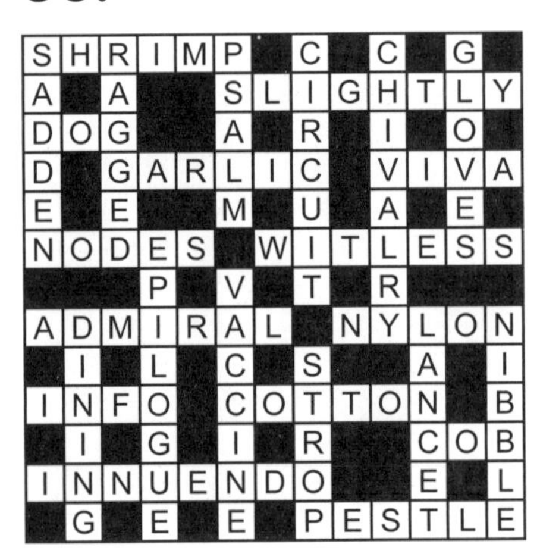

Solutions

91.

92.

93.

94.

E	G	G	S		U	N	I	F	O	R	M	S
N		R		N		I		R		E		I
T	E	A	S	I	N	G		U	P	S	E	T
H		I		G		G		I		T		E
A	N	N	I	H	I	L	A	T	I	O	N	
L				T		E		F		R		H
P	U	M	I	C	E		T	U	X	E	D	O
Y		I		L		E		L				S
	I	N	C	O	N	V	E	N	I	E	N	T
E		U		T		E		E		A		E
B	U	T	C	H		N	O	S	T	R	I	L
O		I		E		E		S		E		R
R	H	A	P	S	O	D	Y		I	D	L	Y

95.

96.

97.

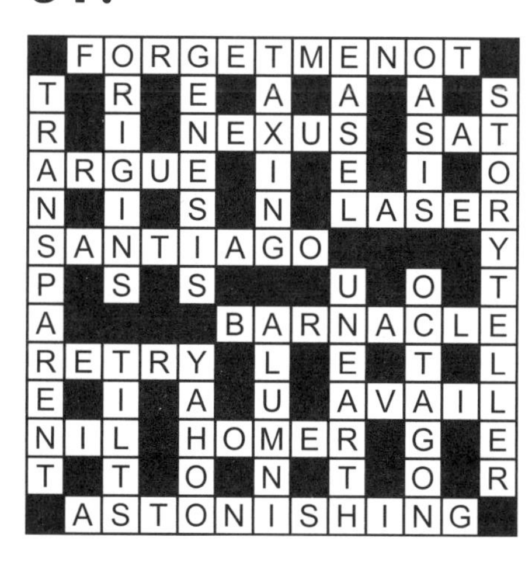

98.

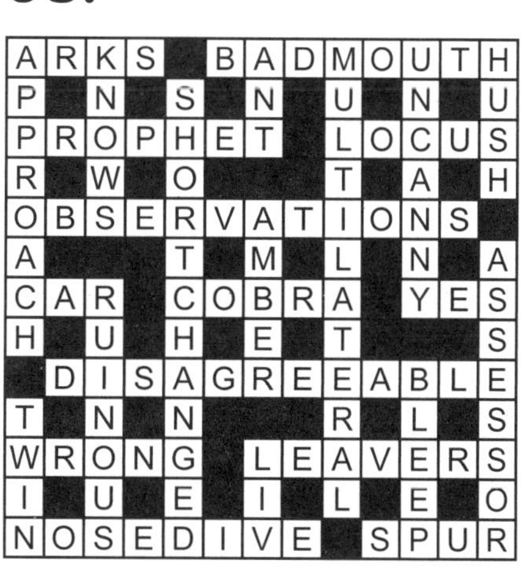

99.

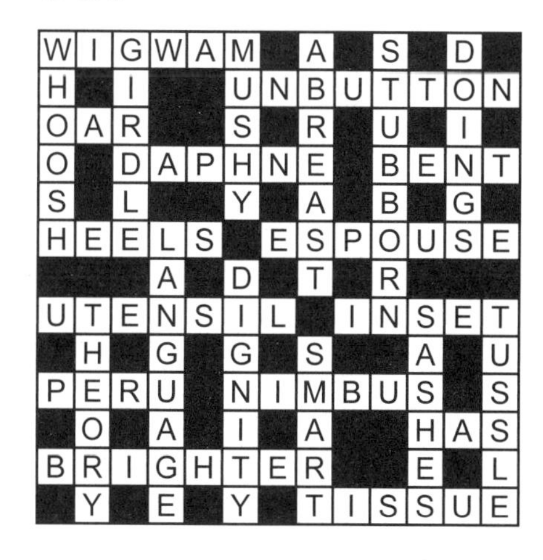

100.

B	U	F	F		P	L	E	A	S	I	N	G
E		I		O		I		B		N		A
T	H	R	I	V	E	D		S	U	S	A	N
R		S		E				O		I		G
A	N	T	H	R	O	P	O	L	O	G	Y	
Y				C		L		U		H		I
A	U	K		A	D	A	P	T		T	E	N
L		I		U		Z		E				D
	U	N	A	T	T	A	I	N	A	B	L	E
W		G		I				E		L		N
A	U	D	I	O		D	E	S	C	A	N	T
I		O		U		O		S		M		E
F	A	M	I	S	H	E	D		N	E	E	D

101.

S	A	P	S		S	P	E	A	K	I	N	G
P		E		S		O		G		N		O
L	E	C	T	U	R	E		R	O	D	E	O
I		A		P		T		I		O		D
T	E	N	S	E		R	A	C	C	O	O	N
D				R		Y		U		R		A
E	B	B	I	N	G		C	L	O	S	E	T
C		R		A		P		T				U
I	N	E	R	T	I	A		U	S	H	E	R
S		A		U		T		R		A		E
I	N	T	E	R		R	O	A	S	T	E	D
O		H		A		O		L		E		L
N	E	E	D	L	I	N	G		E	S	P	Y

102.

103.

104.

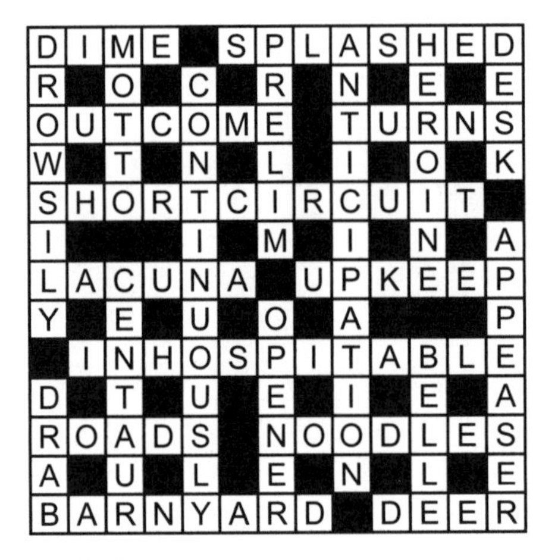

105.

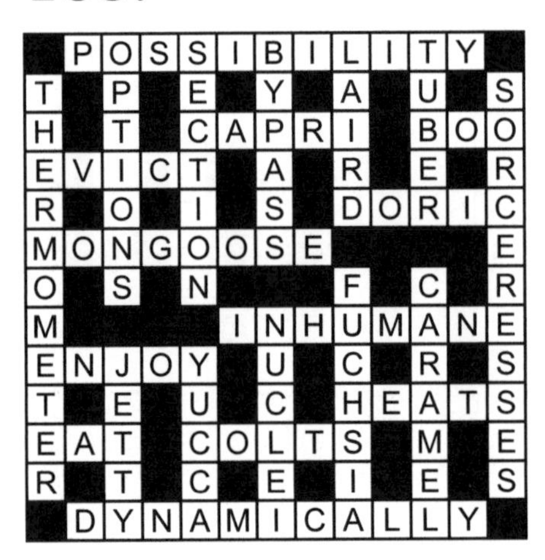

106.

107.

108.

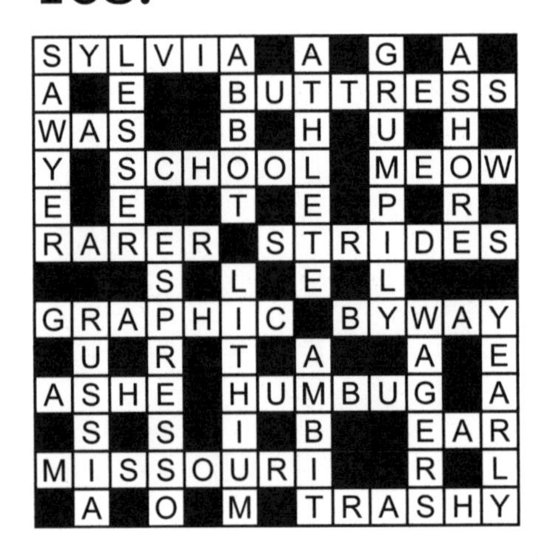

Solutions

109.

S	I	M	I	L	E		R	E	P	A	I	R
T		O		O		C		A		L		A
U	N	D	E	R	G	O		S		E		N
F		I		R		N	O	T	I	C	E	S
F	I	F	T	Y		S		E				O
S		I				T		R	E	A	R	M
		E		B	A	R	O	N		C		
M	I	D	G	E		I				R		S
O				E		C		C	R	O	F	T
H	A	B	I	T	A	T		H		S		A
A		E		L		O	M	I	T	T	E	D
I		T		E		R		N		I		I
R	E	S	I	S	T		F	A	S	C	I	A

110.

111.

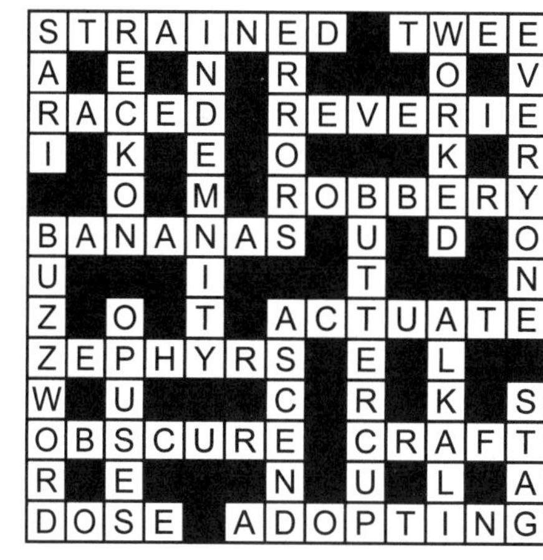

112.

113.

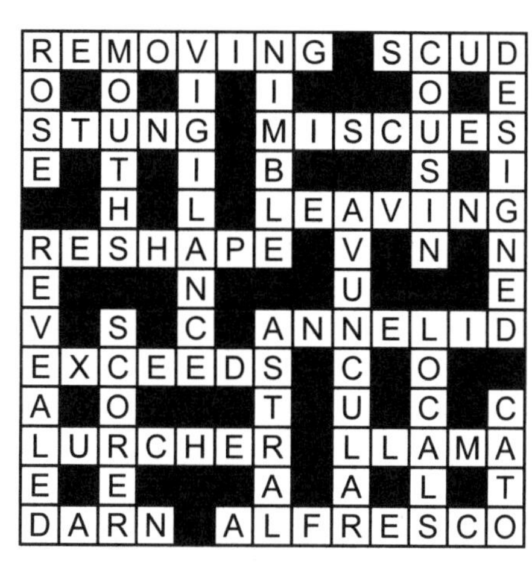

114.

115.

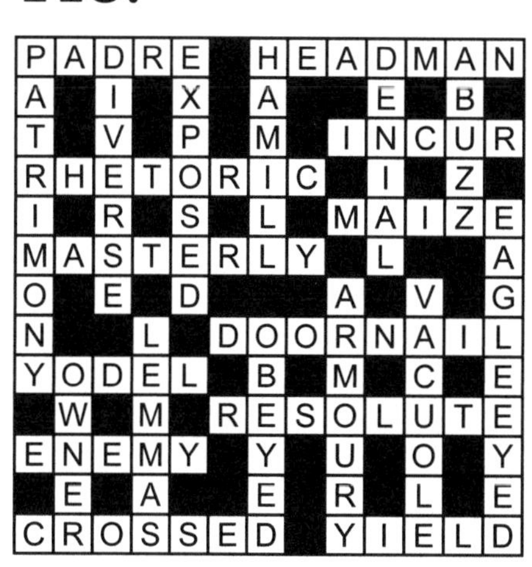

116.

117.

118.

U	N	M	A	S	K		C		U		U	
N		A			N	E	A	T	N	E	S	S
S	K	Y			O		R		W		U	
E		H	I	C	C	U	P		A	U	R	A
A		E			K		O		S		E	
T	E	M	P	O		A	R	C	H	E	R	Y
			R		B		T		E			
C	H	E	E	T	A	H		A	D	L	I	B
	A		C		B		C			I		U
B	R	I	E		Y	E	O	M	A	N		M
	R		D		I		A			I	M	P
F	O	R	E	N	S	I	C			N		E
	W		S		H		H	U	N	G	E	R

119.

F	U	M	E		V	E	N	T	U	R	E	D
E		I		C		A		O		E		A
B	A	T	T	L	E	R		G	I	V	E	R
R		E		O		N		E		E		E
U	N	S	U	S	P	E	C	T	I	N	G	
A				E		D		H		G		H
R	E	V	A	M	P		G	E	N	E	V	A
Y		E		O		F		R				P
	F	R	E	U	D	I	A	N	S	L	I	P
I		N		T		D		E		A		I
S	W	I	S	H		G	E	S	T	U	R	E
L		E		E		E		S		R		S
A	C	R	I	D	I	T	Y		V	A	S	T

120.

M	U	T	T	E	R	E	D		R	U	F	F
A		U		N		L		I		N		L
M	A	G	I	C		I		N	E	W	L	Y
A		S		H		X		C		A		P
			C	A	L	I	F	O	R	N	I	A
S		P		N		R		M		T		P
E	V	E	N	T	S		A	P	I	E	C	E
R		L		I		B		A		D		R
V	O	L	U	N	T	E	E	R	S			
I		M		G		L		A		T		A
C	R	E	E	L		U		B	O	A	R	D
E		L		Y		G		L		X		Z
S	O	L	O		L	A	D	Y	L	I	K	E

121.

O	N	E	O	F	F		A	S	P	E	C	T
R		C		L		A		E		V		R
D	I	S	T	U	R	B		T		I		O
E		T		E		O	U	T	F	L	O	W
R	O	A	R	S		M		E				E
S		T				I		E	X	P	E	L
		I		A	U	N	T	S		L		
D	U	C	K	S		A				A		N
I				C		T		L	A	T	T	E
S	A	M	U	R	A	I		O		O		V
U		O		I		O	R	G	A	N	Z	A
S		A		B		N		I		I		D
E	I	T	H	E	R		A	C	A	C	I	A

122.

C	A	S	E	Y		W	O	R	N	O	U	T
O		P		A		H			O		R	
S		A		W		I		M	U	M	B	A
P	E	N	K	N	I	F	E		G		A	
O		I		I		F		T	H	I	N	K
N	O	S	I	N	E	S	S		T			N
S		H		G				I		P		O
O			A		H	E	D	G	E	R	O	W
R	O	U	N	D		S		N		O		L
	A		G		O	S	B	O	U	R	N	E
S	T	O	O	P		A		R		A		D
	H		R			Y		E		T		G
I	S	L	A	N	D	S		D	R	A	K	E

123.

C	O	M	E		S	H	E	P	H	E	R	D
L		I		D		A		R		L		A
A	L	C	H	E	M	Y		E	M	E	R	Y
P		R		M				C		V		S
P	R	O	P	O	R	T	I	O	N	A	L	
I				N		H		G		T		I
N	O	R		S	P	U	R	N		E	L	M
G		A		T		M		I				P
	D	I	S	R	E	P	U	T	A	B	L	E
S		N		A				I		O		L
H	A	B	I	T		F	R	O	N	T	A	L
U		O		O		O		N		C		E
T	H	W	A	R	T	E	D		S	H	E	D

124.

F	I	G	U	R	I	N	E		U	S	E	S
O		A		E		O				Q		T
U	N	L	I	T		B	E	R	M	U	D	A
L		L		A		O				A		N
		O		L		D	R	I	L	L	E	D
H	A	N	D	I	L	Y		N		L		A
E				A				C				R
S		S		T		S	T	A	L	L	E	D
I	N	Q	U	E	S	T		P		A		
T		U				E		A		Z		P
A	M	I	A	B	L	E		B	R	U	T	E
T		R				P		L		L		E
E	M	M	Y		A	S	T	E	R	I	S	K

125.

U	R	G	E		A	S	S	E	M	B	L	E
N		O		O		P		X		R		X
P	A	I	S	L	E	Y		P	A	I	N	T
R		N		D		I		E		G		R
E	I	G	H	T		N	I	R	V	A	N	A
T				E		G		I		D		V
E	X	C	U	S	E		G	E	N	E	R	A
N		R		T		S		N				G
T	R	A	V	A	I	L		T	I	B	I	A
I		N		M		A		I		E		N
O	L	I	V	E		L	E	A	F	L	E	T
U		U		N		O		L		I		L
S	O	M	E	T	I	M	E		B	E	V	Y

126.

S	H	R	E	D	D	E	D		W	O	A	D
P		H		E		Y				R		E
A	M	I	G	O		R	E	M	O	D	E	L
N		N		D		I				A		E
		A		O		E	T	C	H	I	N	G
P	O	L	A	R	I	S		U		N		A
O				A				R				T
T		B		N		T	H	I	S	T	L	E
T	R	E	S	T	L	E		O		R		
E		H				N		S		U		A
R	E	A	C	T	E	D		I	N	D	E	X
E		L				E		T		G		E
D	A	F	T		G	R	E	Y	N	E	S	S

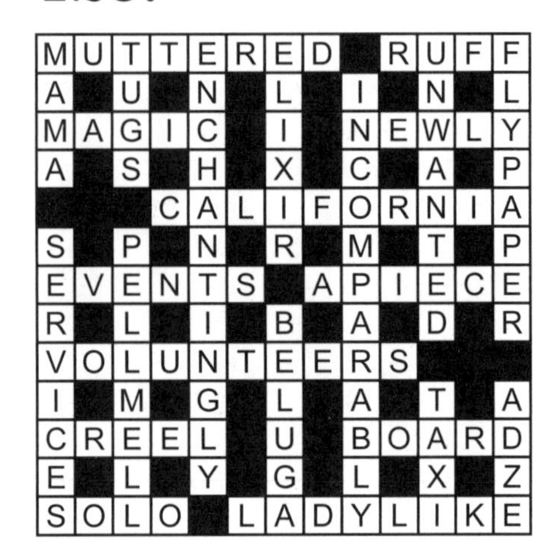

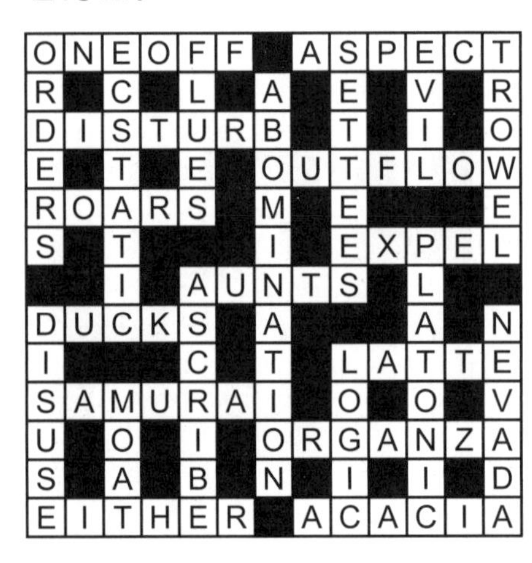

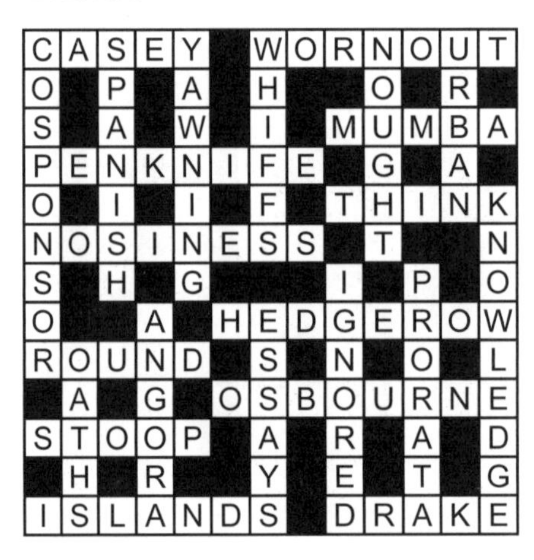

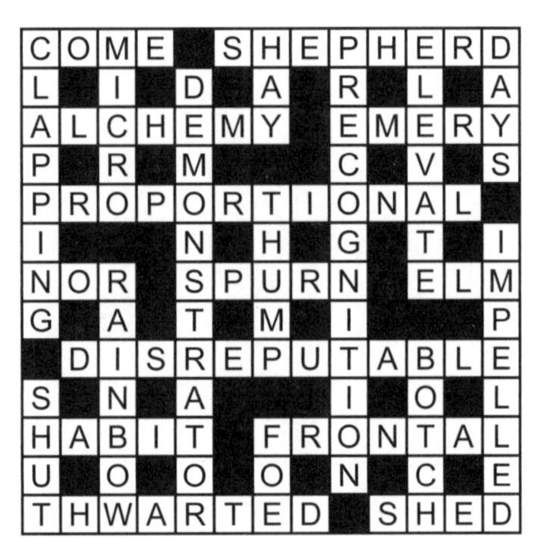

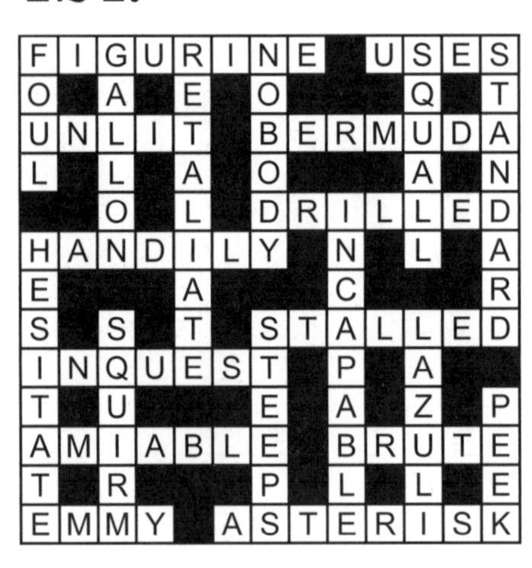

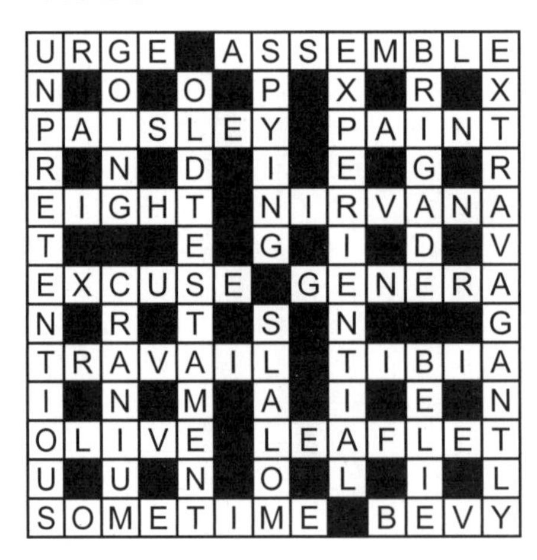

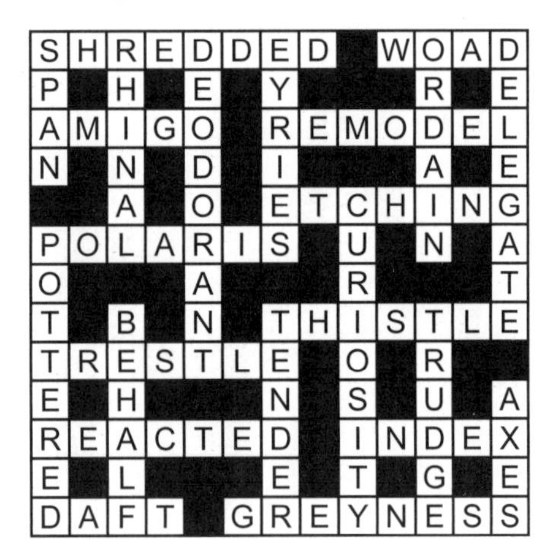

Solutions

127.

T	E	N	D	E	R	E	D		S	C	A	R
I		O		X		I		P		L		E
M	U	S	I	C		G		R	E	A	R	S
E		H		R		H		E		V		I
			M	U	L	T	I	P	L	I	E	D
W		S		C		Y		O		C		U
R	E	C	O	I	L		A	N	G	L	I	A
E		R		A		A		D		E		L
S	P	E	C	T	A	C	L	E	S			
T		A		I		C		R		N		B
L	U	M	E	N		E		A	D	E	L	E
E		E		G		N		N		R		D
R	E	D	S		S	T	A	T	I	O	N	S

128.

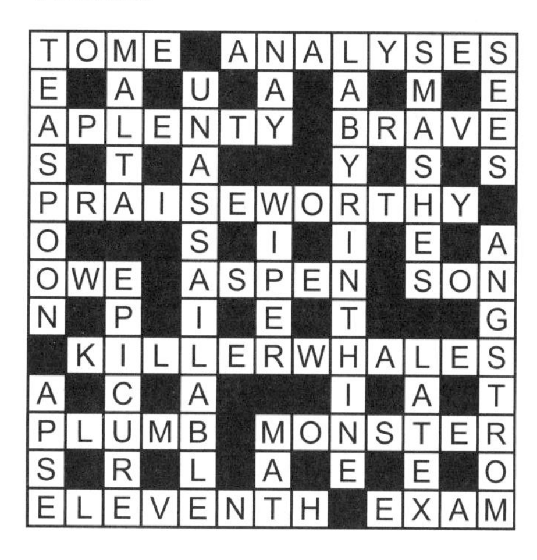

129.

130.

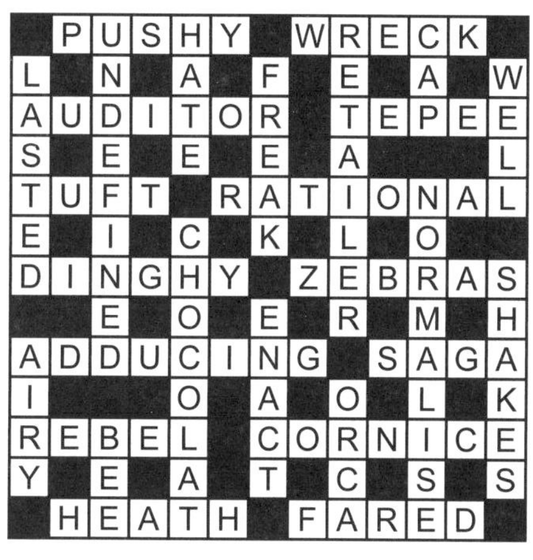

131.

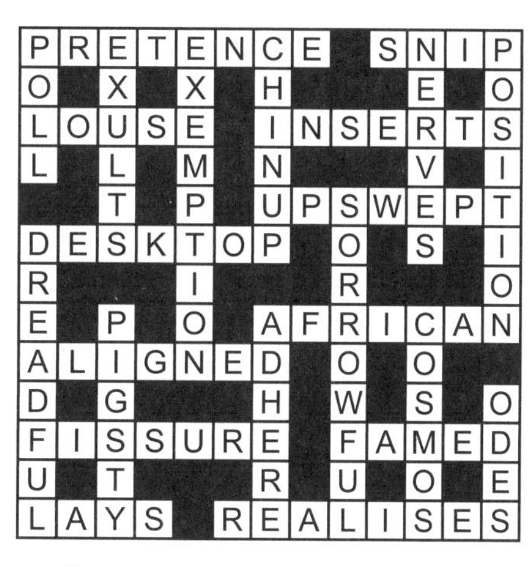

132.

133.

134.

135.

R	E	F	U	E	L		A	B	L	A	Z	E
E		A		X		E		A		X		X
F	A	N	T	A	S	Y		G		O		P
U		D		L		E	X	P	U	N	G	E
G	R	A	N	T		C		I				L
E		N				A		P	E	S	T	S
		G		M	I	T	R	E		C		
C	R	O	W	E		C				O		D
O				L		H		C	A	R	G	O
R	A	V	I	O	L	I		R		N		L
O		E		D		N	E	E	D	F	U	L
N		S		I		G		D		U		A
A	T	T	A	C	K		C	O	L	L	A	R

Solutions

136.

E	N	J	O	Y	S		U		S		G	
X		O			W	E	S	T	W	A	R	D
P	S	I			I		U		I		U	
O		S	E	N	S	O	R		N	O	N	E
R		T			S		P		D		G	
T	U	S	K	S		J	E	L	L	I	E	S
			E		M		R		E			
H	O	A	R	D	E	D		A	R	R	O	W
	R		C		R		G			W		A
F	I	S	H		M	A	N	T	R	A		R
	S		I		A		A			N	I	B
P	O	L	E	M	I	C	S			D		L
	N		F		D		H	O	M	A	G	E

137.

A	D	O	R	N		N	A	R	R	O	W	S
L		P		O		E			E		I	
O		E		U		U		S	M	I	R	K
O	M	N	I	V	O	R	E		I		E	
F		E		E		A		S	N	A	R	E
N	O	R	M	A	L	L	Y		D			M
E		S		U				G		A		A
S			C		C	H	E	R	U	B	I	C
S	T	O	O	D		O		A		S		I
	A		B		P	L	E	T	H	O	R	A
K	N	O	W	N		L		I		L		T
	G		E			E		N		V		E
D	O	U	B	T	E	R		G	R	E	E	D

138.

139.

140.

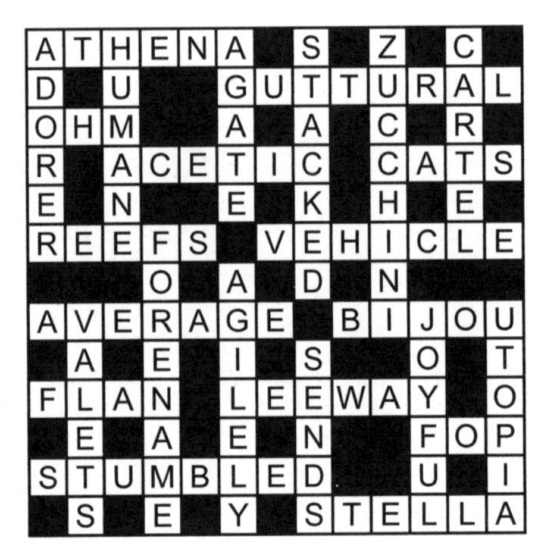

141.

142.

143.

D	A	D	O		T	H	U	M	B	S	U	P
I		O		P		O		A		T		H
S	P	L	U	R	G	E		S	H	A	M	E
T		C		E				T		R		W
U	N	E	X	P	E	C	T	E	D	L	Y	
R				O		A		R		E		R
B	A	R		S	I	N	U	S		T	I	E
S		E		T		O		T				T
	S	C	R	E	E	N	W	R	I	T	E	R
S		Y		R				O		R		O
M	A	C	R	O		T	A	K	E	O	F	F
O		L		U		I		E		P		I
G	U	E	S	S	I	N	G		B	E	A	T

144.

A	L	S	O		D	I	S	C	L	A	I	M
M		L		B		G		O		M		I
B	R	I	T	A	I	N		N	A	M	E	S
E		N		N		O		S		O		M
R	I	G	H	T		R	O	T	U	N	D	A
V				A		E		I		I		N
A	U	T	U	M	N		O	T	T	A	W	A
L		E		W		A		U				G
L	A	R	D	E	R	S		E	L	A	T	E
E		R		I		S		N		N		M
T	H	I	N	G		I	N	C	E	N	S	E
T		E		H		S		Y		E		N
A	I	R	S	T	R	I	P		E	X	I	T

Solutions

145.

146.

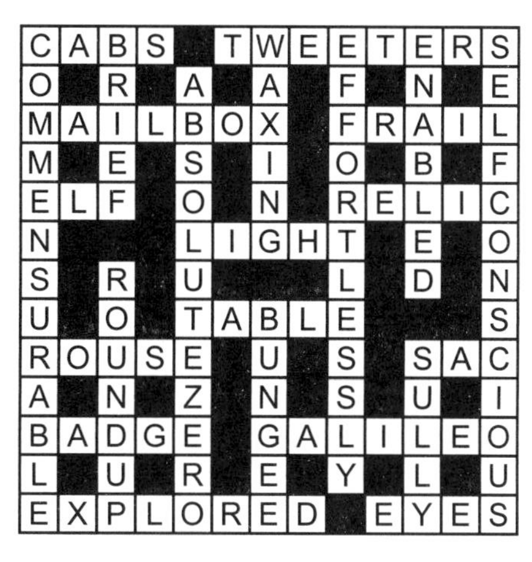

147.

148.

149.

150.

151.

152.

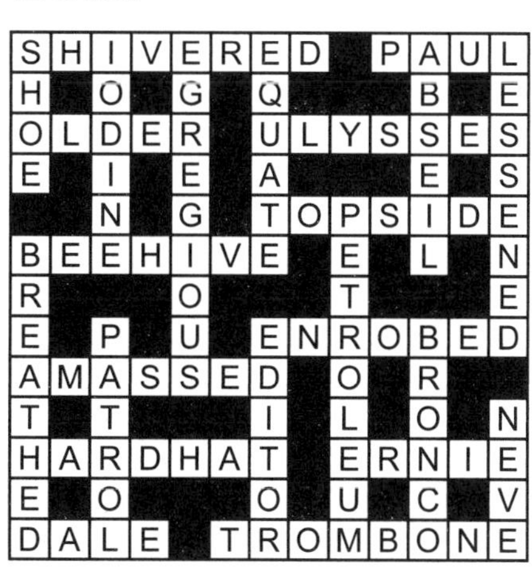

153.

Solutions

154.

```
RELIGION■DIPS
I■U■O■B■I■N■A
LIMBO■L■NAVEL
E■P■D■O■D■O■I
■■■STENTORIAN
S■M■E■G■C■C■I
CINEMA■ATTEST
I■E■P■E■R■S■Y
MEMBERSHIP■■■
I■O■R■T■N■G■D
TINGE■E■ALONE
A■I■D■E■T■B■A
ROCK■IMPERIAL
```

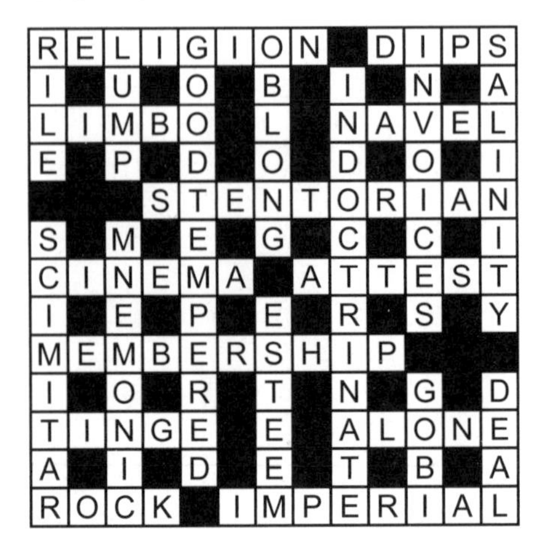

155.

```
OHMS■MISSPEND
U■A■D■O■E■X■O
TAMARIN■LOHAN
S■B■A■■■F■A■E
INADMISSIBLE■
D■■■A■H■N■E■H
ETA■TROUT■DYE
R■E■I■W■E■■■A
■CONCENTRATED
L■L■A■■■E■W■I
ARIEL■BASTION
N■A■L■U■T■N■G
ANNOYING■ZEUS
```

156.

```
OCHE■PRODUCER
V■I■I■E■I■E■U
ERRANDS■SUDAN
R■E■S■I■C■I■E
CURMUDGEONLY■
A■■■F■N■N■L■D
MODIFY■ENRAGE
E■O■I■U■E■■■S
■SUBCONSCIOUS
R■B■I■U■T■L■E
HALVE■SLENDER
E■E■N■E■D■E■T
APTITUDE■ONUS
```

157.

```
TURNPIKE■BROW
I■I■R■N■O■U■O
DRONE■O■VIPER
Y■T■M■T■E■T■S
■■■SEETHROUGH
H■D■D■Y■E■R■I
ORIGIN■ASLEEP
T■V■T■H■T■S■S
PRIMAFACIE■■■
L■D■T■V■M■S■H
ALIKE■A■AMPLE
T■N■D■N■T■I■A
EDGE■PATERNAL
```

158.

```
ADDLED■THRIVE
R■E■D■E■O■O■V
RUSSIAN■T■T■O
E■T■C■GOSHAWK
STRUT■I■P■■■E
T■U■■■N■OVENS
■■C■CHEAT■M■■
CATCH■E■■■O■P
O■■■O■R■ULTRA
SCHERZI■N■I■U
M■A■A■NATIONS
I■L■L■G■I■N■E
COFFER■CLOSED
```

159.

```
CULL■ECLIPSES
O■I■C■U■N■H■U
CONCORD■DRAPE
O■E■L■■■I■L■S
NONFLAMMABLE■
U■■■Y■O■N■O■O
TAP■WOODS■WAR
S■O■O■S■U■■■C
■BLABBERMOUTH
S■E■B■■■M■N■A
CAMEL■SPENDER
A■I■E■A■R■E■D
BACKSIDE■BRAS
```

160.

```
DECKS■ATHEISM
I■O■E■N■■N■A■
S■M■R■G■STATE
REMAINED■A■Y■
U■U■A■L■FIERY
PITILESS■L■■A
T■E■S■■■A■H■C
E■■A■FLATFISH
DODGE■Y■H■L■T
■U■O■ARTICLES
ISSUE■I■R■O■M
■T■T■■C■S■C■E
ASSISTS■TOKEN
```

161.

```
DEBT■KEYSTONE
O■A■S■R■O■U■N
UNLOCKS■METRE
B■S■A■A■N■L■R
LEAST■THAWING
E■■■T■Z■M■V■E
JAGGED■ABJECT
O■E■R■G■U■■■I
IGNOBLE■LILAC
N■E■R■N■I■O■A
TERRA■INSTALL
E■I■I■A■M■T■L
DECENTLY■WHEY
```

162.

```
■STAVE■STUBS■
B■A■E■K■O■I■L
AVIGNON■MANNA
N■L■T■O■A■■■S
TIPS■ALTHOUGH
E■I■D■L■A■P■■
REEKED■SWIRLS
■■C■F■V■K■O■P
SKELETON■ROAR
A■■■R■I■S■T■I
LOWER■CHEWING
T■E■A■E■A■N■S
■BELLS■DREGS■
```

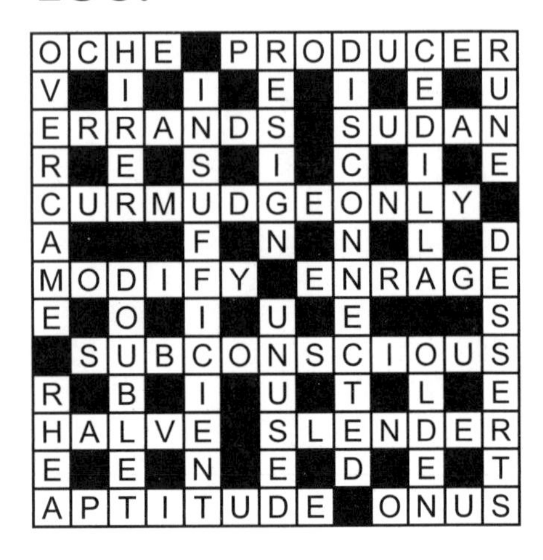

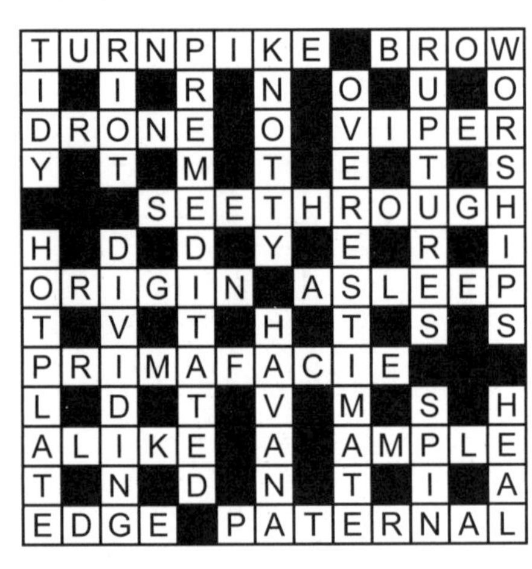

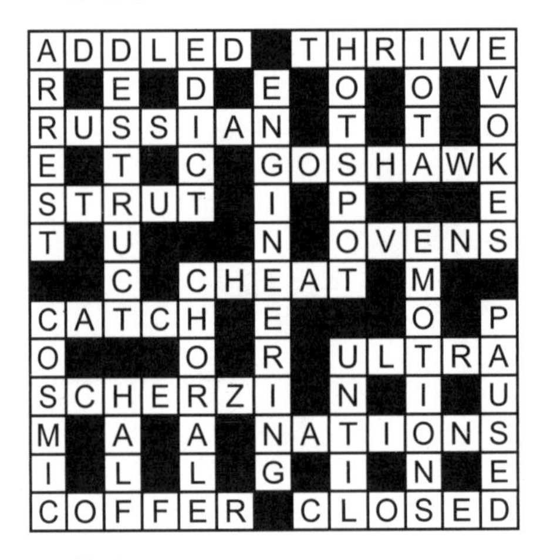

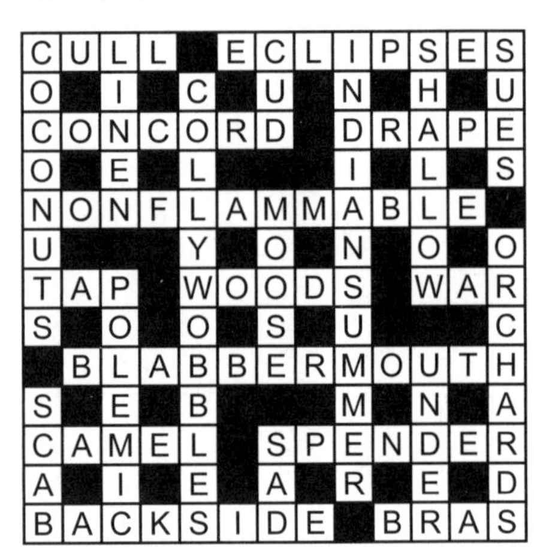

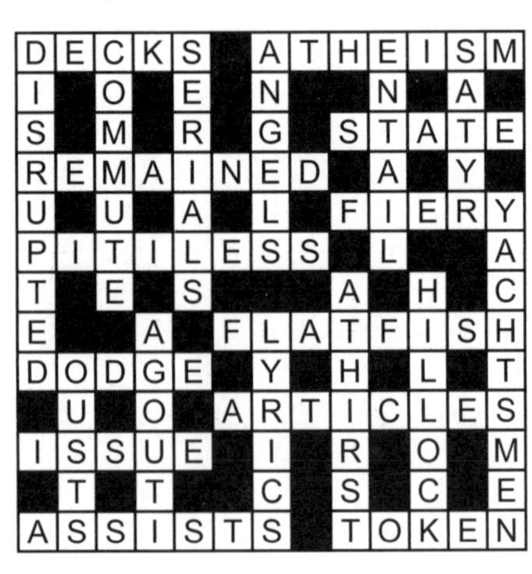

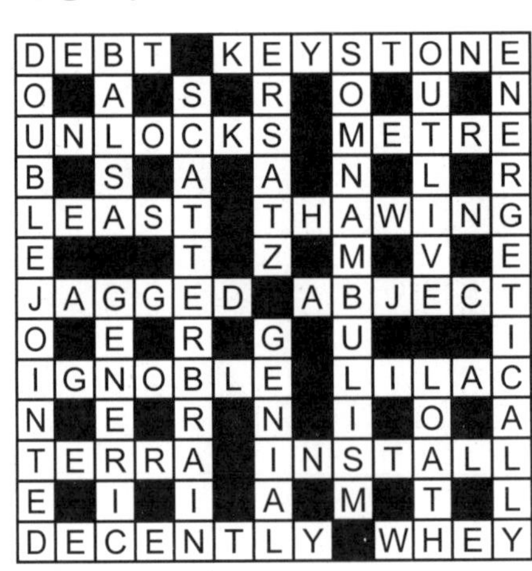

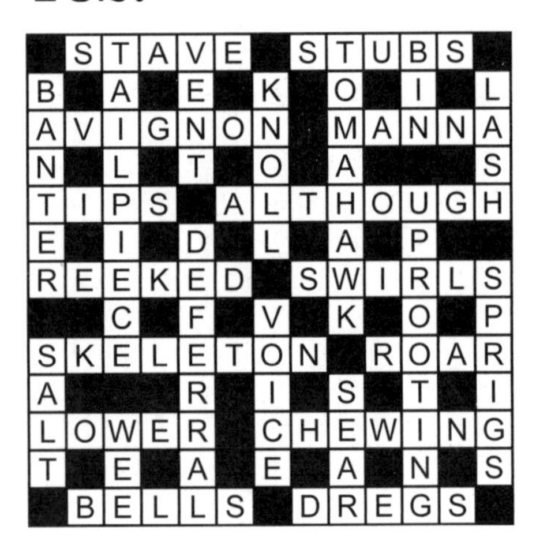

Solutions

163.

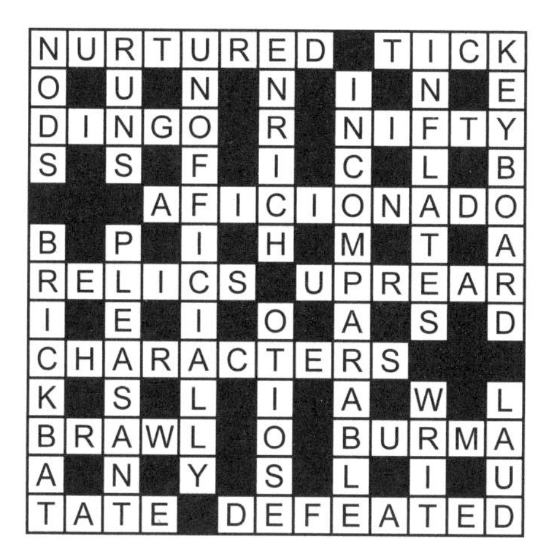

164.

165.

166.

U	R	N	S	■	S	P	O	R	A	D	I	C
N	■	A	■	C	■	O	■	E	■	E	■	H
P	U	N	C	H	E	S	■	P	E	T	E	R
A	■	N	■	O	■	E	■	R	■	E	■	Y
S	T	Y	■	R	■	U	■	E	A	S	E	S
T	■	■	■	E	A	R	L	S	■	T	■	A
E	■	B	■	O	■	■	■	E	■	S	■	N
U	■	I	■	G	R	O	A	N	■	■	■	T
R	O	V	E	R	■	R	■	T	■	A	A	H
I	■	O	■	A	■	A	■	I	■	C	■	E
S	L	U	R	P	■	T	A	N	T	R	U	M
E	■	A	■	H	■	O	■	G	■	I	■	U
D	O	C	K	Y	A	R	D	■	A	D	A	M

167.

168.

169.

170.

171.

A	B	U	T	■	D	E	S	O	L	A	T	E
P	■	S	■	S	■	X	■	B	■	M	■	X
P	R	I	M	A	T	E	■	S	C	U	B	A
R	■	N	■	C	■	M	■	C	■	S	■	G
E	L	G	A	R	■	P	O	U	R	I	N	G
H	■	■	■	I	■	T	■	R	■	N	■	E
E	N	A	B	L	E	■	H	A	N	G	A	R
N	■	R	■	E	■	P	■	N	■	■	■	A
S	C	R	A	G	G	Y	■	T	H	E	F	T
I	■	A	■	I	■	T	■	I	■	R	■	E
B	I	N	G	O	■	H	U	S	B	A	N	D
L	■	G	■	U	■	O	■	M	■	S	■	L
E	V	E	N	S	O	N	G	■	D	E	F	Y

172.

S	I	N	E	W	S			A		M	A	Y
	D			A		S	A	M	B	A		A
M	I	L	K	S	O	P		I		R		R
	O			H		O		D	O	T	E	D
S	T	I	L	E	T	T	O			I		A
	I			D		S		T		N		G
I	C	A	R	U	S		P	O	L	I	C	E
M		M		P		T		W			O	
P		I			O	R	D	N	A	N	C	E
O	P	A	L	S		A		H			K	
U		B		O		W	E	A	R	I	N	G
N		L	I	B	E	L		L			E	
D	R	Y		S			A	L	W	A	Y	S

173.

B	R	A	N	D	N	E	W		E	A	R	N
A		C		I		N		C		L		O
K	I	N	G	S		V		A	S	L	A	N
U		E		A		I		R		U		S
			A	F	T	E	R	T	A	S	T	E
P		S		F		S		O		I		N
A	P	O	G	E	E		I	G	L	O	O	S
L		U		C		A		R		N		E
P	O	L	I	T	I	C	I	A	N			
A		M		I		T		P		B		A
B	R	A	V	O		I		H	O	U	S	E
L		T		N		O		E		Z		O
E	V	E	R		U	N	F	R	O	Z	E	N

174.

S	A	L	A	M	I		A		C		S	
I		A			D	I	V	O	R	C	E	D
T	A	U			Y		E		O		A	
U		G	O	B	L	I	N		S	U	D	S
P		H			L		U		S		O	
S	A	S	S	Y		B	E	D	B	U	G	S
			H		C		S		O			
E	S	T	U	A	R	Y		T	W	I	C	E
	H		T		O		C			D		A
M	E	A	D		U	N	R	O	L	L		R
	L		O		T		U			I	A	N
G	L	O	W	W	O	R	M			N		E
	S		N		N		B	I	G	G	E	R

175.

T	H	E	O	L	O	G	Y		V	A	M	P
R		N		A		I				V		A
O	F	T	E	N		V	A	R	I	A	N	T
D		I		D		E				T		I
		C		S		U	P	H	E	A	V	E
K	N	E	E	C	A	P		O		R		N
A				A				I				C
M		O		P		A	P	P	R	O	V	E
I	M	P	R	E	S	S		O		P		
K		E				S		L		T		H
A	U	R	I	C	L	E		L	A	I	T	Y
Z		A				S		O		M		P
E	A	S	E		E	S	T	I	M	A	T	E

176.

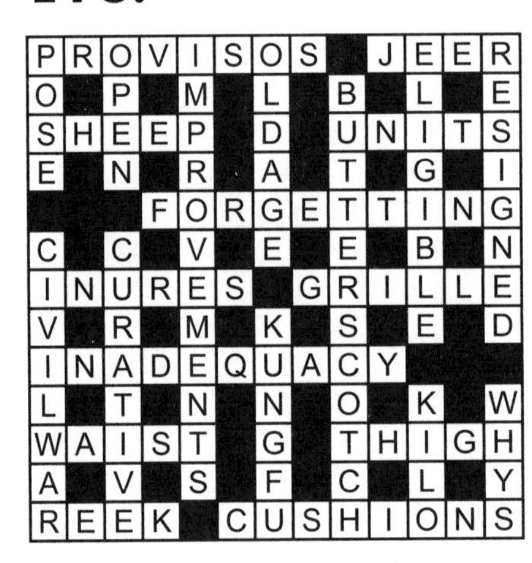

P	R	O	V	I	S	O	S		J	E	E	R
O		P		M		L		B		L		E
S	H	E	E	P		D		U	N	I	T	S
E		N		R		A		T		G		I
			F	O	R	G	E	T	T	I	N	G
C		C		V		E		E		B		N
I	N	U	R	E	S		G	R	I	L	L	E
V		R		M		K		S		E		D
I	N	A	D	E	Q	U	A	C	Y			
L		T		N		N		O		K		W
W	A	I	S	T		G		T	H	I	G	H
A		V		S		F		C		L		Y
R	E	E	K		C	U	S	H	I	O	N	S

177.

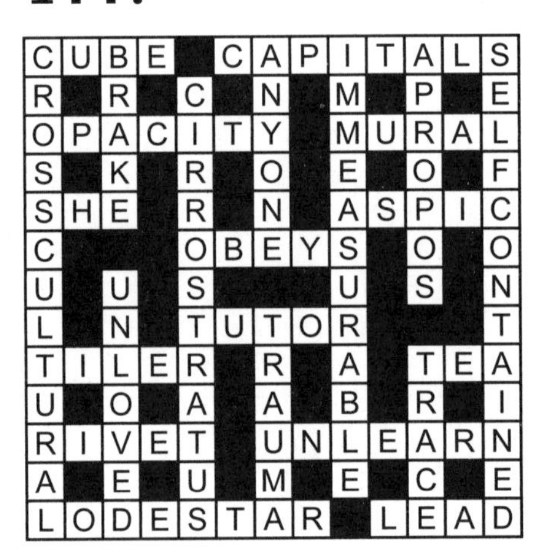

C	U	B	E		C	A	P	I	T	A	L	S
R		R		C		N		M		P		E
O	P	A	C	I	T	Y		M	U	R	A	L
S		K		R		O		E		O		F
S	H	E		R		N		A	S	P	I	C
C				O	B	E	Y	S		O		O
U		U		S				U		S		N
L		N		T	U	T	O	R				T
T	I	L	E	R		R		A		T	E	A
U		O		A		A		B		R		I
R	I	V	E	T		U	N	L	E	A	R	N
A		E		U		M		E		C		E
L	O	D	E	S	T	A	R		L	E	A	D

178.

P	U	F	F		S	P	E	C	I	O	U	S
O		I		S		S		A		D		E
R	E	E	N	T	R	Y		R	I	D	G	E
P		N		R		C		B		M		R
O	L	D	F	A	S	H	I	O	N	E	D	
I				I		E		H		N		P
S	H	A	G	G	Y		O	Y	S	T	E	R
E		R		H		S		D				O
	D	I	C	T	A	T	O	R	S	H	I	P
A		Z		E		I		A		E		E
G	R	O	W	N		C	A	T	E	R	E	R
E		N		E		K		E		O		L
S	T	A	R	D	U	S	T		O	N	L	Y

179.

E	N	T	R	A	N	C	E		A	G	A	R
L		H		S		R				A		E
A	T	O	M	S		E	N	G	U	L	F	S
N		R		O		D				A		I
		N		C		I	N	D	E	X	E	S
S	T	Y	L	I	S	T		I		Y		T
W				A				P				E
E		S		T		A	S	H	A	M	E	D
E	N	T	R	E	A	T		T		U		
T		A				T		H		D		E
P	E	T	U	N	I	A		O	G	D	E	N
E		E				I		N		L		D
A	I	D	S		S	N	U	G	N	E	S	S

180.

N	E	P	H	E	W		U	P	S	H	O	T
A		R		N		C		R		A		E
T	R	O	T	T	E	R		I		L		N
U		P		R		E	N	V	I	O	U	S
R	O	O	M	Y		S		A				O
E		S				T		T	O	W	E	R
		E		G	A	F	F	E		I		
E	L	D	E	R		A				Z		T
U				A		L		U	S	A	G	E
R	E	C	I	T	A	L		S		R		R
E		Y		I		E	C	U	A	D	O	R
K		A		F		N		A		R		O
A	N	N	O	Y	S		P	L	A	Y	E	R

Solutions

181.

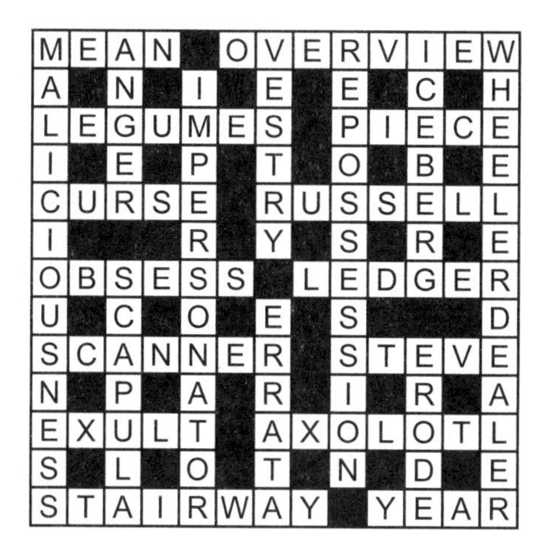

182.

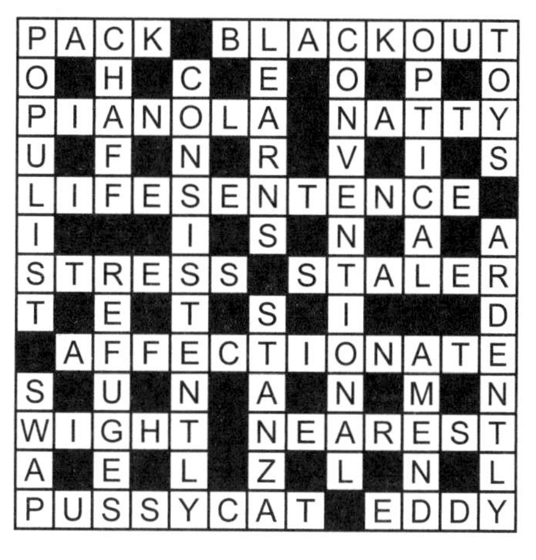

183.

184.

185.

186.

187.

188.

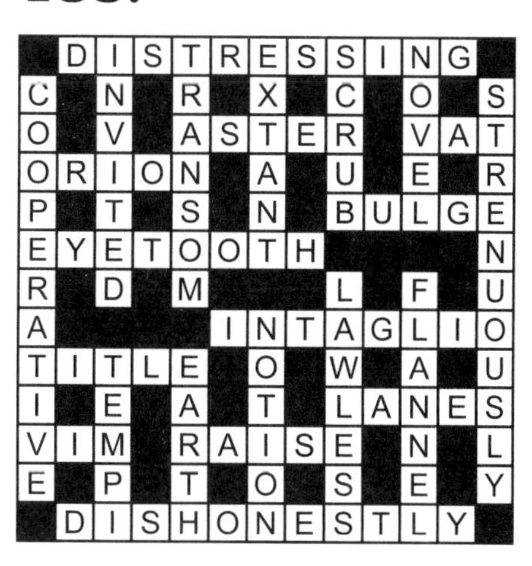

189.

190.

B	U	M	P	■	P	R	O	T	E	C	T	S
A	■	A	■	P	■	O	■	H	■	H	■	U
C	O	R	P	O	R	A	■	I	D	I	O	M
K	■	G	■	S	■	S	■	C	■	G	■	O
B	R	E	A	T	H	T	A	K	I	N	G	■
I	■	■	■	G	■	S	■	S	■	O	■	H
T	H	E	I	R	S	■	S	K	I	N	N	Y
E	■	X	■	A	■	A	■	I	■	■	■	P
■	R	H	O	D	O	D	E	N	D	R	O	N
C	■	O	■	U	■	J	■	N	■	E	■	O
A	O	R	T	A	■	U	S	E	L	E	S	S
L	■	T	■	T	■	R	■	D	■	V	■	I
F	A	S	T	E	N	E	R	■	S	E	A	S

191.

192.

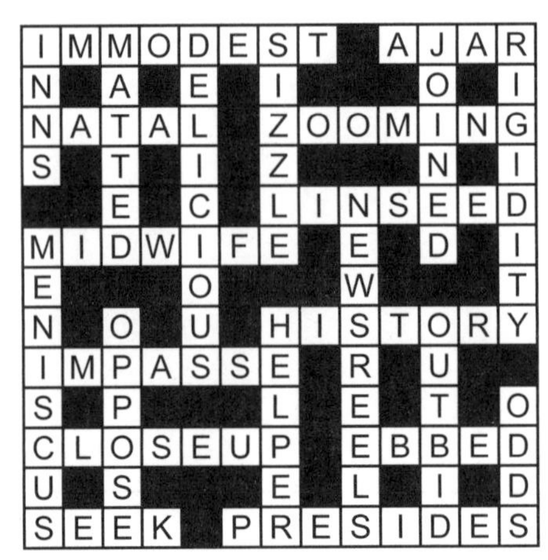

193.

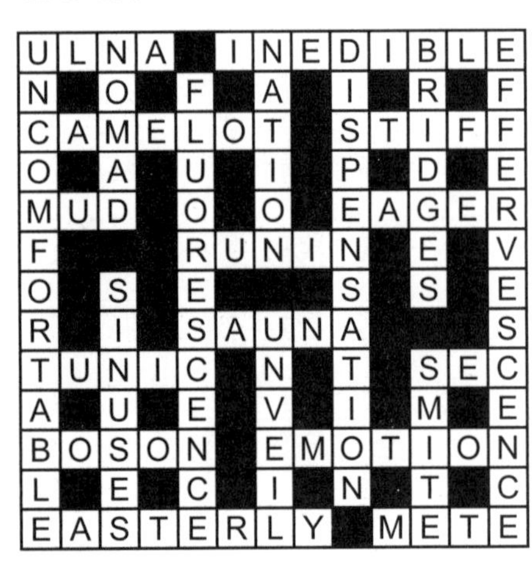

194.

195.

196.

197.

198.

Solutions

199.

A	U	D	I		C	E	R	B	E	R	U	S
N		A		D		N		I		E		A
T	E	M	P	E	R	S		O	R	D	E	R
I		P		C		U		D		R		A
B	A	S	I	L		E	P	I	T	A	P	H
A				A		S		V		F		F
C	Y	B	O	R	G		S	E	E	T	H	E
T		A		A		E		R				R
E	R	R	A	T	I	C		S	T	I	N	G
R		R		I		H		I		V		U
I	M	A	G	O		O	U	T	D	O	E	S
A		C		N		E		Y		R		O
L	A	K	E	S	I	D	E		R	Y	A	N

200.

201.

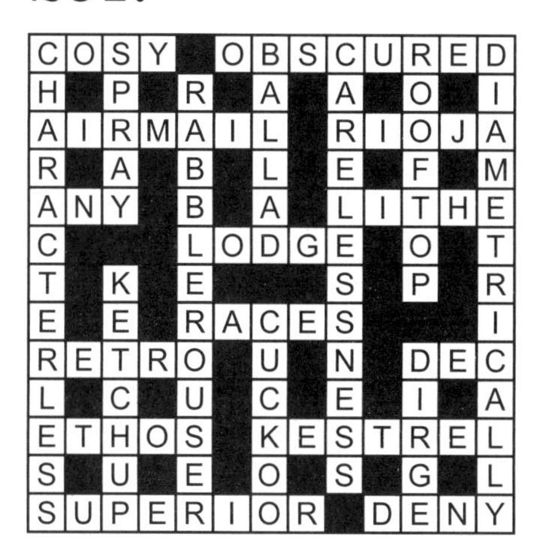

202.

203.

204.

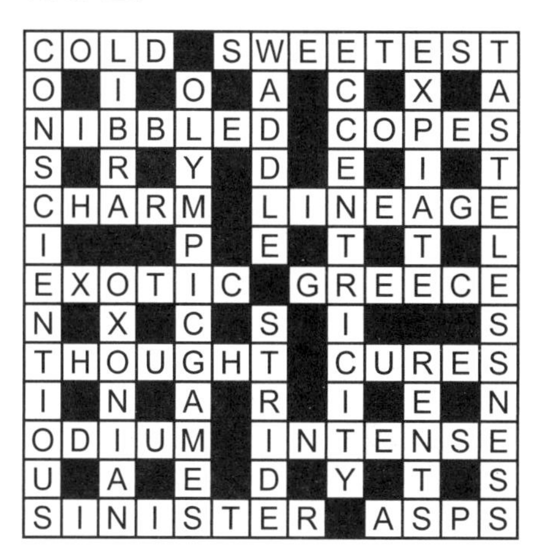

205.

206.

207.

208.

209.

210.

211.

212.

213.

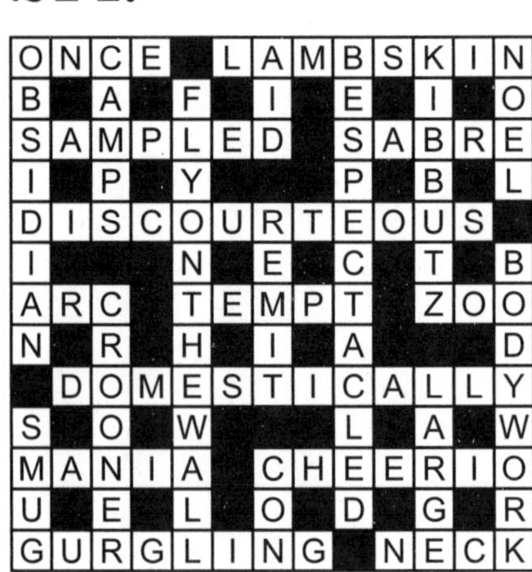

214.

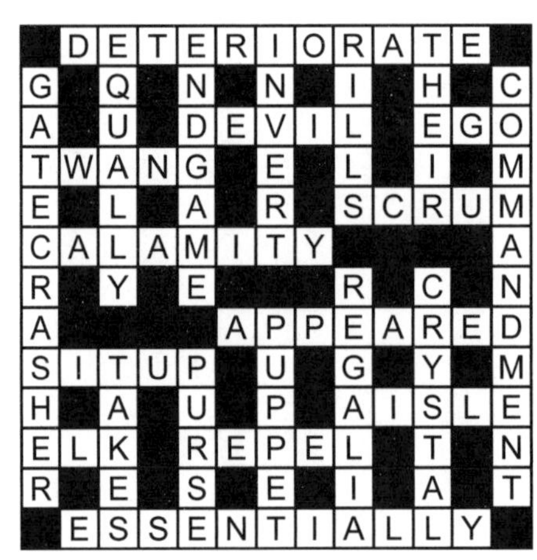

215.

216.

Solutions

217.

218.

219.

220.

221.

222.

223.

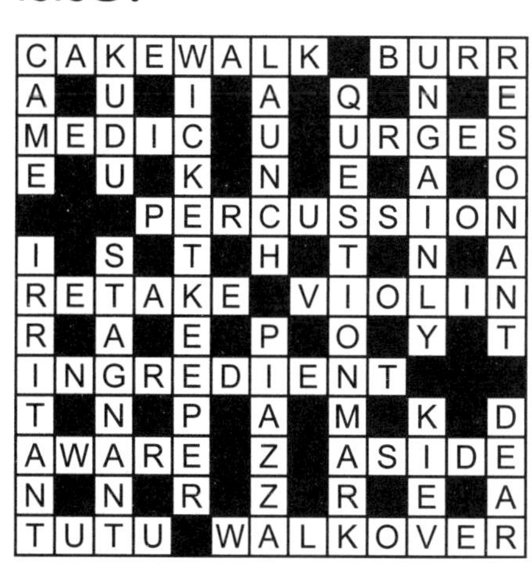

224.

225.

226.

S	A	F	E	■	A	L	L	E	Y	W	A	Y
O	■	L	■	M	■	I	■	L	■	H	■	O
L	E	A	V	E	N	S	■	E	P	O	X	Y
D	■	I	■	A	■	T	■	C	■	E	■	O
I	R	R	E	S	P	E	C	T	I	V	E	■
E	■	■	■	U	■	N	■	R	■	E	■	P
R	E	G	A	R	D	■	S	I	E	R	R	A
S	■	O	■	E	■	G	■	F	■	■	■	R
■	U	N	E	M	P	L	O	Y	M	E	N	T
F	■	D	■	E	■	O	■	I	■	S	■	I
A	C	O	R	N	■	B	O	N	U	S	E	S
I	■	L	■	T	■	E	■	G	■	E	■	A
R	E	A	S	S	E	S	S	■	O	X	E	N

227.

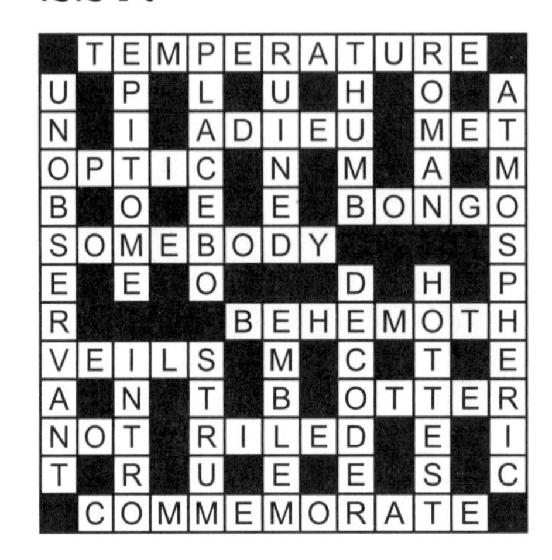

228.

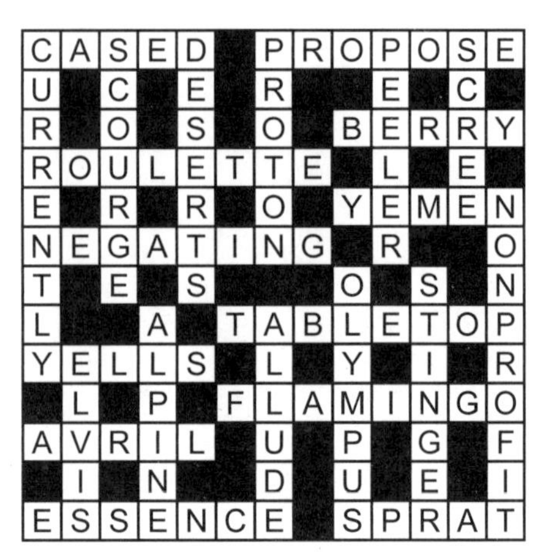

229.

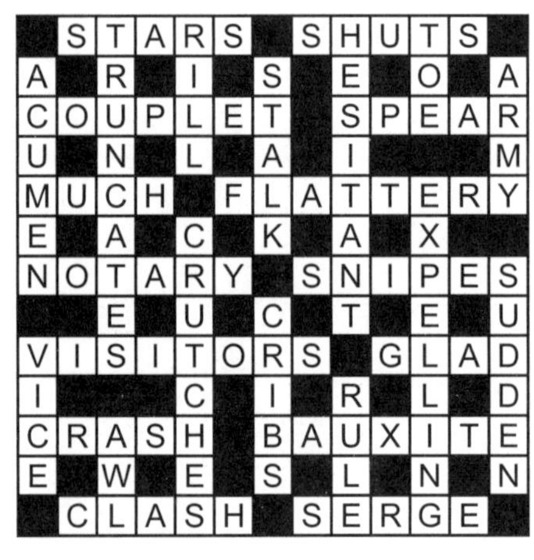

230.

231.

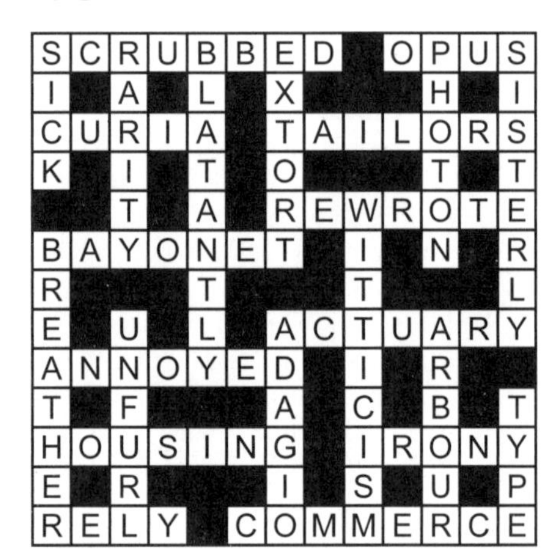

232.

233.

234.

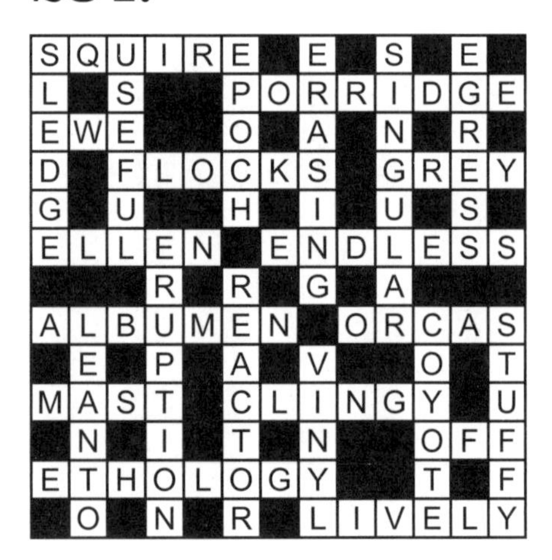

Solutions

235.

B	O	U	N	C	Y		E	M	B	O	S	S
R		N		H		W		I		R		U
O	R	I	G	A	M	I		C		A		N
L		C		I		T	U	R	T	L	E	S
L	A	Y	E	R		C		O				E
Y		C				H		B	U	R	N	T
		L		C	A	D	G	E		E		
S	H	E	L	L		O				S		B
A				A		C		E	A	T	E	R
C	U	L	P	R	I	T		P		R		O
K		O		I		O	P	I	N	I	O	N
E		L		F		R		C		C		Z
D	E	L	A	Y	S		T	S	E	T	S	E

236.

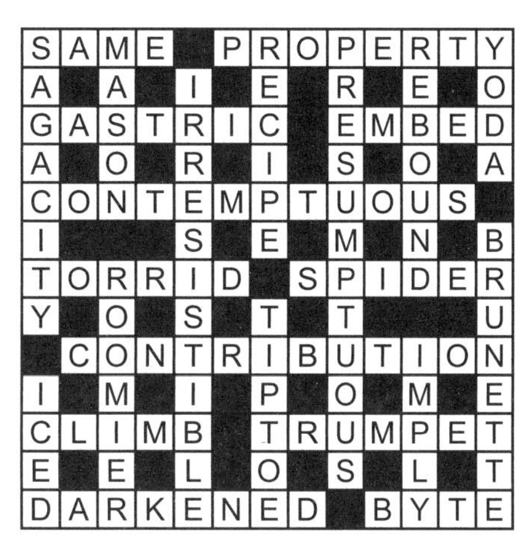

S	A	M	E		P	R	O	P	E	R	T	Y
A		A		I		E		R		E		O
G	A	S	T	R	I	C		E	M	B	E	D
A		O		R		I		S		O		A
C	O	N	T	E	M	P	T	U	O	U	S	
I				S		E		M		N		B
T	O	R	R	I	D		S	P	I	D	E	R
Y		O		S		T		T				U
	C	O	N	T	R	I	B	U	T	I	O	N
I		M		I		P		O		M		E
C	L	I	M	B		T	R	U	M	P	E	T
E		E		L		O		S		L		T
D	A	R	K	E	N	E	D		B	Y	T	E

237.

W	I	N	O	N	A		I		O		I	
O		U			V	A	G	A	B	O	N	D
M	A	R			I		N		S		T	
B		S	A	F	A	R	I		T	H	E	N
A		E			N		T		A		R	
T	I	D	E	S		R	E	S	C	I	N	D
			L		S		S		L			
E	F	F	E	C	T	S		R	E	E	D	S
	I		C		E		T			S		I
N	E	S	T		N	E	W	E	S	T		E
	N		R		C		I			A	W	N
A	D	M	I	R	I	N	G			T		N
	S		C		L		S	C	H	E	M	A

238.

I	M	P	S		M	I	S	H	M	A	S	H
L		E		S		N		E		P		E
L	O	A	D	I	N	G		N	E	P	A	L
U		R		G		O		C		E		T
S	A	L	O	N		T	E	E	N	A	G	E
T				I		S		F		S		R
R	E	B	U	F	F		V	O	W	E	L	S
A		R		I		T		R				K
T	R	A	M	C	A	R		W	O	R	S	E
I		G		A		O		A		E		L
O	R	G	A	N		U	P	R	I	G	H	T
N		E		C		P		D		A		E
S	C	R	E	E	N	E	D		S	L	U	R

239.

A	L	P	A	C	A		C		C		T	
S		A			S	O	U	T	H	E	R	N
T	A	R			H		C		E		E	
E		S	T	R	E	A	K		R	I	M	S
R		O			N		O		O		O	
N	I	N	O	N		S	O	J	O	U	R	N
			B		O		S		T			
P	A	R	V	E	N	U		I	S	A	A	C
	C		I		E		S			V		R
A	Q	U	A		N	E	T	T	L	E		A
	U		T		E		A			R	O	T
L	I	C	E	N	S	E	S			S		E
	T		D		S		H	O	V	E	R	S

240.

D	O	G	S		R	E	D	C	O	A	T	S
E		L		I		D		A		R		H
F	R	O	W	N	E	D		L	O	T	T	O
E		O		F		I		L		D		R
R	U	M	E	R		E	X	I	G	E	N	T
E				I		S		G		C		T
N	A	D	I	N	E		G	R	O	O	V	E
T		R		G		T		A				M
I	M	A	G	E	R	Y		P	O	P	U	P
A		S		M		C		H		H		E
L	I	T	R	E		O	P	E	N	A	I	R
L		I		N		O		R		S		E
Y	A	C	H	T	I	N	G		W	E	E	D

241.

L	I	F	E	P	E	E	R		B	A	L	M
A		O		R		N		E		B		I
C	O	N	G	O		C		X	E	N	O	N
E		T		F		O		P		E		S
			D	E	A	D	W	E	I	G	H	T
B		P		S		E		R		A		R
R	E	L	I	S	H		L	I	T	T	L	E
O		A		I		P		M		E		L
A	S	T	R	O	N	O	M	E	R			
D		I		N		T		N		P		E
W	A	N	D	A		A		T	A	U	N	T
A		U		L		S		A		R		O
Y	A	M	S		C	H	I	L	D	R	E	N

242.

C	A	G	E		C	O	N	C	E	D	E	D
H		R		C		W		A		E		I
E	Y	E	B	A	L	L		N	E	V	I	S
A		E		N				O		I		H
P	Y	R	O	T	E	C	H	N	I	C	S	
E				A		Y		I		E		E
S	U	M		N	I	C	K	S		S	I	X
T		I		K		L		A				C
	U	N	D	E	T	E	C	T	A	B	L	E
E		U		R				I		R		S
M	E	T	R	O		R	I	O	T	E	R	S
I		E		U		I		N		V		E
R	E	S	I	S	T	O	R		W	E	T	S

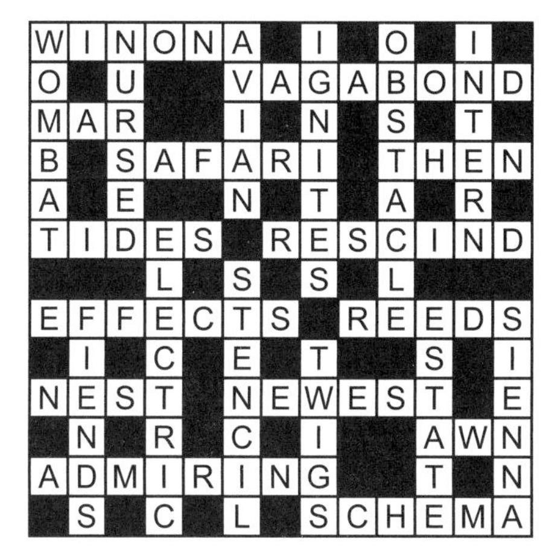

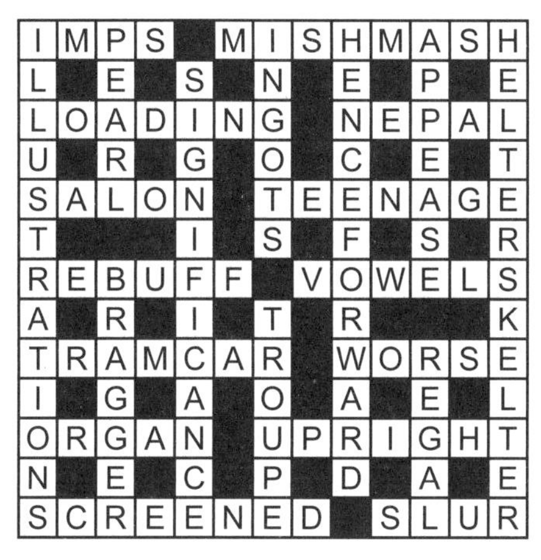

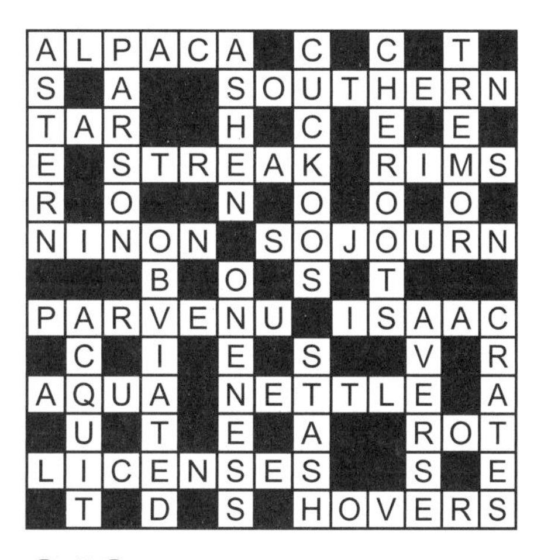

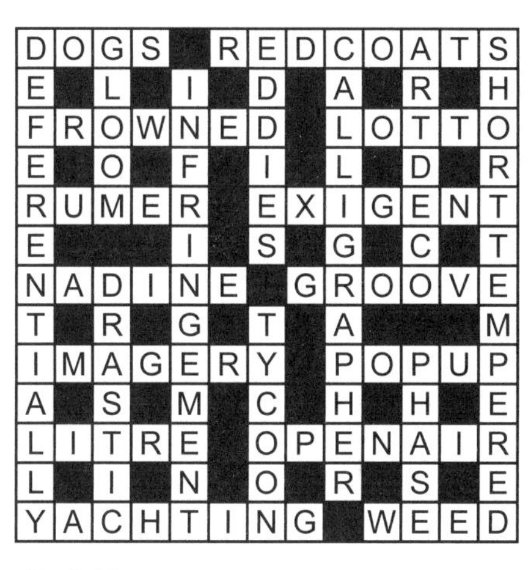

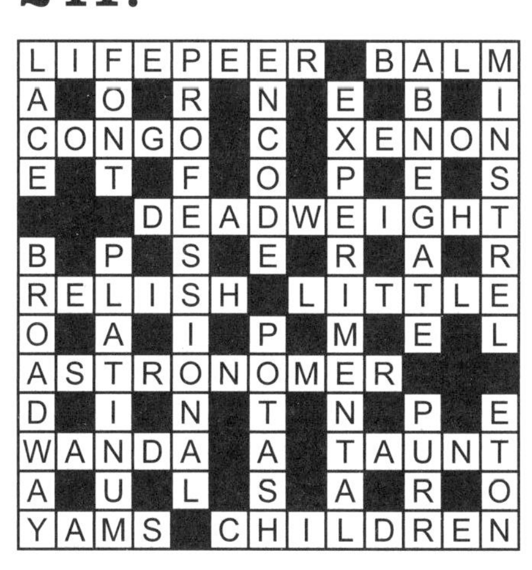

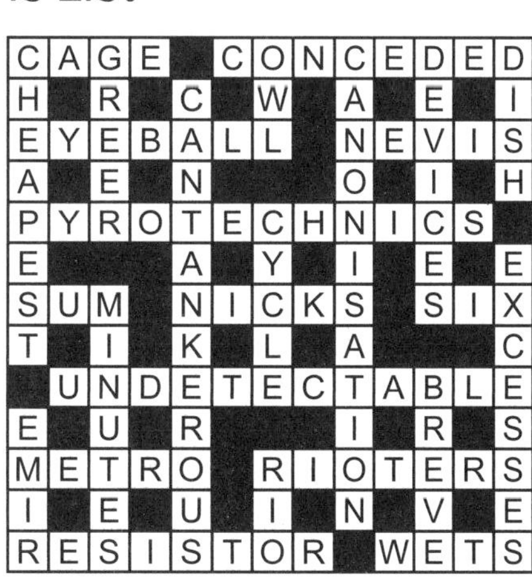

243.

R	E	N	O	W	N		G	L	O	B	A	L
E		O		I		P		E		E		A
A	R	B	I	T	E	R		A		A		W
P		L		T		O	R	D	E	R	L	Y
E	L	E	G	Y		G		E				E
R		M				R		R	A	Z	O	R
		A		W	E	E	D	S		I		
J	U	N	T	A		S				M		P
E				R		S		T	A	B	O	O
J	U	M	A	N	J	I		I		A		U
U		I		I		O	C	T	O	B	E	R
N		T		N		N		A		W		E
E	N	E	R	G	Y		U	N	B	E	N	D

Solutions

244.

D	A	H	L	■	A	S	S	E	S	S	E	S
O	■	E	■	F	■	L	■	F	■	A	■	U
U	N	A	L	I	K	E	■	F	R	Y	U	P
B	■	V	■	E	■	E	■	E	■	I	■	E
L	O	Y	A	L	■	P	A	R	T	N	E	R
E	■	■	■	D	■	S	■	V	■	G	■	F
C	R	A	G	G	Y	■	W	E	A	S	E	L
H	■	U	■	L	■	S	■	S	■	■	■	U
E	N	T	R	A	N	T	■	C	H	I	N	O
C	■	O	■	S	■	R	■	E	■	R	■	U
K	I	C	K	S	■	A	N	N	U	A	L	S
E	■	U	■	E	■	I	■	T	■	T	■	L
D	R	E	S	S	I	N	G	■	V	E	R	Y

245.

246.

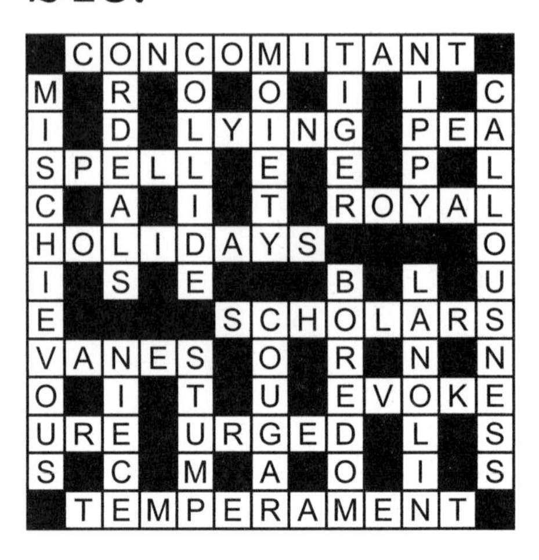

247.

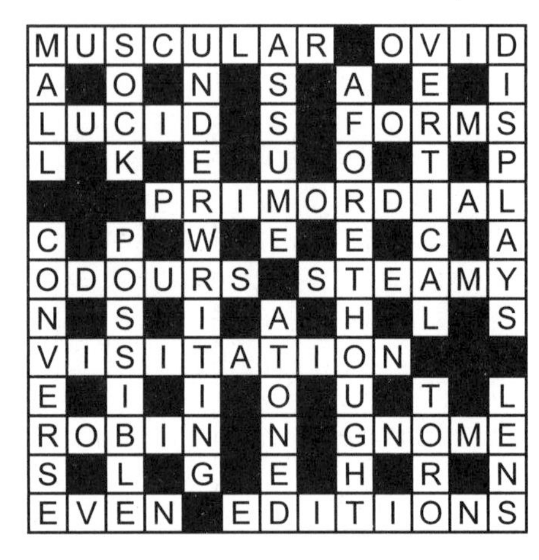

248.

249.

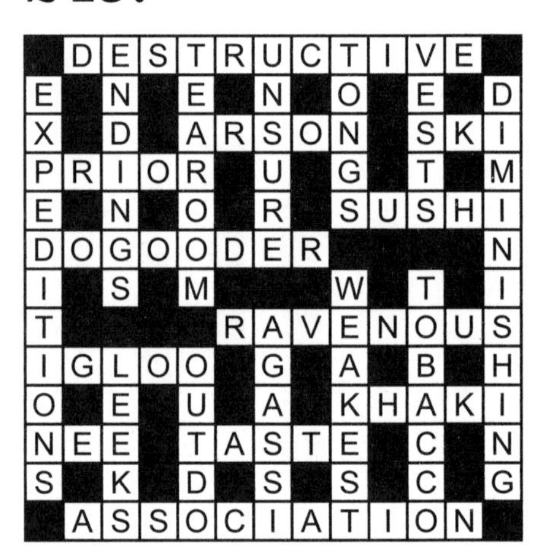

250.

251.

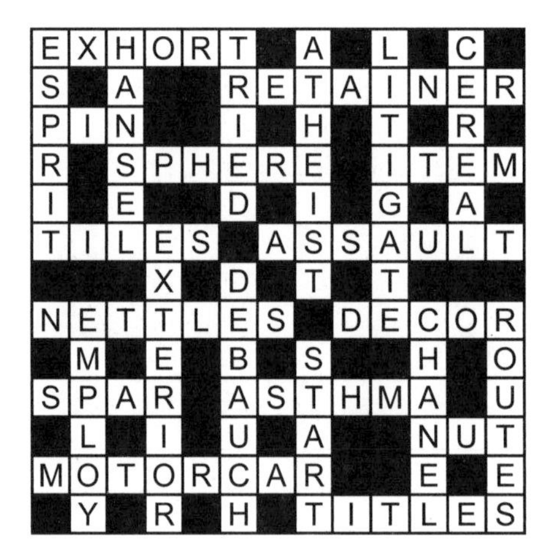

252.

Solutions

253.

254.

255.

256.

257.

258.

259.

260.

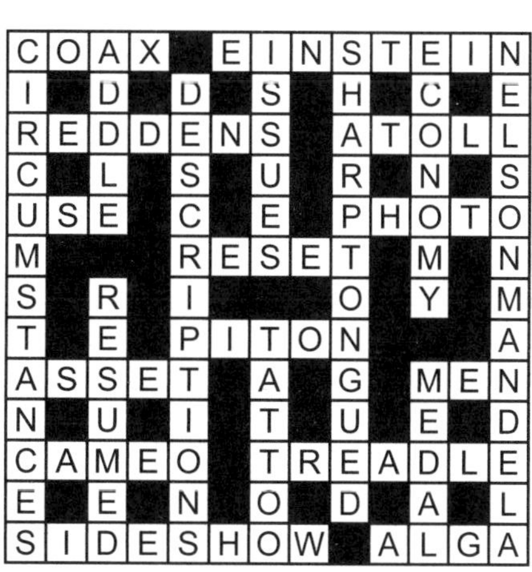

261.

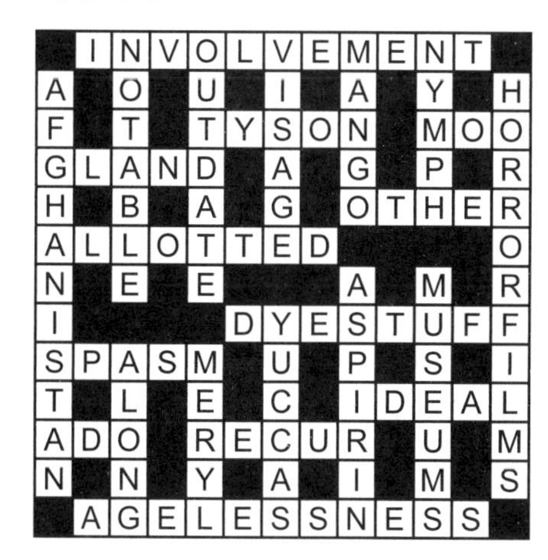

262.

R	E	T	I	N	A		M		D		M	
E		H			P	R	E	C	E	D	E	D
A	R	E			P		M		J		R	
S		S	H	E	L	V	E		E	N	I	D
O		I			Y		N		C		N	
N	A	S	T	Y		S	T	E	T	S	O	N
			E		E		O		E			
I	S	O	N	O	M	Y		E	D	D	I	E
	C		D		B		E			A		R
C	H	E	R		R	E	D	E	E	M		M
	I		I		O		I			P	H	I
P	S	A	L	M	I	S	T			E		N
	T		S		L		S	E	A	N	C	E

263.

I	N	C	A		O	B	E	D	I	E	N	T
N		R		H		U		E		X		H
C	O	O	P	E	R	S		M	A	P	L	E
O		W		A		H		O		E		O
R	U	N		D		E		N	I	C	E	R
R				M	E	L	T	S		T		E
U		P		I				T		S		T
P		R		S	U	G	A	R				I
T	R	E	A	T		A		A		S	I	C
I		S		R		T		B		A		A
B	A	S	T	E		H	E	L	P	F	U	L
L		U		S		E		E		E		L
E	X	P	O	S	U	R	E		P	R	A	Y

264.

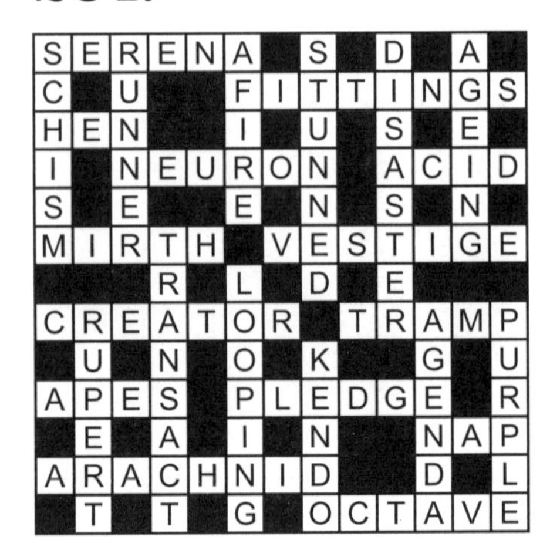

S	E	R	E	N	A		S		D		A	
C		U			F	I	T	T	I	N	G	S
H	E	N			I		U		S		E	
I		N	E	U	R	O	N		A	C	I	D
S		E			E		N		S		N	
M	I	R	T	H		V	E	S	T	I	G	E
			R		L		D		E			
C	R	E	A	T	O	R		T	R	A	M	P
	U		N		O		K			G		U
A	P	E	S		P	L	E	D	G	E		R
	E		A		I		N			N	A	P
A	R	A	C	H	N	I	D			D		L
	T		T		G		O	C	T	A	V	E

265.

B	A	C	H		U	G	L	I	N	E	S	S
U		A		M		R		N		N		I
T	O	R	P	E	D	O		D	R	O	L	L
T		O		T		T		E		U		V
E	L	L		A		T		F	E	N	C	E
R				P	R	O	S	E		C		R
F		F		H				N		E		J
I		L		Y	A	R	D	S				U
N	A	I	L	S		I		I		R	O	B
G		G		I		G		B		O		I
E	T	H	I	C		H	O	L	D	A	L	L
R		T		A		T		E		S		E
S	P	Y	G	L	A	S	S		S	T	Y	E

266.

L	O	S	E		U	N	K	N	O	W	N	S
A		Y		M		A		O		A		O
C	O	L	L	I	E	R		N	E	R	V	Y
R		P		S		R		A		B		A
O	T	H	E	R	W	O	R	L	D	L	Y	
S				E		W		C		E		C
S	C	U	L	P	T		P	O	O	R	E	R
E		N		R		S		H				I
	R	E	C	E	P	T	I	O	N	I	S	T
D		Q		S		E		L		M		E
R	O	U	G	E		W	H	I	S	P	E	R
E		A		N		E		C		E		I
W	E	L	L	T	O	D	O		F	L	E	A

267.

	S	C	O	U	T	M	A	S	T	E	R	
H		A		T		O		L		A		A
E		L		I	N	A	N	E		R	U	B
L	O	C	A	L		N		E		L		S
I		I		I		E		T	R	Y	S	T
C	L	U	S	T	E	R	S					R
O		M		Y				S		S		A
P					A	N	A	L	Y	T	I	C
T	R	A	I	N		A		A		I		T
E		N		A		M		M	U	F	T	I
R	U	G		D	E	I	S	M		F		O
S		L		A		N		E		E		N
	B	E	L	L	I	G	E	R	E	N	T	

268.

E	X	P	O		A	M	I	C	A	B	L	E
X		A		W		O		O		U		T
P	U	N	C	H	E	D		N	O	L	I	N
E		I		O		E		S		L		A
D	E	C	E	L	E	R	A	T	I	O	N	
I				E		N		R		C		R
T	O	U	C	H	Y		B	U	C	K	L	E
E		P		E		S		C				V
	B	R	E	A	S	T	S	T	R	O	K	E
B		A		R		A		I		P		R
E	L	I	O	T		R	U	N	N	E	R	S
T		S		E		V		G		R		A
A	B	E	R	D	E	E	N		G	A	L	L

269.

C	A	F	E		E	L	E	M	E	N	T	S
A		L		I		A		O		E		T
T	O	U	R	N	E	Y		T	H	E	T	A
E		N		F		I		I		D		C
B	U	G	L	E		N	O	V	E	L	T	Y
L				C		G		A		E		F
A	G	E	N	T	S		S	T	O	D	G	E
N		A		I		A		I				R
C	U	R	I	O	U	S		O	W	I	N	G
H		L		U		S		N		L		U
E	M	I	T	S		I	T	A	L	I	C	S
T		E		L		G		L		A		O
T	A	R	R	Y	I	N	G		E	D	E	N

270.

E	A	S	Y		S	N	A	P	S	H	O	T
X		H		H		E		R		E		I
P	R	O	L	O	N	G		E	R	R	E	D
L		U		P		A		S		E		E
A	U	T	H	E	N	T	I	C	I	T	Y	
I				L		E		R		I		H
N	E	A	R	E	R		M	I	S	C	U	E
S		S		S		A		P				A
	O	U	T	S	T	R	E	T	C	H	E	D
C		N		N		A		I		E		R
H	E	D	G	E		B	I	V	A	L	V	E
U		E		S		L		E		L		S
M	O	R	A	S	S	E	S		M	O	O	T

Solutions

271.

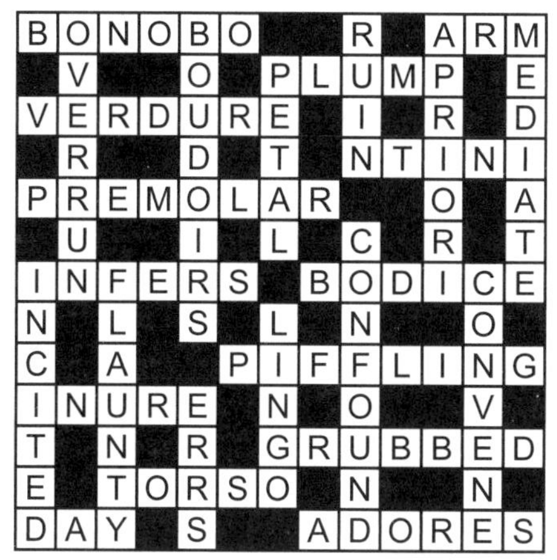

272.

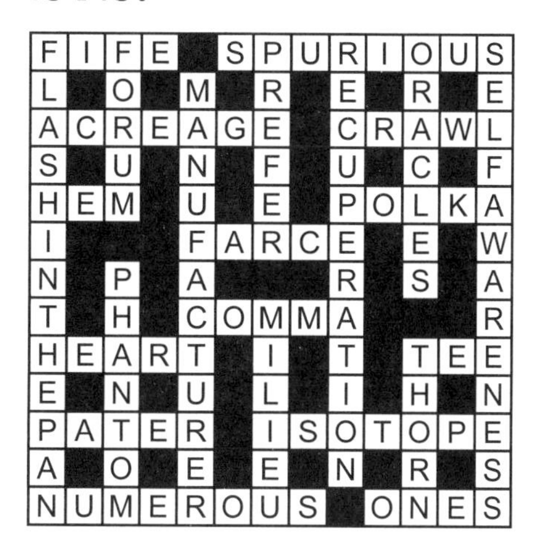

273.

274.

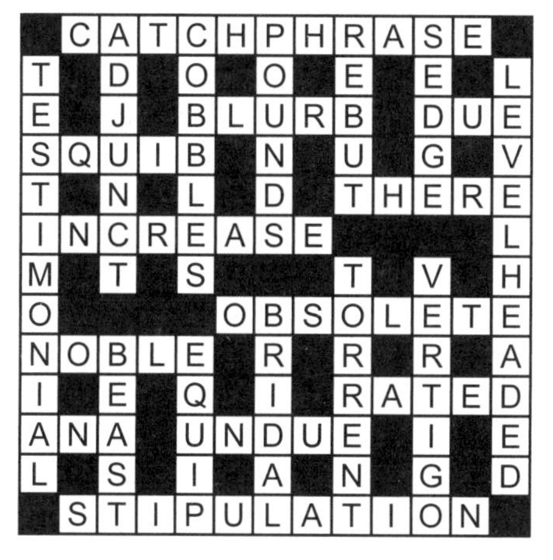

275.

276.

277.

278.

279.

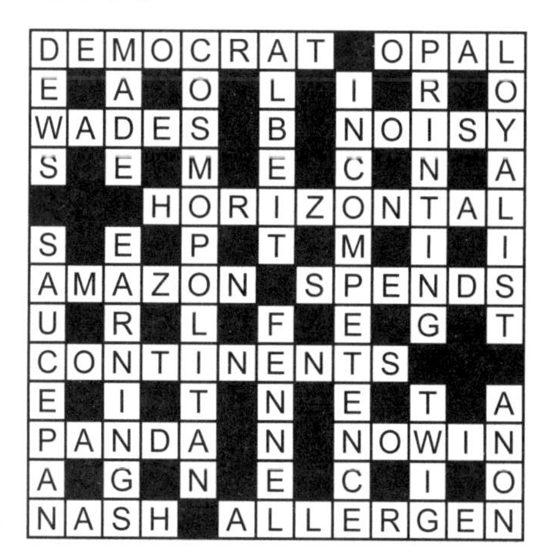

Solutions

280.

■	S	M	A	L	L	M	I	N	D	E	D	■
C	■	A	■	O	■	E	■	E	■	V	■	S
O	■	N	■	W	I	D	E	R	■	I	V	Y
R	A	D	A	R	■	I	■	V	■	T	■	N
P	■	A	■	I	■	A	■	E	L	A	N	D
O	B	T	U	S	E	L	Y	■	■	■	■	I
R	■	E	■	E	■	■	■	P	■	E	■	C
A	■	■	■	■	H	A	C	I	E	N	D	A
T	O	P	I	C	■	R	■	T	■	S	■	T
I	■	I	■	O	■	D	■	F	U	N	G	I
O	I	L	■	V	I	O	L	A	■	A	■	O
N	■	A	■	E	■	U	■	L	■	R	■	N
■	B	U	T	T	E	R	F	L	I	E	S	■

281.

282.

283.

284.

285.

286.

287.

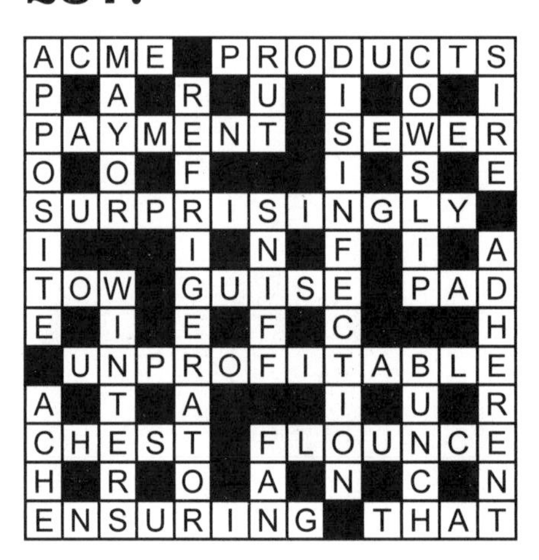